Miss Annie

God sent a 3¢ stamp and more. . .

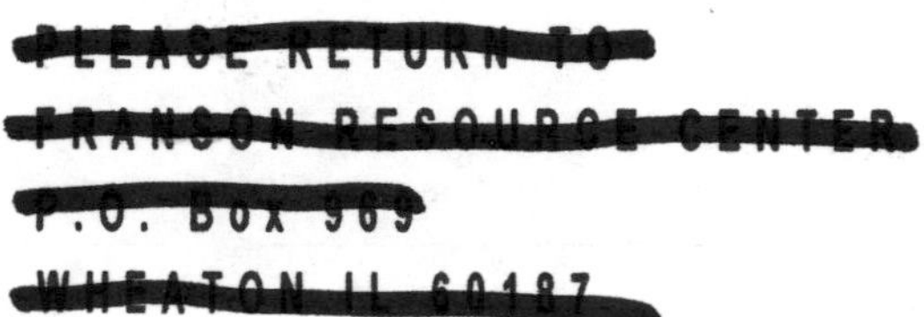

Annie Goertz

Canadian Cataloguing in Publication Data

Goertz, Annie, 1919-
Miss Annie

ISBN 0-9687449-0-7

1. Goertz, Annie, 1919- 2. Missionaries--India--Biography. I. Title.
BV3269.G59A3 2000 266'.0092 C00-910786-X

Order office:
135-2279 McCallum Road
Abbotsford, BC
V2S 6J1
Canada

Printed in Canada

Contents

Dedication

First of all, to my Lord and Savior Jesus Christ.

My parents Peter and Catherine Goertz.

My thirteen sisters and brothers - six of whom are with the Lord.

Sixty-nine nephews and nieces.

A host of great nieces and great nephews and also great greats. I'd like to mention each but you know who you are.

To all my Pastors: in Saskatchewan, British Columbia, Port Huron, Mich. and in India. You have faithfully taught me God's Word.

Acknowledgements

My sincere thanks to my editor Victoria Capell. We had never met till the day you picked up my manuscript. But we have become friends. You have managed to make it read much more smoothly. Some of my writing jumped so much from subject to subject, and still does. We had a time limit so I was not able to allow you to revamp the whole story. So my apologies to you Victoria. You were very patient with me.

My thanks especially to Frances and Howard Hall for constantly nudging me to write it all down and for saving all my letters.

My brother Edwin, you graciously read every page as I wrote it and encouraged me to keep on.

To all my family and special friends who kept asking how far along I was and volunteering to buy a book. Thank you, you are brave souls indeed.

Gratitude to Peter Hanks for setting up my computer and so patiently teaching me how to use it.

A very loving thank you to all my faithful financial and prayer supporters. Especially to Ross Bible Church which was my sole supporter for at least fifteen years. Then others came on board but you continued. God bless and reward you all.

A very warm thank you to each one of you. Without any of you this book would not be in print. God bless you.

Foreword

Through the years some of my friends have urged me to put on paper the story of my life. In particular, a very dear friend, Mrs. Frances (Howard) Hall has been more insistent than others. When I retired she handed me all the letters I had written to her family during my years in India. I kept a diary throughout that time as well. However, I never seriously considered writing a book. Most of the entries in my diaries were too sketchy I thought, besides I had forgotten so much.

Then others began to urge me to consider it. Now and then, I'd catch myself putting a few pictures or clippings into a file I called, "In case I write a book." But no, I should have done it soon after I retired in 1984.

About two years ago, while reading the obituaries in our local paper, I came across a line (at the end of a lady's obituary) that I could not get out of my mind. It read, "EACH TIME A PERSON DIES, A LIBRARY IS BURNED." That means once a person is gone, you can never, ever ask him/her anything again about their life. It is too late!

That hit me like a ton of bricks. My life had been so full and so rewarding. But to whom could I pass on those experiences? I never married so there were no children to pass them on to while they were growing up. But yes, I have many dear nephews and nieces, great nephews and nieces and even great greats! Why not write something down for them? In turn they can pass the information on to their posterity.

One day, I actually sat down in front of my typewriter and typed a few paragraphs. I sat back and reread it. I did not like it. Some sentences needed to be switched around. I tried. How much white out would I use to erase so much? It was hopeless (it wasn't before the invention of the computer though!). So I gave up on the book idea.

I visited my brother Edwin and he gave me a demonstration of what a computer could do. I saw those lines of print running around on the screen. He could pull out a word or a sentence and place it somewhere else!! He pulled up a letter he had written months before and showed me how he could change it. That was magic!

Could I get a computer and learn to use it? Very likely not. Then it came to me this way, "Annie, everything you know, you have learned. You can learn to operate a computer too, if you try." Then I mentioned to Edwin that my friends had asked me to write a book on my life. He picked up on that and greatly encouraged me to go ahead with it. So I started. When I let up on the writing he would call and urge me to keep going. "Keep going, Annie" he would say, "it always takes longer than you think." I kept at it and now it is finished.

Why was it important to write down my stories and experiences for my family, supporters, friends and relatives? I believe my main reason was to affirm to them that God can be trusted implicitly. He keeps His word. He never changes. He never leaves us alone for one second. He loves us more than we can fathom.

Second, I trust that by telling of my conversion others will come to know my Jesus, too.

Third, that young people might hear the call of God to become ambassadors to wherever He may lead and whenever He may call. God pays the highest dividends here and hereafter.

Fourth, that we will all be spurred on to pray more for our family and our missionaries. In the pages to follow you will see how important prayer is.

If you are helped in any way by my narrative, it would rejoice my heart to hear about it. God bless you as only He can.

Annie Goertz

I can be contacted by either of the following methods:

Mailing office:

Annie Goertz
135-2279 McCallum Road
Abbotsford, BC
V2S 6J1
Canada

Email:

orphanann@telus.net

Introduction

It was the year 1919. In world news were many important headlines such as some of the following: GERMANY SIGNS PEACE TREATY ENDING WORLD WAR (World war I had begun in 1914). TROTSKY'S ARMY DEFEATS WHITE RUSSIANS. AMERICAN LEGION FORMED IN PARIS. 388 CARAT DIAMOND FOUND IN SOUTH AFRICA. FIRST COMMERCIAL PARIS-LONDON FLIGHT ESTABLISHED.

A few more highlights of that year are that Arc Welding was invented. The beloved gospel singer Tennessee Ernie Ford was born. Incidently, Ernie went to be with the Lord in 1991 at age 72. Life expectancy was only 54.4 years. The Stanley Cup games were halted due to influenza, from which thousands died. Movie titles were very tame compared to now. Popular music during that era included a Lullaby. It would be interesting to know the title. The first Remembrance Day was held on November 11, 1919 but it was known as Armistice Day.

The government of Canada in Ottawa, Ontario looked like this: the Prime Minister was Sir Robert L. Borden, the Governor General was the Duke of Devonshire and to my surprise the ruling party was not the Liberal Party nor the Conservative but the Unionist Party.

That same year in the United States, one of the headlines was TEDDY ROOSEVELT DIES IN HIS SLEEP AT AGE SIXTY. Next Woodrow Wilson became President.

What was the economy like in 1919? Here are some sample prices:

Average income	$ 1,914.00
New car	$ 466.00
New house	$ 5,626.00
Loaf of bread	$ .10
Gallon of milk	$ .62
Gallon of gasoline	$ .15
Gold per ounce	$ 20.67
Silver per ounce	$ .54
Dow Jones Average	$ 107.00

As of the day of writing (early 1999) the Dow Jones Averages $7,842.43.

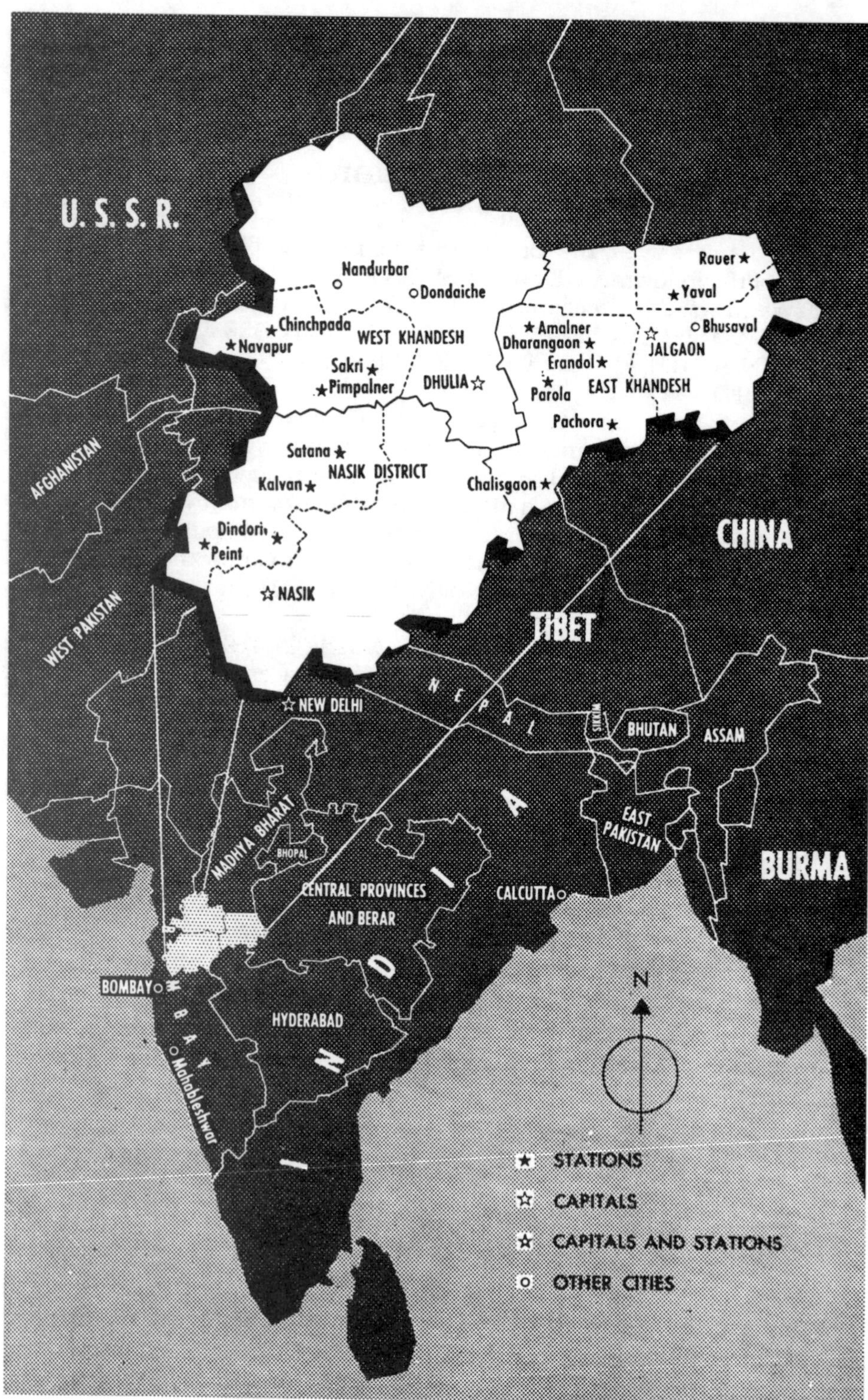
U. S. S. R.
Nandurbar
Dondaiche
Chinchpada
Navapur
WEST KHANDESH
Sakri
Pimpalner
DHULIA
Raver
Yaval
Bhusaval
Amalner
Dharangaon
Erandol
Parola
JALGAON
EAST KHANDESH
Pachora
Satana
NASIK DISTRICT
Kalvan
Chalisgaon
Dindori
Peint
NASIK
AFGHANISTAN
WEST PAKISTAN
CHINA
TIBET
NEW DELHI
NEPAL
SIKKIM
BHUTAN
ASSAM
MADHYA BHARAT
BHOPAL
EAST PAKISTAN
BURMA
CENTRAL PROVINCES AND BERAR
CALCUTTA
BOMBAY
HYDERABAD
Mahableshwar
INDIA
N
STATIONS
CAPITALS
CAPITALS AND STATIONS
OTHER CITIES

CHAPTER 1

Beginnings

The Goertz household was all astir on Tuesday, June 17, 1919. The seven children which graced their home at that time were Isaac, Jacob (Jake), Hulda, Mary, Martha, Matilda (Tillie) and Samuel (Sam). Suddenly they were all hustled off to the neighbours as it was time for the arrival of the eighth child. The midwife was immediately summoned to the home and before long the cries of a baby daughter echoed through the house. I was named Annie after my Grandmother Anna Peters Heppner, paternal aunt Annie (Goertz) Ratzlaff, and maternal aunt Annie (Heppner) Lowen. Customarily when a baby was named after a person, that individual would present the baby in question with a gift. Aunt Annie Lowen responded by crocheting a beautiful wee vest for me. I remember wearing that vest, which was sewn on to the top of a petticoat, till I was at least 6 years old even though the bottom had to be replaced several times and the top became stretched with my increase in size.

Mother holding a squirming me and Father holding Sam. See text for the names of front six.

Annie, about 1 year old.

My mother often told me that I was very sick as an infant and she feared for my life. She had her own explanations as to why I was sick but she prayed that God would spare my life. Years later doctors discovered that my problem was a congenital deformity - spina bifida occulta; how they dealt with this will be related in a later chapter.

The farm, where I was born, is located in Saskatchewan, Canada, about nine miles southwest of Waldheim and about seven miles northwest of

Hepburn. My birth was not registered in the Waldheim post office till July 18 as there appeared to be no rush to register a child in those days. Years later it was discovered that my brother Isaac had not been registered at all when he applied for a passport before embarking on a trip to other countries, including Israel, as he was unable to get a birth certificate. Since my brother was born in the middle of a cold winter when it was hard to travel to town the matter of registration eventually was totally forgotten. Occasionally, a child would be registered by a neighbour and end up with a name different than what the parents had selected because the neighbour had not remembered the name accurately. By the way, our parents were able to get Isaac registered at that late date, so he did receive his birth certificate and passport to make that trip.

Mother's parents and family. Our mother marked by X.

My parents, Peter Sievert and Catherine (Heppner) Goertz, were married on November 6, 1904. Father was born in Marion, South Dakota, USA, on September 29, 1882 and died October 24, 1973. Mother was born in a village near Blumstein, Manitoba, Canada, on June 30, 1885 and died November 6, 1976.

Grandfather Rev. Sievert Goertz and his family had migrated to Saskatchewan in 1898. My Father was sixteen at the time and adapted very well to life on the homestead in an area that would eventually be named the Waldheim District. When our Dad turned 18 his Father applied for some acreage on Dad's behalf. On the application papers he stated, "my son Peter is only 18 but he is very strong and he is a very hard worker. Please be so kind and sell it to him". The Lands Office granted the request with remarkable efficiency. The application had been submitted March 2nd and the title for the land was issued on March 24th of the same month!

When my Mother was almost six years old her Mother died while giving birth to her fifth child, a son whom they named John (Heppner). Grandfather Anton Heppner decided he could not care for a new born as well as the four older children so he gave the baby to his wife's parents to raise. He then married a single woman by the name of Pauline Spieser who had a young daughter.

My Mother's family immigrated to Saskatchewan from Manitoba, probably in 1892. They evidently travelled by train, and with them were Mother's grandparents (also Anton Heppners by name) and the senior Heppner's son David. Another couple Mr. and Mrs. George Enns were also in that party. The

Enns couple later, or as soon as possible, opened up a general grocery store in the town of Rosthern. This party's boxcar in which they had travelled, was detached from the train and left in Rosthern. They lived in one boxcar, all of them as far as we know. When they arrived there were NO buildings in Rosthern, only a water tank which was there for the train. So it made sense to leave the families near some water.

My mother and these families lived in the boxcar for about one month. They must have brought a team of oxen with them for the men scouted around in the oxcart to look for land day after day. Finally, they came upon some Homestead Land which they were able to buy at the rate of $10.00 per 160 acres! While living in the boxcar they enjoyed (?) a free ride to the town of Duck Lake once a week. The reason being there was no siding or switch at the time. When the train had delivered the goods they returned it to it's resting place till next time. The children were all warned as soon as they heard the train whistle in the distance, they were to climb up into their 'home' as fast as possible. If they did not, they would be left by themselves in the open prairie until the train returned hours later. Mother told us they all in turn got left only ONCE!

Mother remembers vividly seeing her step-mother take seed from little bundles of cloth in which she had tied them. She evidently had no hoe so she took a regular kitchen knife and went outside beside the house. She stuck it into the sod, lifted it a little and slipped in some watermelon seeds. Then she pulled out the knife and stepped on the spot. Mother said it was amazing how quickly everything grew. Of course, it was virgin soil.

After I was born, doting aunts, uncles, and cousins came to see me, as they did whenever a baby was born. It seemed the thing to do at such occasions was to ask the next oldest child if they might take the new brother or sister home with them. They thought it was fun to argue with the child. I was told many times by my Aunt Nettie (Heppner) Spieser that when my brother Herbert (Herb) was born two years later she asked me if she could take my baby brother home. The reason she gave was that our family had enough children. She said my answer was, "Oh no, we don't have too many. We do not even have enough yet!" Somebody else must have agreed with me(?!) For after Herb, came Rosie (Rosa Mae), Otto, Edwin, Miriam, and Jona (Joe). That made a grand total of 14 children - seven sons and seven daughters. Everyone grew to adulthood.

One of my earliest memories is of sitting on Dad's lap in church playing with a small aluminum comb he always carried in his suit pocket. I have never seen an aluminum comb anywhere since then. We all in turn got to play with that in church to keep us quiet. It was very special.

Another of my very early memories is of having a headache. It seems to me I must have been about one and a half years old, if it's possible to remember when one is that young. I stood by my mother while she was standing by the stove cooking and put my hand on my head and said, 'hurts' and cried. This happened so often. She would then put two kitchen chairs together and lift me on to the chairs so I could lie close beside her. Somehow it felt better then. Those headaches continued till I was sixteen. Mother had a little business of her own of fitting people with eye glasses. She made a little extra money that way. One day she asked me to come and be tested for the fun of it. To her amazement, I needed glasses badly. She ordered them at once and ever since then my headaches vanished. I believe that first pair cost five dollars.

In those early years, there were no gravel roads in the country. When it rained the roads were very muddy. Even when going by horse and buggy, or by what we called a Bennet Wagon, it was very slippery. It made me much afraid, but not too bad, as long as Dad was the driver. When my brothers would drive I was so afraid but never said a word. I was sure we would slide into the ditch and be turned upside down. That never happened though since they were careful drivers. This was several years before I went to school.

Before I go any farther, I want to make a disclaimer. While writing my life story I am writing about experiences the way I remember them. We, sisters and brothers, all grew up in the same home but not everyone will have the same memory of a particular incident or time. So, if my version is a little different than theirs, I ask them to bear with me. The same goes for my fellow missionaries in India or anyone else. I only wish I had undertaken this task years earlier when experiences and incidents would have been clearer in my mind. Hence, you will read expressions like this here and there, "as I remember . . ." I also want to thank my parents, sisters and brothers for their love, support and influence on my life.

Our parents loved us all very much. Though I do not remember them ever telling us that they loved us. They just showed it. There never was a lot of hugging and kissing except when someone was going on a trip or for serious surgery. In later years though, we showed our affection more that way and still do. We also were never told, 'You are very special,' in that many words, as seems to be the custom now. We just knew we were all special to our parents.

My birth took place in a three room house on a farm. One bedroom, livingroom and kitchen cum diningroom and a small attic. I remember lying awake sometimes listening to the whole family breathing deeply in their sleep. We had a wood heater in the livingroom and on very cold mornings we sat around it eating our bowls of porridge. Behind the heater was the wood box. It was a comfortable spot to sit and get warm. That heater supplied heat for the whole house.

In the kitchen was a range with a large firebox. Right next to the firebox quite a large tank was attached which we filled with water. It was always real hot, at least when the stove was in use. So though our house had no plumbing we always had hot water. Behind the range was another wood box. The oven too, was always hot and ready for baking anytime. And bake we did every day! That is, bread had to be baked every day except Sunday. So on Saturday, a bigger batch was made as well as a large batch of buns. We did no cooking on Sunday. Food for Sunday was prepared the day before. Often we boiled potatoes with their skins on for salad as well as eggs. Farmer sausage was fried, or fruit soup made which we called 'mousse'. It had to be something that would keep without a refrigerator.

On Sunday, relatives or friends would drop by for lunch. No one needed to be invited it seemed. It was probably more common to come over for a meal we call 'faspa'. It's a lighter meal which is served earlier than supper. Buns or bread would be served with butter and jam, cookies or cake and coffee. A special treat might be some cheese or cinnamon buns. Our turn came too, to go to an Auntie's place for a meal or faspa. Those times were times of great enjoyment. It seems we have lost that spontaneous way of visiting friends and neighbours.

Most of us remember so well occasions when Mother had just dished out all the food on our plates. Before we could say grace and start to eat we saw a car appear on the yard. So quickly Mother would bring out another plate. Take a wee bit out of each of our portion and the plate was ready for the guest. The guest never knew that we all had a part in that donation. Sometimes there had not been too much on our plates. I mean of the main food because it might have been left from the noon meal. But we always had enough bread so we did not go hungry. At such times Mother would quote a saying or proverb while she was filling the plate. "Wass vier einem kaum genieget macht ein kaestlich fest vier zwei." Translation - what's barely enough for one, makes a lovely feast for two. In that way she taught us how to share what we had. She had many wonderful sayings with which she taught us a lot and I will quote more of these as my story unfolds.

If you had been in a large family like ours, you would soon know why Mother dished out the food. Everyone was hungry and hungry tummies cause the eyes to see big. So there might not have been enough to go around for everyone. She always seemed to know exactly how many pieces of chicken or whatever she had so everyone always got enough and fair. There were exceptions of course. When we had corn on the cob (which was from our huge garden) we could eat as much as we wanted. Then we were allowed to pile up the empty cobs sort of pagoda style and see whose pile was the tallest. That was fun. Also at Easter we would boil a huge kettle of eggs and we could eat as many as we wanted to. That was possible because we had our own chickens.

A custom among the Mennonites is to make portzilka (fruit fritters) for New Year's. We used dried prunes and raisins. Some of our acquaintances put very little fruit in the batter. Mother would say, "if we're going to make it, it must be good." So she instructed us to put lots of fruit in. It was the same with almost any dessert we made. It had to be tasty and lots of it. When we made our own ice cream we usually made it with pure cream in buckets (with a custard base) and two gallons of it for one meal. Yummy!

Some other dishes that we made were veranika (you could call them perogies) with cottage cheese and eggs. No potatoes or cheese in them like you buy in the store. We ate them with cream gravy and sugar. Some eat veranika with farmer sausage and gravy. Roll kuchen is something else we enjoyed a lot in the summer time when the watermelons were ripe. Roll cookies are fried in deep fat. For soups we had noodle soup (homemade noodles), cabbage borscht, green leaves soup (I think the English name for it is Sorrel). Butter soup made with potatoes, a bit of onion and spice. Salmon soup is something I just could not eat. It smelled too fishy. I used to eat bread and butter that meal. Then one day Mother set the bowl of soup on the table and announced, 'Today we are all going to eat salmon soup.' She didn't look at anyone in particular, but I and everyone else knew whom she had in mind. She served me along with the rest and I just started to eat. To my great amazement it tasted really good. I ate it ever since. Oh yes, I nearly forgot I also did not try borscht. One day when our parents were away some of my older sisters decided to teach me to eat it. They fed it to me. We struggled a bit but some did get into my mouth and to my great amazement it too tasted delicious. Thanks to my sisters I have been very fond of it ever since.

Another time when our parents were away my brothers caught a rabbit- probably shot it. They brought it home and my older sisters fried it. I can't remember if I ate any or not. Seems to me I did because they said it tasted like chicken.

We had a lot of gophers and they ruined the crops. So the municipality offered a penny or maybe even a nickel for every gopher tail we'd bring in. We'd tie them on a string and hang them up in the shed until we had enough to take in for our money. Usually two people were needed to catch the gopher. One would pour a bucket of water into one hole while the other stood at the other hole with a big stick. As a rule one wallop would finish the gopher off when he came out.

Sometimes when our parents were gone for the evening in the summer, some of us did not really want to go to bed before they returned. So we took old blankets or jackets and lay on our backs out in the front yard. We'd talk and talk about all kinds of things. We'd try to see formations in the clouds as they floated in the sky. Some clouds went faster than others. Some darker, some lighter and fluffy like cotton. We'd look at the stars and find the big and small dippers, also the soldier. When the conversation came to a lull my mind would go to the God who made it all and kept it all in place. I often wondered why the stars did not fall on us. Though sometimes we saw a falling star but we knew that was a natural happening. Then I thought about Eternity. How long would Eternity be? Our parents told us and we heard it in church too that it means forever and ever and ever. But there had to be an end somewhere! I was very small at the time but I knew I was not ready to spend Eternity in Heaven and that was where I wanted to go. Later we went to bed and that thought still lingered in my mind for a while and many times after that.

Our parents spoke Plaut Dietsch (some call it Low German) and so that was the first language we learned. At that time it was not reduced to writing but now it is. However, we heard only German in Church and Sunday School. We heard it as babies and just picked it up. I understood it all and could read it because the only Bibles and hymn books we had were in German. I learned a lot of the hymns by heart and remember some of them to this day. Later in school we learned to write German as well.

Our church was the Brotherfield Mennonite Brethren Church. In churches the men and boys sat on one side and the women and girls on the other with an aisle between. My first recollection of church was that we (women) came in on the south side entrance which opened to what must have been the first chapel they had since it was very small. There were several rows of long pews - two and two pushed together. I soon discovered they were pushed together that way so that the mothers could put their babies on those benches to sleep. Older children slept there too. It made a safe place so they could not fall off. I remember Mother carrying her baby wrapped in a woolen maroon coloured blanket. It had a nice soft cotton lining as well as flannel blankets. The baby usually fell asleep during the drive to church so was gently put down on the bench so he or she would not awaken.

In the winter time we had the worship service in the morning and we all stayed for lunch. Each family brought their own - which usually consisted of fried farmer sausage, buns and cold coffee in a crock with a cork stopper. Oh, I can close my eyes and still remember how good it tasted. We had cloth napkins so as to protect our Sunday-go-to-meeting clothes. Then after lunch we had Sunday School. One of my teachers was Mr. Pete Jantzen and he was good. Then it was time to go home and do the chores all over again. Perhaps there was an evening service or else a Yugendverien (put on by the young people) but everyone came. In the summer we had both Sunday School and the service in the morning.

On certain Sundays the church observed foot washing, probably once a quarter. Then, the curtains in the aisle, which were there to separate Sunday School classes, were drawn so that the men and women could not see each other. One woman would take a basin of water and a towel and go to another woman and wash and dry her feet. I always felt it was a very serious matter as I watched them. Sometimes I'd see a woman cry when she saw another woman approach her with the basin. Sometimes I saw them embrace first and say something. I asked Mother about it and she said that they probably were asking each other for forgiveness before they could truly wash each other's feet. That left a deep impression on me. I don't think that I was any more than five years old at the time. As far as I know foot washing is not observed anymore in any churches.

There were not many missionaries when I was a child. My mother's younger sister Helen Heppner was a missionary in China and she came to visit us. She told us stories which I do not remember anymore but they made an impression on me. One thing I do remember is a small pair of very tiny leather shoes which she gave us. She told us that the Chinese women bind their feet so that they cannot grow past a certain length and will fit into tiny shoes.

I believe two or maybe three missionary couples visited our church and told us about those that had never heard about Jesus. They showed us slides in black and white. Some of the faces were taken real close up and the sad face almost covered the whole screen. I can still see it in my mind's eye. If I were an artist I could draw it from memory. Those pictures are forever etched in my mind. I felt very sorry for them and was so glad that those missionaries were willing to go and tell them about Jesus. I did not know at that time that the Lord would call me also to go to a foreign country as a missionary, specifically to India.

We were all taught early to work. We heard it said around the house that, 'Work makes life sweet.' Sometimes one or the other of us decided we did not want to do a certain chore then and there. The response was, 'The bible says that whoever does not work should not eat.' That settled it for us for we certainly wanted to enjoy the next meal.

Our family did mixed farming. We had wheat, oats and barley. As for animals we had lots of horses, cows, pigs, sheep, guinea hens, chickens, geese, turkeys and ducks. We would slaughter cows for beef and also sheep. Pork we never ate. Our parents had always eaten pork in their parent's homes. Then they got married and in the fall they butchered a pig. They cooked and ate some of the pork but both got deadly sick. Since they had only been Christians a few months they thought perhaps it was God telling them that pork was not to be eaten like in the Old Testament. So they gave ALL the meat away to their friends and never had any more pork in their house ever, and never ate it anywhere else. Consequently, we did not eat it either. However, I learned to eat it many years later and enjoy it. I believe all my sisters and brothers did the same.

I mentioned butchering an animal in the fall. Well, it was a big day in the community for everyone did the same. Neighbours took turns helping each other for that day. I remember so well that I could not stand the sight or smell of fresh meat in the house. So on that day, I would ask mother if I could have a sandwich to take to school so I did not have to see it. She agreed.

You must know we did not have deep freezers in those days. No, not even electricity. So how was the meat to be preserved for the winter months? One or two barrels were set up on the north side of our house and they became our 'deep freezers.' And it was 'deep' indeed because in those years the temperature dropped very low. It often went to 50° below zero in what we called the REAUMUR way of measuring temperature. Some readers may not have heard of REAUMUR. It was invented by a man by that name in 1730. Zero marks the freezing point and 80° the boiling point of water. Later the Fahrenheit method came into use and it took me a long time to get used to it. Then in India, Fahrenheit changed to the Celsius method. Took me a while too, and of course that is what is used in Canada now and in various parts of the world.

Now going back to the meat - one layer of snow was put on the bottom of the barrel, then a layer of meat. That was continued until the barrel was full. The meat was covered with a wooden lid and on it a big stone to secure it from dogs. It never entered our mind that someone might steal it and no one ever did. That meat always lasted till spring.

As I said before, we grew our own grain. Dad had a Hammer Mill and he was able to put different knives and screens in for different grains. So he ground the wheat for flour, cream of wheat, whole wheat and bran. That stood our family in good stead for that meant we always had bread and porridge. Dad used to grind our neighbours grain for them too. The mill also shredded hay for fodder. I should tell you right here that one day my brother Jake was feeding some sheaves into the mill when his mittens got caught in the knives. His right arm was pulled into the machine a way but somehow by the grace of God, he managed to disengage the rollers with his shoulder. As I remember, that reversed the rollers and he was able to pull out his hand only to see that half of the mitten was eaten off. That meant that his four fingers were cut off at the second knuckle. His first thought was, "I can still play the fiddle because there is enough left of my fingers!" The doctor came out from town and sewed it up by stretching the skin over the ends of the bone. There was no anaesthesia used. The pain was so bad he almost twisted the metal bed frame with his left hand. The doctor showed Mother how to put

Ozonol ointment on it and she dressed the fingers faithfully for weeks.

Our garden provided us with all the potatoes, vegetables, rhubarb, gooseberries and red currants we needed. To preserve our vegetables we stored them is a cellar (not a basement) under our house. We had a trapdoor in the floor of our pantry. Rough wooden stairs led down to what was more or less a huge hole in the ground. No finished walls and the floor was of dirt. We did have one dividing wooden wall though which divided it in two areas. Shelves were put up on that wall. In that area we stored our canned vegetables and fruit, etc. In the other area a load of sand had been dumped. In it we buried carrots, parsnips and red beets. The sand seemed to preserve them better. The potatoes were on piles in a different spot. In winter we would be sent down there to dig out carrots or beets, or whatever was needed for the next meal. I remember how too often toward spring some of the vegetables would get soft or even rot. But there were always enough firm ones. It was not very pleasant then for once in a while something would feel too soft and clammy and cold. It was not a vegetable but a salamander! That would send us screaming up the stairs. Then someone older would come down with a lantern and help.

For food we hardly needed to go to town, we had almost everything we needed. But for salt, sugar, cocoa, and spices we would need to go.

As for clothes, they were a little harder to come by. There was not money for cloth but we had flour sacks. They made strong dresses for us girls and shirts for the boys as well as pillow cases and even bed sheets. We were poor, I guess, but we did not really know that for everyone was in the same situation. It taught us to make do with what we had and it was good for us.

Annie back row middle, Rosa left front row

The flour sacks had to be prepared by washing out the print and then bleaching them in the sun. The sun would take out the last traces of lettering and colour. When they were pure white we dyed some sacks one colour for school dresses and the rest a different colour for church dresses. The pattern of the dresses was changed from time to time according to the prevalent style. I was so proud when I got a new one.

Because of our large family, we were later given used clothes but they did not fit. They had to be made over. So I learned to sew at an early age from watching my older sisters. We made our own patterns by laying paper on our old clothes. Winter coats would start looking shabby after a few years. Our parents could not afford new ones. I imagine again that I learned from my sisters how to take all the seams apart, brush away all the loose threads and then to sew up the pieces by reversing the cloth. The finished product looked like

Joe feeding lamb, Herb holding nephew Cliff, Edwin with niece Elma, Otto, Miriam feeding lamb.

a new coat. It was a lot of work but it was well worth it for Mother praised me very much. Dresses and coats were sometimes handed down from one to another. I was always glad for a hand-me-down because it was new to me and I loved the sister that gave it to me. She needed a new one because she grew taller.

We had sheep so the wool was used for making quilts, socks, stockings, house slippers, mittens and gloves. But first the sheep had to be sheared. I was so proud when I was deemed old enough to help. The first few I sheared, I knicked the skin a bit and it bled. But the sheep held still as it says in the Bible. But I felt so bad. We washed the wool and hung it out on the line to dry. The washing matted it so it had to be loosened up by pulling it gently apart with our fingers. The next step was to learn how to spin yarn for knitting or crocheting. We had our own spinning wheel. It was hard at first to co-ordinate feet and hands. We had to pedal with our feet and then twist and stretch the wool in just the right way. The finished product was wound in large balls ready for the next step. For quilts we had to card the wool by hand with wooden carders. A carder was a metal toothed instrument of which we needed two to do the job. We placed a small amount of wool on one carder and then combed it, as it were, with the other carder. When it was a nice piece of thick smooth wool we removed it carefully and laid it aside in a box until there was enough for a quilt. I still have a woolen quilt. The stockings were so warm but s-o-o-o very itchy.

In the early thirties, the great depression set in and the necessities of life were harder to come by. When there was no rain there was no grain. Father and the boys would plant the fields and then they prayed and waited for rain. I remember Dad asking Mother to come with him in the car to go and see what condition the crops were like. They came back looking sad because the crop was so sparse coming up. I sensed the concern they had as to how to make it through the fall and winter with their family. Come harvest time there may have been a wee bit to cut just for fodder for the animals but none for flour. The cows also could not give milk in the winter time because of lack of fodder. That meant there was no milk for porridge or postum, let alone to drink.

A lovely picture of my parents

For a year, or probably longer, we and all our neighbours, were on what was then called Government Relief. They provided some necessities but all I can remember distinctly is the dried fish. Boxes of it. Oh yes, they sent us some canned fish too. It was called Chicken Haddie. It was quite a novelty at first. Mother boiled the dried fish, baked it and fried it. We even ground it up for hamburgers, rather fishburgers. I must say McDonald's tastes better! We were very thankful but sometimes it all seemed too fishy. I never heard our parents complain. They prayed a lot.

We heard of some people using the big slabs or fillet of fish to nail on their outhouse walls to make them more wind proof. I don't know if they actually did or not. Made for a good story anyway!

CHAPTER 2

The Family Moves

Rosa, Otto, Edwin, Annie (in tires) playing in the sand, yellow house in background.

When I was seven years old our family moved two miles north to a much larger home. This one was painted sort of a yellow colour. The old house was never painted but we used to give it a coat of diesel oil once in a while and paint around the windows and doors which made it look nice. It also helped preserve the wood. The new house was a two storey building. It had a large kitchen/dining room, a living room, an entrance, a nice sized pantry and a bathroom. The upstairs was nicely finished and divided into sleeping quarters for us children. Oh yes, there was a bedroom downstairs for our parents and the baby.

There was a summer kitchen apart from the house. It had an old wood stove in it, some counters, a working area and a huge, what we called, Russian stove. It was built of bricks. We used it to bake our bread and buns in. There was a large fireplace at the bottom where we built a big fire. When the wood was burned up, we pushed an iron rack into it with 7 or 8 loaves of bread placed on it. When the door closed the bread or buns baked beautifully in it just from the heat of the bricks. That kept our house cooler in summer time. We did our canning out there too and often our cooking.

We sometimes had men come around to see us, we called them bums. They came for food which we gave them. One time just after we had cooked our meal a "bum" came and before knocking on our door he went into that kitchen. Our parents were not home and we did not know what he might have put into our food. We were afraid to eat it but I am sure we did. For the time being it was a bit of a scary story to add to the spice of life. As far as we younger ones were concerned it was a big story. Once in a while these men would spend the night in our home. Our parents were very hospitable and one of my brothers would give up his bed for him. Sad to say sometimes they left behind some bedbugs. If we thought of checking the bed soon enough we could contain them in that bed only. We used kerosene on the mattress and that took care of it. Woe to us if we didn't check right away. I am sure my generation of readers will know exactly what I am talking about.

We lived right next door to the school-Rose River School. Now it was my turn to start school. Since we lived so close it meant we could always walk to school and come home for lunch too. I have always been very fond of sandwiches. The previous school where all my older sisters and brothers attended was Carson School. When they came home in the afternoon I would quickly look in their lunch pail for left-over sandwiches. Sometimes there were some and I enjoyed them. Now in the new school there was no need for lunches. Consequently, to this day I feel 'jipped' because I never got to carry a lunch pail and sandwiches.

I knew no English except a few nursery rhymes. Jack Spratt had a cat, it said Meow-Meow. Another:

Jack and Jill went up a hill
To fetch a pail of water
Jack fell down and broke his crown
And Jill came tumbling after.

I had learned them from listening to my sisters and brothers. The rule in school was that no one was to speak Plat Deutsch but only English. How else would we learn English? Makes sense. My first teacher was Mr. John Gossen. He was very kind. When he said a word or sentence we were to repeat it. Well, they all did except I. This went on for several months. I was afraid to say it wrong so I said nothing.

Unknown to me, Mr. Gossen had talked to my parents. We had smart parents. They invited my teacher for supper. I thought that was wonderful until supper was over. Then Mr. Gossen told my parents in my presence that I refused to say a word in school. My Dad asked me if that was so. I nodded. "Well, why don't you talk?" he asked. I told them that I did not know English, so how could I talk? My Dad explained to me that I would learn it word by word if I would only repeat after the teacher. Then he turned to the teacher and said, "Tomorrow Annie will repeat after you." And I did! I had been so afraid of making a mistake.

A few months later my friend Clara Kasper fell down and got a nose bleed. I ran to tell the teacher, "Clara's nose is bleeding, no blooding, no bleeding." He smiled and told me that I had it correct the first time. I enjoyed our school text books. They had such lovely stories with morals. I often wish I

My school - the X marks me

had been able to keep them. In fact I did, but our parent's house burned years later and all that any of us had in the house was gone. The books were not the most important either.

Mr. Gossen was our teacher only for one year. Then Miss Nettie Schmor came. I was to have gone into Grade 2 but because I was good in reading and spelling I was put right into Grade 3. Our school was a one room school house. So one advantage was that we learned by listening to the other grades. If my memory is correct Miss Schmor also stayed only one year. For Grade 4 I had Miss Tena Welk, who later married Mr. Frank Wiens. By the way, Mrs. Wiens is in her nineties and lives in a nursing home in Maple Ridge, BC. That is as of May 2000. Then I skipped Grade 5. I still had Mrs. Wiens for Grade 6. Skipped Grade 7 and then my teacher was Mr. Ed Harms for Grade 8. So that made only 5 years for my schooling and I was 12 years old. I later regretted the fact my schooling was cut so short. More about that later.

In those years, the crops were better. We had lots of milk, butter and cream. Often on Saturday before going to bed, Mother would pour us each a cup of cream and we'd eat a fresh bun with it. It was delicious. Every evening after milking the cows, (in the summer only) we'd strain fresh milk into a two-gallon syrup pail. Then we would tie a long rope to the handle and lower it into our deep well. After a few hours it was nice and cold and we all drank some before going to bed. That seems to have given us all strong bones. None of us is prone to broken bones.

We also made our own cheese. We bought Rennet tablets which were added to the milk to cause it to thicken and turn into curds. We added butter colouring to it and pressed the mixture into large pans or moulds. When they finished dripping we turned out the cheese heads and placed them outside on the fence posts in front of our house to dry. It was good. We even sold some to relatives or neighbours.

In the winter we were able to keep our milk, cream and butter cool in our pantry. But in summer it was a different matter. My Father and brothers dug a big hole about 8 feet deep in the ground near our fruit garden. A pointed roof was built over the hole. Then in the spring before the break-up of the ice in the river, the men folk went to the river with a sleigh. They chopped or sawed huge chunks of ice and brought it home. They put a layer of saw-dust down in the ice cellar, then a layer of ice blocks, then more saw-dust and ice until it was full. A crude ladder was placed inside just in front of the little door. We made little holes in the ice and set our milk and cream in there. The ice usually lasted till the fall.

Many times in the summer we'd make our own ice cream. We had a two gallon metal ice cream can which we fastened inside a wooden pail. Then we took turns turning the handle. It would freeze rapidly. On days when the whole family was at home, we made four gallons of it. Seems to me we ate as much as we wanted. It was so rich so I imagine we could not handle too much.

However, one day my brother Herb got very sick during the night. He blamed it on the ice cream which we had for supper. It turned out that he was actually coming down with the flu. After that he always put his ice cream in an enamel cup and melted it on the back of the stove before he ate it. Many years later, however he was able to eat regular ice cream again and enjoyed it.

Father would sometimes tell people that he and Mother need not quarrel about which one had more help. While Dad had seven sons to help on the farm, Mother had seven daughters to help in the house. We needed a big garden so that was the girl's job. Of course, those jobs were not always that well defined. I am very thankful for what I learned from Dad while working on the field or helping with carpentry or even masonry when we built an addition on to our first house years later. More about that to come.

I remember so well how wonderful it was when at this time I was given some jobs to do that adults do. I cannot put into words how I felt when my parents trusted me. I took the responsibility and their trust very seriously. I felt I could do anything when they trusted me and did not want to disappoint them.

The first such incident was when one winter someone needed to go to the town of Waldheim to get the mail and buy some groceries. I volunteered and was allowed to go. It was very cold, so Mother put some stones or bricks into the old kitchen stove oven to warm up. Dad hitched a horse to the little sleigh which we called a cutter. It had only one seat. The dictionary describes it as, "a light sleigh." I wore warm clothes and double mittens, and a scarf around my cap and neck. The hot stones were wrapped in gunny sacks and placed on the floor of the sleigh, I put my feet on them and a big blanket over my lap completed the outfit. No queen could have been any happier than I when Dad handed me the reins. Dad trusted me with that big horse and to do the family business! What joy!

After I travelled nine miles I reached town and drove up to the row of hitching posts. I found my way out of the blankets as if it had been a cacoon and carefully covered the stone and seats to keep it all warm for my return trip. I tied the horse up to the post like I had seen Dad do and gave it the hay that I had brought. I knew Dad would be so pleased if he could see me.

As I remember, there were no more than four or five places of business on the street and only on one side. There was Mr. Siemens General Store, and Mr. Abrams store - I think he sold cloth. There was the Post Office and A Weisenamt Building. The latter being a sort of Trust for orphans. Then there was the "Pool" where men played pool. There was some other business in the same building so once in a while we had to go in there. I remember the air inside looked blue from the cigarette smoke. To this day when I enter a room or building where people have been smoking I say, "This smells like a pool room."

Having completed all the business, I hitched up the horse and sleigh again and started on my way home. I had been admonished I must try to be back home before dark and I was. As I drove up to our front door Dad came out with a big smile and a 'well done' for me. Dad unhitched the horse for me as it was cold. Whenever we were sent on an errand in a sleigh or buggy with horses we were given instructions as to what to do if a sudden snow or rainstorm should blow up. In a blinding snowstorm we might not be able to see the road Dad said. So he told us to never forget that the horses always know the way home. We were to slacken the reins and let the horses go for they would always bring us back home safely. When leaving home, we had to pull the reins right or left to guide the horses for they had no idea where we wanted to go. But coming home was different. Also the horses always wanted to go faster on the way home.

I said I worked in the fields with my Dad and brothers. I believe all of us girls did. During harvesting we all stooked the sheaves of grain. When it was a good crop the sheaves were very heavy. We'd stand two sheaves up first leaning against each other. Then one on each side of those two and maybe two or four more. The air and sun were to get through and dry the grain for threshing later. I was proud even if tired, to look out over the field and see all the neat piles of sheaves.

After a few weeks they were dry and were then thrown onto a hayrack. The threshing machine was set up on the field and a crew of men operated the affair. A tractor was hitched to the threshing machine to run it. But Dad had a big steam engine and mostly used it instead as it was cheaper to run. Then the hay-racks of sheaves were brought to the machine one after another until all the grain had been threshed. The grain came out of a spout and was blown into a wagon-box. We children took turns in the wagon to shovel the grain along evenly.

Some of the grain was stored in granaries till the price might go up or be sold later when we had need of cash. I remember shovelling grain in there and can still smell the dust. On one such occasion I came out of the granary with a very dirty face from the dust and perspiration. I did not wash my face but when I sat down to have supper I was asked why I did not wash my face. I said, "Well, won't I get a bigger piece of pie when Mother sees how hard I worked?" Mother never let me forget that. And years later on occasion would give me a bigger piece as she smiled.

Most of our grain though was hauled directly from the field to the Grain Elevator in town. At first, I rode with my brother or older sister on these trips. Then when I 'knew the ropes' I did it by myself. Again I was very proud to be trusted with two horses and a wagon load of grain. I was scared though to drive the wagon up the steep incline into the elevator. So I would dismount and go inside and kindly ask the 'elevator man' if he would do it for me. He always did it very graciously. I must have been eleven or twelve years old. We also used the horses to haul fodder home from the field in big hayracks.

At one such time when I was going back to the field (which was about two miles) with an empty hayrack, one of the reins tore. That scared me because I had no idea where the horses would take me so I jumped off. No sooner did I jump off when the neighbours dogs heard us and barked very hard. Now I was sure they would tear me in pieces and I was very afraid of strange dogs. So I started to run as fast as I could (fear helped me along) and managed to grab a hold of the rack to get back on just as the dogs reached me. I knew I could not guide the horses but they knew the road so well they just went on and stopped at the usual place. So I tied the reins together and was able to go back home again after the rack was loaded.

Dad was the only farmer with a steam engine for miles and miles. So he used to go to the neighbours to help with their threshing. Always at 12:00 noon Dad would blow the whistle. That was the signal that it was time to stop and eat, not only for our crew but also for the neighbouring farmers. Come to think of it, Dad had quite a pioneering spirit. Not only did he have the first steam engine, but also the first radio, gramophone and car in the area.

As to the radio, it had tubes in it. There were two Christian radio speakers that I remember from those days. One was Oscar Lowry and the other Dr. Charles Fuller. When the program came on all of us children were summoned to the living room and we all sat and listened. I don't remember anyone objecting. The gramophone had records that looked like a sleeve. We slipped them onto a shaft-like thing. There was a big horn from which the music came. It was a wind-up machine.

Our first car was a Ford that had cloth windows. Or were they of a celluloid substance? The second car I think was a Whippet make. It had glass windows. So when we talked about which car we would go in we asked if it was the 'glass car' or the Ford. For a while we went to church in two cars but each one was instructed to come back in the same car he had gone in. That way no one would be left. Twice a child was left at church sleeping on the back bench because each driver thought that he must have decided to go home in the other car. A quick search or roll call indicated the child was left at church. A trip was made back and the still sleeping child was unaware of being left.

Going back to the field work again for a bit. I want to mention that after some of my older brothers were away from home going to Bible School or whatever, I accompanied our Dad to the field. It meant getting up at 4:00 in the morning and coming back after dark. Mother had prepared a lunch and a big crock of coffee with a cork stopper. The coffee of course, was all cold by lunch time but that did not matter. That's how everybody drank it, there were no thermoses then. I still think of it as having a very special flavour which went along with sitting down from our labour and being refreshed by it and the food. I never heard anyone ever say, "That coffee is c-o-l-d."

I mentioned earlier that we used to lower a pail of milk into the well to get cold before we drank it at bedtime. I want to say something about our well. It was very deep and we had a hand pump. But no matter how much you worked that handle up and down you could not get any water. You had to pour in some water first to prime the pump. For that reason we always kept a can of water near the pump. Each one had to remember to refill it again after using it.

One Saturday after my sister and I had peeled the boiled potatoes for salad the next day, we went out to play. We were trying to set up a table between two trees. The huge board platform we were trying to lift was very heavy and I let my end fall. It fell on my right foot. Unfortunately there were several nails sticking out on the under side and they went right through my foot in three places. We screamed and Dad came to pull the nails out of my foot. Now there was dirt on my foot too. Dad carried meinto the house and Mother put my foot in a pail of warm skimmed milk and I soaked it in that for a long time. As far as I remember I never got any infection in it. That milk bath was probably not what the doctor would order nowadays. But Mother always had a remedy for everything and it helped. She was always so loving. Just a stroke of her hand across our fevered brow would help a lot.

I believe all of us had a lot of earache when we were small. I remember I had my share of them and it was always worse at night. Poor Mother, she must have been so tired but when we trudged downstairs in the middle of the night she never complained. She got up and warmed a spoonful of thick cream over the kerosene lamp and poured it into my ear. She plugged it with a bit of cotton and sent me upstairs again with a hot water bottle to put on my ear. It always seemed to help. Bless her!

My Mother, Aunt Nettie, Aunt Helen. (who went to China)

We had our share of childhood diseases too, like mumps, chicken pox, measles, flu and colds. When one of us got sick, Mother would sometimes say that we might as well all hurry up and get it because sooner or later we all had to. And the younger we got it the better. There were no vaccinations for years. But when they were introduced we were told not to have them because they knew someone had died after one. I, for one, was not anxious to have anyone give me a needle because it might hurt. I discovered years later that I could not go overseas without them and they were not as bad as I imagined.

CHAPTER 3

My Conversion

Our parents became Christians about six months or so after they were married. Mother had assurance of salvation first and she often told me how she tried to help Dad. She would tell him what she did and asked him to do the same, namely ask Jesus for forgiveness and then believe that He had done so. She also told him, "If only I could I would feed it to you with a spoon." He did receive assurance of salvation and they were both baptized right away. So we were all born into a Christian home and for this we are eternally grateful.

Dad did not have very much money when they got married but he did buy a fifty cent gold wedding ring for each of them. But after they were saved they felt it was wrong to wear jewellery. So they took them off and threw them in the fire and watched them burn. Mother used to say she wished they had not done that. But I don't think she ever got another. Oh, by the way, after the ring purchases were made Dad still had fifty cents in his pocket on their wedding day.

Now I must go back a bit. Dad had been able to purchase a small section of homestead land from the government and built a small one room house on it, probably made of sod. They had no furniture except a bed. So Dad cut a large tree into pieces that would be about the right height to sit on since they had no chairs. I suppose one or two of those were cut a little longer to serve as a table. That's all they had for the first year. When Mother neared the end of her first pregnancy they had a nice surprise one day when they came home. There were two new chairs standing by their front door. Her parents had done it and they appreciated it very much.

Dad had been given a team of horses by his parents and probably a buggy. Then Mother's parents gave her a cow which was tied behind the buggy and brought to their new home. But one other gift she received from them was a frying pan. No farmer's wife could do without one. How they got their dishes I do not remember. I forgot to say that our parents were married in a newly constructed barn. Her father decided that before he brought the cattle into it for the winter it might as well be used for the wedding. Mother made her wedding dress of dark brown material with a tight waist band as was the custom.

As soon as they became Christians they established a family altar. They read the Bible together and prayed every morning before breakfast and again before bed. They kept this up till their dying days.

When the children came along each one was introduced to the same twice daily custom. Mother taught each of us a short prayer that her mother had taught her. It was in German but translated it would read something like this, "Fear God little child, God sees and knows all things. Amen." It was not really a prayer as such. In later years I thought I came to understand it better and her reason for teaching it to us. I believe it was to help us realize that God saw us all the time, even when we did wrong. But also if we might be in danger or lost we were to remember that God could see us and was with us. Also if we told a lie or took something that was not ours God saw and heard even if Mother and Dad did not. Another lesson I learned from that prayer was that whenever we called on Him, He would hear us.

Our parents having devotions.

As more children were born, the custom in devotions was changed a little. After we all sat down to breakfast Dad would read a chapter from the Bible and then he prayed alone. But in the evening before going to bed we all gathered in one room and Dad would read another chapter in the Bible. Sometimes Dad would go to one or the other whom he felt he had wronged during the day and ask for forgiveness. That left a deep impression on all of us, I'm sure. Then we all knelt down to pray. First Dad, then Mother, then the children in turn according to our age down to the youngest that was old enough to talk.

When we were a bit older, probably 5 years old, Mother taught us a longer German prayer. It went something like this. "Christ's blood and righteousness, this be my adorned and honoured dress. That will be sufficient when I go to Heaven and stand before God. Amen." I remember praying that prayer every night when it came my turn. One night when I was about 8 years old it came my turn to pray I could not and did not. Finally the next one prayed and I was relieved.

I had always known that I was a sinner and could not go to Heaven. But that night it suddenly hit me, as it were, that I was really lying every time I prayed that prayer. I knew it was a sin to lie, too. So I never prayed again with the family till years later when I became a Christian. Then I prayed my own prayer as did my sisters and brothers as soon as they were saved. After I quit praying with the family, Mother would often mention my name in prayer which made me feel very uncomfortable. However, she and Dad always prayed for us. One sentence Mother often prayed during those evening prayer times was, "Lord, grant that when we get to Heaven, we may be able to say, 'Lord, here are we and the children you entrusted to us'".

Whenever, Mother or any family member asked me why I did not pray anymore I would not answer, just cry. I felt no one would be able to help me.

I very much wanted to be saved and often asked the Lord to save me even when I was a very small child. I knew I had to ask Jesus to come into my heart and I did that very often. Sometimes every night but nothing happened. I wanted to feel I was saved, how else would I know? Often I would wait till my sisters were asleep and I would get up and pray. Then I'd wait for something to happen though I did not know what. If nothing happened, then I'd close my eyes really tight and pray again. Then I'd open my eyes to see if I could see a light. Or I'd listen carefully for Jesus to say "Annie, your sins are forgiven." Sometimes I'd look for a vision of Jesus on the cross. I had heard older people in our church tell of such things that had happened to them and that they knew for sure that they were saved.

I always liked testimony meetings in hopes that I might get some help. However, I also heard some of the older church members tell how they were saved and then add, "I hope I can hold out till the end." and that puzzled me. I thought if they didn't know for sure, then how could I?

Other times I thought about all God had to do and all the people on this world He had to take care of. Adults had big problems and they needed God's help. Besides how many people were there in the world that were dying and each one needed God to take them to Heaven. How could He listen to a little girl pray or see her cry? I must be patient and let Him take care of serious things first. My parents could have helped me but I thought nobody had my problem, so how could anyone help?

I attended prayer meetings. When I heard of a missionary conference in the area or even farther away I would go. Surely the missionaries that knew how to explain it so simply so even the uneducated heathen could understand would say something in their speech so that I could understand.

When I was about 11 years old, Rev. Edwin Erickson came to the school I was attending. He worked with the Canadian Sunday School Mission (CSSM). The teacher gave permission for him to talk to the whole school (which was a one room school). He told us if we would memorize 500 verses from the Gospel of John and be able to recite them, we could attend Bible Camp free for one week. He gave us the list which we took home. Two of my older sisters, Martha and Matilda (Tillie) memorized them too.

It was explained to us that after we memorized the first twenty verses we could recite them to our teacher (how things have changed), then he would report it to the mission. Then they would send us a button to pin on our dresses. For the next forty verses, we were given a book from Moody Colportage. I believe we did that till we received 5 books. Then during summer holidays we went to camp at Wakaw Lake, Saskatchewan.

We slept on straw in tents. We, boys and girls, were divided into groups with a leader. My leader was Miss Roxie Menzies. Rev. Erickson did most of the preaching, though there were others like Mr. Lloyd Hunter and Mr. D. N. Aikenhead. At one morning service I was very convicted when the altar call was given. But I was such a shy child, I did not have the courage to go forward with the others. I prayed, "Dear God, please send Roxie over to talk to me." As soon as we were dismissed I saw Roxie making her way to me. God had answered my prayer so He must have time for me! Roxie took me to nearby bushes where we could talk alone. She explained to me how to be saved. I told her I had done that probably hundreds of times and nothing had happened. She realized I was looking for feelings and explained to me I must trust God's word because feelings would change from day to day. How wonderful it was! I was HAPPY!

Then we walked back to the tents but on the way I heard a voice which I did not recognize as Satan's. He told me I was saved but that I must not tell anyone. I should try out my joy for two weeks. If it were still there then I could tell others. If not, then it was just as well I had not told anyone only to make a fool of myself. That sounded very logical so that's what I decided to do. What a big mistake. The next morning I awakened with a painful boil on my arm. My joy was gone for sure.

My sisters probably saw me go off with Roxie and expected me to say something. But I did not tell anyone that I was saved. Now I was back to square one, wondering if I would ever be saved. Sometimes I thought I must have committed the unpardonable sin, whatever that was. I must have done it unknowingly and now there was no hope for me. That was a terrible plight to be in. I later learned that the unpardonable sin is when a person willfully rejects Jesus Christ until he dies. All other sin is pardonable. Praise God!

I kept going to conferences still holding out dim hope. When my brother Sam graduated from Millar Memorial Bible Institute in Pambrun, SK I accompanied my parents to the event. Sam had told one of the students, Edna Abrams (she later married Ed Ratzliff), that I was coming in hopes she would talk to me. Well, she did and she was so very concerned and kind. Somehow I was not able to pray with her. I felt so bad to disappoint her for I knew she really cared.

When I was 13 years old, I went to another camp held by the CSSM. This time my group leader was Miss Helen M. Peters who later became a missionary to Africa. One night I was under such conviction I could not sleep and was trembling. I got up and awakened Helen. She so kindly got up and took me into a car that was parked nearby. By the light of her flashlight she read again from God's word. None of the verses said I had to feel saved. So I understood that and went back to bed really happy.

But that did not last either and I was back to my routine of begging God to forgive my sins. When attending revival meetings I would often go forward only to go home the same as before. My sister Martha sang for me sometimes, "He was not willing that Annie (any) should perish." I was under deep conviction but I did not want her to know. So I turned around and sang for her the only love song I knew, which was the "Dear John" song. She cried because she thought I was so hard.

One of my older sisters told me a few years ago that she had thought, that I thought I was good enough and did not need to be saved. That was far from the truth. Outwardly, I probably was a good girl. The reason being that when I did something wrong I felt so very guilty and could not sleep. I did not want to go and confess it so I tried to be good. But inwardly, I felt I was a very great sinner.

A few years went by and I was still not a Christian. Every fall when we dug the potatoes, carrots, and beets I thought of a verse from the Old Testament, Jeremiah 8:20, "The harvest is past, the summer is ended, and we (I) are not saved." It was usually windy and cold at that time and the leaves were falling. It all added to my grief - so hopeless.

One time I was so desperate I decided to fast till I knew whether I was saved or not. I kept on working and only drank water and homemade postum. Mother was very concerned because I did not eat and begged me not to work. But I guess I thought I needed to punish myself. Probably the sixth or seventh day into my fast when I was in the outhouse something happened. A voice clearly spoke to me in my heart, it was the Holy Spirit. It was a verse from the New Testament, 2 John 5:13, "These things have I written unto you that believe on the name of the Son of God; that ye may know that ye have eternal life, and that ye may believe on the name of the Son of God."

Joy flooded my soul when I realized that meant me. But, it was short-lived as before! Would you like to know why? Well, how could I, for the rest of my life, tell folks I was born again in an outhouse?! But I was satisfied that God had revealed to me that I was saved. I gave up my fast at once and ate the next meal. I can only imagine how concerned and puzzled my family must have been because I did not tell them what had happened. The Bible tells us that we believe with our hearts and confess with our mouth, (Romans 10:9). I did not confess so I did not grow and therefore again I deducted that I was not saved. What a roller-coaster life!

In July of 1940 just after I had turned 20 we heard of a Young People's camp coming up near Langham, SK. Nine of my sisters and brothers were planning to attend. I did not. Mother kept urging me to go too. I knew she was concerned about my spiritual condition. I felt it was too late for me and also I did not want our parents to have to do the chores. I told her I would rather stay home to help.

I know she prayed hard. Lo and behold, the morning that Dad was going to take them all to the camp in our truck I suddenly decided I would go too. It was the Holy Spirit for sure. It did not take me many minutes to put some clothes in a bag and off we went. If I remember correctly the camp was to last a week. Rev. Edwin Erickson was the main speaker again. I attended all the meetings but nothing seemed to touch my heart, no conviction as I had experienced before. But on July 27, 1940 I sat between two of my sisters during the final meeting on the last day of camp and it was different.

Rev. Erickson announced his text was Exodus chapter 12 and read it. Then he proceeded to imagine that we were all going to Egypt that night to visit some of the homes of the Israelites just prior to their sitting down to the Passover meal. "Let's see how they feel," he said. So we knocked at the first door and they swung the door wide open and said to come and join them. They were singing they told us. When we inquired why, they told us how happy they were for the provision God had made. It was the blood on the doorpost. The Death Angel would see it and pass over their home. Their first-born would not die. After a bit we left.

We knocked at the second home once, twice, thrice and the door opened just a few inches. A mother was at the door wiping her tears with the corner of her apron. We asked what was wrong. She wondered how come we did not know what was happening that night for it was so terrible. Yes, we had heard but why was she crying. Have you not put the blood on the doorpost and is the whole family inside? She assured us of both but with fresh sobs she said, 'but what if the Death Angel does not see it in the dark?'

Then he left the conversation there and asked us a question. 'Which house do you think was the safest, the happy one or where the Mother was crying?' I knew for sure the first one was but I was too shy to raise my hand. Then after the show of hands he shocked me by telling us that both were safe. I was puzzled for a bit. Then suddenly light flooded my mind and soul. It was not their feelings but the blood that mattered.

I saw it! I saw it! I had pled the blood of Jesus hundreds of times to wash away my sins. I had prayed, cried and fasted, always hoping for the assurance to come through my feelings. Now through the illustration of visiting those homes I realized I had done exactly what the crying mother had. Then, I realized, Jesus must have forgiven my sins the first time I asked Him and I AM SAVED! At once I turned to my sister Martha who was sitting on my right and whispered almost out loud, "I am saved." She was so happy she cried. Isaac was sitting behind me and I turned around and told him I was saved. He was happy.

Right there I decided that this time I was not going to listen to Satan and try out my joy like I had before. I was going to tell everybody. As soon as we were dismissed I almost ran to Mr. Erickson to tell him my good news and joy. Then I went around the room and shook hands with anyone I could get close enough to and said, "I am saved, I am saved!" It was not enough to say it once. I guess I wanted to be sure Satan heard me. I was one happy girl and yes, there were plenty of feelings. But now they came at the proper time. I praise the Lord, over and over again for saving me!

So, I really do not know how to date the day of my salvation. But I know I received assurance of salvation on July 27, 1940. I used to say to myself if God ever forgives my sin and lets me KNOW they are forgiven, then I'll trust Him for anything and everything. Nothing will ever be too hard for Him after that. And it has not been too hard. Praise The Lord!

On July 28 Dad came to pick us up from camp to bring us home. Nothing was more important to me right then than to tell my parents the good news. I did and they were both overjoyed. They suggested right then that we all kneel down and thank God. They both prayed and then I blurted out my first prayer with the family after all those years. It seemed very strange to hear my own voice.

Now I would like to invite anyone reading my story that is not saved to do as I did. Confess your sin, turn from it to Jesus and ask Him to forgive you. Turn your tangled life over to Him. Believe that He will do what you ask Him to do on the authority of God's Word. For He says, "He that cometh to me I will in no wise cast out." John 6:37. And Romans 10:33 says, "For whosoever shall call upon the name of the Lord shall be saved." No matter what, do not trust your feelings. I tried it for years, they change too often. God's Word does not change. I have tested it too. He can be trusted to be with us in any and all circumstances. He does exactly what He says He will do. Then confess Him before your loved ones and friends.

That last sentence reminds me of a chorus we sang a lot at camp. It goes like this:

Romans ten and nine, is a favourite verse of mine
Confessing Christ as Lord, I am saved by grace divine
For there the words of promise, in golden letters shine
Romans ten and nine!

We children used to sing whenever we were going to church or anywhere else, especially if by sleigh in the winter time. We also sang when riding in the back of the family truck. People told us it was good to hear us sing as we drove by. If we knew people that did not attend church our parents took us there to sing for them. We always hoped that their hearts would be touched as we sang the old hymns. We often sang Mother's favourite which was, "There's No Disappointment in Heaven." Dad's was "The Old Account Was Settled Long Ago." When we all were a bit older we'd also sing a song together after our evening devotions. It was usually a German song like, "Keiner Wird zu Schanden, Welcher Gottes Hart" or "Die Zeit ist Kurz, O Mensch zie Weise." The first means, 'no one will be put to shame who trusts in God.' The other, 'The time is short so use it wisely.'

Talking about riding on the back of the truck I am reminded of a comical experience we had. On one of our trips to Saskatoon a rather stylish young lady wanted a ride. We were glad to take her but what we had not thought of telling her was that we always got very dusty. Well, we went to Eatons store to use the washroom and this dear lady looked in the mirror and was horrified to see how dirty her face was. We were used to the dust and just bent over the sink and washed face, hands and even arms. She looked on. Finally, she told us she had not washed her face with water for years. We had never heard of such but we asked her how she kept clean. She told us she used only cream cleansers. That was news to us poor farm kids. We thought it amusing. She decided no amount of cream would get all that dust off so summing up her courage she bent over the sink and followed our example. Needless to say she did not ride back with us. She somehow found a cleaner way to get home.

That was just an aside. Back to my conversion. As soon as I had that sweet assurance that Jesus was my Saviour, I wanted to be baptized. I told my parents and they contacted the Canadian Sunday School Mission. By the time all this was talked over it must have been about the end of August or even later. It was decided the river would be too cold or whatever, I cannot remember why it was postponed till the following year. On June 22, 1941 I was baptized by Rev. Henry Hildebrandt, President of Briercrest Bible Institute, from Caronport, Saskatchewan. There were several others baptized the same day but to my sorrow I cannot remember their names.

Several men, including Mr. George Elliot, from Langham scouted around for a safe place on the banks of the South Saskatchewan River near Langham. They drove some long poles into the river where it was not too deep and tied ropes from one post to the other. These were for us to hold onto as we walked into the water to Rev. Hildebrandt. Some men helped us walk to him. Oh, how happy I was I could hardly wait my turn. As we came out after we were immersed the group of Christians on shore including my happy parents, sisters and brothers sang for each one of us. It sounded like angels to me for they sang "I Have Decided to Follow Jesus, No Turning Back, No Turning Back." That was certainly my testimony.

There were, of course, no changing rooms on the river banks. But provision had been made for us. Two big trucks with a tarp or something over them were backed up close by. One for us girls and one for the men. We climbed up and changed into dry clothes. I am sure I had a perpetual smile on my face because I was saved, knew it and was now baptized. I knew that the Bible taught baptism, I am also sure our family sang all the way home as we were wont to do. And I was able to sing more lustily than ever. Next to my receiving assurance of salvation, the day of my baptism was my happiest day.

The group at the Ranger Lake camp that I was in. 1940 when I received assurance of salvation. I am at the left, back row.

Somehow, I have no recollection of what took place in my life for the next full year. But I know I loved to read my Bible and go to church and conferences. Some in my family were at Bible School. So I too must have considered but more about that later.

CHAPTER 4

More Childhood Memories

The Goertz family in 1936.

There are still some childhood memories that I want to recount here, one of which was how we spent our Christmas. It was a custom at our house that each family member had their special place around the table. Those sitting next to the wall sat on a long bench, and they were usually the younger ones as more of them fit on the bench. Dad and Mother each sat at one end of the long table. The older ones sat on chairs on the other side. Whenever there was an empty spot everyone knew who it was.

On Christmas Eve, which we always called, "Heilige Ovent" (Holy Night or evening) we put plates at each place on the table before we went to bed. We knew our parents would put something on our plate, not Santa Claus. We did not know about him till we attended school. Our regular dishes would be needed for breakfast and lunch, so we put pie plates out first (they were bigger!) and enamel plates for the rest. That way we could keep our goodies safe even when mealtime rolled around.

We could hardly wait till morning. Usually, there were lots of peanuts in the shell, several kinds of candy, a tangerine, other nuts and a handkerchief in our plates. Some years there might also be a small toy, or hair clip for the girls. What the boys got I do not remember. I know I got a beautiful doll one year. We were always so happy and went to say thank you to our parents.

Some years there might only be peanuts and no candy or hankie. We were just as happy and thanked our parents. We had been taught to be thankful for small mercies or gifts. Sometimes a banana, apple or orange had to be cut into two or more pieces so as to go around for all. We were thankful but very human. When one or the other would say, "Mother, his/her piece is bigger than mine," she would stop and explain that it was impossible to cut each piece exactly the same size. Then there would come a little proverb or saying, "He who does not honour the small is not worthy of something bigger."

However, there came a Heilige Ovend, when Mother said sadly, "Children, this year we have NOTHING to put into your plates. Do not set them out on the table." We put them out anyway. When I was older I realized that our parents probably did not sleep that night. They must have felt very sad and no doubt prayed that the Lord would help their children not be too disappointed in the morning.

Morning came and we rushed downstairs to the table. It was true, there was nothing in the plates. I do not remember that anyone complained or cried. But I do remember Mother coming out of the bedroom to wish us all a happy Christmas. I thought I saw her eyes glisten with a tear or two. In her hand was an ever so tiny brown paper bag. She reached in and said, "We do have a peppermint for each of you." We each took one and said our usual 'thank you for the present.'

Sometimes, when we were having a meal, we were not quite as thankful. Someone would say, 'I do not like that.' Remember I told you I did not like certain soups? I guess we all at one time or other would say those five words. Mother always seemed to have an appropriate proverb on the tip of her tongue. Right about now this one sufficed, "When the little mouse is full the kernel turns bitter." Or another that fit was, "Hunger treibs ein" (when you're hungry it will go in, or down).

In the morning when it was time to get up and get ready for school we usually did not rush downstairs like at Christmas!! So we might have to be called a few times. Dad had a unique 'teaching tool' which I think he only needed to use once on each of us. He would climb the stairs and pour a few drops of ice cold water on our face from an enamel cup. I can still see it! He would laugh and say that would wake us up! It did. After that, Mother would call upstairs once and add that next would come the cold water.

Mother would also give us bits of good advice for our health's sake. When she called us to get out of bed, she often added, 'don't jump too suddenly - stretch first.' I do that almost without fail to this day and have taught it to other children when I had to get them up. I have been rather pleased and surprised to learn that doctors know that too!? "Do not get up too quickly from a lying down position or when getting up from a chair," they faithfully tell their patients. Yes, our Mothers had a lot of wisdom. We thank God for them and the memories we have stored. The same goes for our Fathers, too.

Since water had to be carried into the house from the well we did not waste it. In the winter time we pumped it out of a cistern which was under the house and it had to last till spring. Our drinking water however we carried in even in the winter. So for our weekly Saturday night baths we had to conserve water too. We had a galvanized tub into which a small amount of water was poured. Maybe starting with girls, the youngest would be bathed first, I guess the thinking behind that must have been that they were the cleanest. Then each one in turn, according to age got in (often with a query first about having been to the bathroom or not) and a kettle of hot water was added. That was good strategy because the bigger the person the more water was needed! Then it was the boys turn with a fresh lot of water.

We always walked barefoot all summer long, even to school. For Church we wore shoes. Our feet were dirty from going barefoot and we usually washed them before going to bed. Again, a bit of good advice from Mamma was to be sure to wipe it good and dry between the toes or we might get sores. How true that was for I experienced athletes foot later in India. There it gave me opportunity also to give that bit of advice to many girls there in the boardings. Come spring, we were tired of our shoes and begged to go barefoot. We were told we could go barefoot only after the thermometer showed 70° F. So we all learned to read that thing quickly. It took me much longer to learn to read a clock.

I was known as a very shy child. However, when I was very excited or proud of someone I did talk, as when my oldest sister Hulda wore a hair net for the first time to church. That 'worldly' fashion had just come in. I was so proud of her. I ran ahead of her and opened the door wide and called out, "Here comes our hairnet!" She wished to disappear. I don't remember how old I was, I did it so innocently. If she were not such a kind sister she might have let me have it when we got home.

When it came to eating, I was very shy too. When company came to our house I would eat but if we went somewhere else, especially to a home, I would not eat. The hostess felt sorry for me and put some food on a plate. Then Mother had to take me into the privacy of the bedroom to eat.

As all children, we would get into quarrels or fights. Sometimes if we had been too rough and hurt each other badly we'd get a spanking. Most often Dad had another remedy and that was to have us hug and kiss each other. That was hard to do after we had been so angry. It made us feel foolish in a way and we both ended up laughing. Then it was all over till the next time.

Salesmen would drop by our farm and try to sell Dad various things. After the salesmen gave a good sales pitch, we were sure Dad would buy. Usually he did not and we wondered why. He said if you bend over and talk into an empty barrel it will make a lot of noise.

Some of his other sayings were, 'If I point a finger at someone, I must remember that four fingers point back at me' or, 'the Bible is a road map for our lives. If we follow its direction we won't get on the wrong road.' Toward the end of his life he had bone cancer and was in a wheelchair. He had a lot of pain and could not walk at all. When anyone asked him how he was doing, his answer was, "I am helpless but not hopeless." That was a really good testimony.

Earlier I mentioned how happy I was whenever my parents would teach me how to do something new and then trust me. Their confidence was what I wanted. I remember the first time Mother taught me how to squeeze a piece of dough off the big piece and roll it into a bun and put in on the pans. Later she taught me how to make the dough for buns, also for bread. Her measure was always a big flat lid off a Rogers Golden Syrup pail. The recipe called for so many lids of flour. We had no measuring cup back then. A huge round bowl was placed on a low chair so that as we bent over it we could put more umph into the punches as we kneaded the dough.

I used to taste cake batter and puddings. One day bread pudding had been put into the oven when I was not around. I opened the oven to taste it. No sugar! Mother was glad that time because I rescued the pudding.

CHAPTER 5

Loss of the Farm

Before we moved into that big yellow house I talked about, Dad had borrowed money. He owned a lot of land but to work it properly he needed better and bigger equipment. He borrowed the money for that which was okay because the crops were good when he borrowed it. The other farmers did the same. What no one knew was that crop failures were around the corner. In fact, nine or ten years in a row.

Now there was no money to make payments. Creditors' letters started to arrive at our home. It was very hard for our parents. I was quite young but I remember how sad Dad looked and Mother too. The letters had to be answered. My sister Martha was chosen as his secretary. Then she left home to attend Bible School at Beatty, Saskatchewan.

Now it was my turn to be secretary. I was given a pen and writing pad and Dad and I would go to the living room where it was quiet. There were several letters to write. They went like this, "you loaned me the money in good faith for the plow, tractor or whatever it was and I intended to pay you back. I still do but due to crop failure I cannot at this time. Please be patient with me and I will pay you. I have a wife and a large family of fourteen children. When the crops improve I will pay every cent."

That made me feel very sad too, for I sensed how big a burden it was for my parents. Although I did not think of myself as a Christian and I did not know if God would hear me, I prayed earnestly. Would the Lord please send good crops or give Dad some money from somewhere.

The crops did not improve so eventually Dad lost the farm and the house I've been talking about as the yellow one. We still had the old farm and house where most of us were born. So we moved back there probably in about 1936. I'm not sure of the year. In the meantime my two oldest brothers Isaac and Jake had been baching in that house.

Now to back up a bit to the year 1929 which was before we moved back of course. On November 6 of that year our parents planned to celebrate their 25 wedding anniversary in our home. Just a quiet celebration with a few people being invited. Isaac was attending Hepburn Bible School (in Hepburn, SK) at the time. Two of his teachers had been invited to give a little talk.

What I did not know, was that Mother was expecting their fourteenth child any day (I was ten years old). So there was considerable doubt as to whether the celebration would come off as planned. Isaac (remember he was the oldest in the family) had been instructed to call home first to talk to Mother before he came home with the two teachers. One of which was Mr. Esau. Mother told Isaac that all was GO. The celebration went very well. One of our storekeepers Mr. Siemens, was one of the few guests that had been invited. He brought a nice shiny four gallon aluminum pail as his gift to my parents. It really did look like silver to me and I was impressed. That proved to be a strong pail and we forever referred to it as the 'Siemens pail.'

The baby boy held off his debut till November 6. He knew how to time it. He weighed twelve pounds and was named Jona. He liked his name at first but when he was older he changed it to Joe, but not legally. I do not know why he changed it. But I think he did it because he felt he was a little too much like the Jonah of the Bible who ran away from the Lord. He too did the same for some years. Praise the Lord, he came back to Him and was able to point some of his buddies to the Saviour. Sadly though, he did not live very long. He went to Heaven on January 5, 1987 at the early age of fifty seven years and two months. He left behind his wife Leona and a son Brian.

When my parents lost the farm it was a terrible blow to them and to us the family. The hardest part was that is was a minister who sold it to us and then later reclaimed it when there was only very little left to be paid. Our Father went into depression for a few months and no wonder.

At the time I did not know what to make of it all for I was only about 13 or 14 years old. It kind of made me depressed too. Now as I look back, I know that Dad and Mother encouraged each other and in the Lord. When Dad recovered he started holding Sunday Services in Carson School for we did not go back to the church we had attended for many years. It was hard on everybody. But in retrospect I take my hat off to Dad for having the courage to do what he did and not become bitter at the minister or the Lord.

For the most part, the people in the Carson district did not attend church anywhere as I recall. My parents were very courageous and a good example to us. Dad would take the service himself many times. But he also invited ministers from Langham and Dalmeny, like Rev. Jake Lepp and Rev. Henry Schultz to speak. Also Rev. George Buhler from Waldheim helped out along with others.

But that was not all. Our parents were concerned because many in the area were not Christians as far as we knew. So Dad arranged for evangelistic meetings to be held in the school on week nights. Evangelists like Rev. Edwin Erickson and his brother Olaf, Rev. Herb Peeler, Kenneth Robbins, Ewald Schmidt, John Parschauer and others were the speakers.

Praise God quite a few were born again. I remember specifically how convicted I was. We'd stand to sing invitation hymns like, 'Just as I Am,' and others. I would grab the bench in front of me because I was trembling so much. Sometimes I'd go forward during the invitation but usually not.

Those services continued for many years, probably till my parents sold their farm and moved to British Columbia. What happened after that I do not know. But the Lord really blessed those efforts. My folks were faithful rain, shine or snow. The Lord called some young people from that group to go to the foreign fields as missionaries.

My Dad was probably not even aware of how far reaching his efforts would be. I do not think that he thought of himself as a church planter but that is what he was. His Father, as I told you before, started a church in Marion, South Dakota and when it was going good he started the Salem Church in SK, along with another minister. So our Dad followed in his Father's footsteps.

When the farm was taken away from our parents the owner may have meant it for evil, I don't know that and I am not the judge but certainly Satan meant it for evil but God meant it for good.

Before I leave this chapter I want to recount a few more things from my childhood. I said Mother had lots of wisdom. When she called us to get up in the morning she often added, "don't make your beds right away. Leave the blankets turned back till after you dress." The reason, to let the germs crawl out of our beds. I guess it really was to let it cool off first!

We had a very bad scare one lovely summer day. Our parents had gone to Saskatoon (forty miles away) for the day on business. Usually they took some of us along but not that day as far as I remember. We children were all busy with something or other. Suddenly someone called out, "Where is Edwin?" He was about 2 years old.

We all ran in different directions to try to find him. We felt very responsible because we had not kept our eyes on the little ones. One ran into the barn to look, another to the chicken coop, another to the pasture. We looked under every bed and in every room. Someone very hesitantly went to look in the huge water trough thinking he might have tried to look and fell in! No little brother Edwin! Some of us cried. We were really in a panic for there was no other place to look. If only Mom and Dad would come home right then we wished.

Suddenly the phone rang. Our neighbours about two miles away called and asked if we were missing a child. YES, we were! We hitched up the horse and buggy and Mary went to the Funk's as fast as the horse would go. They told her that some Doukhobors had seen him on the road by himself and picked him up and brought him to their place. Edwin was crying very hard by then. They gave him a cookie and some milk. He refused everything. Of course he was very scared and wanted to go home. Finally one of them said that this little boy looked like he could belong to the Goertz'.

My, was he happy when he saw his sister Mary and quickly was helped up into the buggy. Mary said he put his head on her lap and stayed that way till they arrived home. Then the story unfolded. He had wanted to go with our parents but was not allowed to. So he, thinking they had gone to Waldheim and that he knew the way, started out after them. He really did take the right road too.

We were all overjoyed that our little brother was back home safely. When our parents returned that evening the first item of news of course was that Edwin had tried to follow them. It really gave them a terrible scare too. Mother said her heart almost stopped and that she was not able to sleep that night. She imagined what would have happened if Edwin had not kicked and screamed in the car like he did so that the Doukhobours dropped him off at the Funks. She was pretty sure that they would have taken him back with them across the river on the Petrofka Ferry and we might never have seen or heard from him again. We were all given very stern warning that no one else should ever try to follow them like he had done. We knew what the consequences would be if we did and anyone picked us up.

In the fall, we would fill the back of our truck with potatoes, cabbage, carrots, corn, bottles of milk, cream and butter. Of course the milk and cream were not pasteurised. Off to Saskatoon we would go to peddle our wares. Quite often I went along to help sell. I enjoyed it because people would readily buy. Mother would go to one door and I to the next. Dad would sit in the back of the truck to dole out the stuff to us and we took it back to the customers.

Edwin. Taken about the time of the story.

People were always very kind and I remember being given a cookie now and then. One day when the lady of the house opened her door out rushed a wee dog. Before I knew what was going on, the pooch had gone around behind me and bit my heel. That really scared me and ever since I have had an aversion to dogs.

I mentioned earlier that we had geese and turkeys on the farm. The gobblers sometimes got upset and would come after us. We were also warned the gander could be obstreperous at times. Well, one day I was walking in the yard minding my own business (I must have been about 5 or 6 years old) when suddenly the gander came for me. He grabbed my little apron with his beak and beat on me with his huge hard wings. Fortunately, Dad was within seeing distance otherwise I would have been severely hurt. Dad grabbed the gander from behind and pulled him off of me. It really scared Dad and he decided to finish the gander off. He wrung it's neck till he was sure he would not hurt another of his children.

He took the bird to the kitchen and told Mother he thought we'd better have roasted goose for supper. He explained to her what had happened and we had a lovely dinner.

CHAPTER 6

Off to Bible School

Now I will pick up the story from where I received assurance of salvation and was baptized. I am trying to think of the song we sang years ago about heaven above being a brighter blue . . . since as now I know I am His and He is mine. That was my experience for sure. Actually nothing around me had changed to brighter colours. I looked at everything in a different light. How wonderful to be born again and know it!

My desire now was to be a Sunday School teacher so as to be able to teach little children like my Sunday School teachers taught me. I knew Bible School would be the place to learn that.

During the summer of 1941, I applied to Miller Memorial Bible Institute at Pambrun, SK. That is where several of my brothers had studied as well as one sister for a short time. I was turned down because the G.I.'s were returning after the war and they wanted to reserve the space for those young men. I understood that since they had interrupted their studies in order to go to war. I was advised to apply again the next year. That would have made me 22 years old by then.

My brother Isaac thought I should not wait a whole year. He told me about a school in Alberta that he had heard about through an acquaintance. He got me the address and it was Prairie Bible Institute in Three Hills. I believe he had also visited there and liked the President, Rev. L. E. Maxwell. So I applied and had my acceptance very quickly. I was overjoyed that now I could devote my whole day, every day to nothing but the study of God's Word, the Bible for six months.

I was asked naturally, to bring my own bedding and towels. I believe I had only one towel and washcloth. But that was enough, I could only use one at a time anyway. My clothes presented a different story. Specifications were that dresses had to be 12 inches from the floor and I possessed only one that qualified. There was no money to buy another. But Isaac knew of a girl from Waldheim, SK that had attended the year before and he knew she did not plan on returning. I think he asked her if I could have one of hers. That worked because she said she did not intend to wear it anymore for it was too long.

Now my outfit was ready. But there was an important item that had not entered my mind - money. I needed money for a bus ticket to travel to school and my tuition, room, board and books when I got there. I had said to myself before I was saved that if the Lord would ever forgive my sins and let me KNOW they were forgiven then there was nothing I needed to be concerned about. All other things would be easy for the Lord to care for, for nothing was too hard for Him after that.

The day in October arrived for me to be on my way to school. My parents said nothing about any money I would need but I am positive they must have prayed earnestly. Mother packed a lunch in a small box for my journey. It contained a whole fried chicken, a dozen buns and some cinnamon rolls. How blessed I was! After my goodbyes to sisters and brothers, my parents took me to Saskatoon to board the bus. I did not have any money but Isaac had given me a $20.00 bill. Isaac gave us girls each a one way ticket to Bible School but not the boys. After helping them make a little suitcase out of an orange box, took them to a corner on the highway, dropped them off and said to hitch a ride. But in one way or another he made sure we got to Bible School. Bless him!

If I remember correctly my bus ticket was about $19.85. I sent Isaac the change because I knew he needed it. He really could not afford to give me the $20.00. My bus rode off into the night. I already missed my family for it was my first time away from home. My lunch smelled so good and I dug into it pretty soon. In those days we did not get out at every stop for a cup of coffee either.

My bus trip ended in Calgary, AB. From there I, along with a few other students, took the train the last 80 miles of the journey. In Three Hills we were met by students who helped us with our baggage to our respective rooms. My roommate was already in the room and welcomed me very warmly. She was starting her second year. I am not giving her name for reasons that will be clear later. She showed me around the dorm and later to the dining room for our meals.

Our arrival at school had been planned for a Saturday. This gave me time to settle in before school started on Monday. On Sunday, my roommate took me to the Tabernacle for the service and right to the front bench. Well, Mr. L. E. Maxwell spoke on Jonah and acted out some parts as he was apt to do. When it came time for Jonah to be thrown off the ship, he grabbed the wooden railing and pretended to jump. He was so agile I was sure he would land on the floor right in front of us. My heart was touched by the joy and earnestness of this man of God. It was just the beginning of four glorious years sitting under his ministry in church and the classroom.

An aerial view of some of the P.B.I. buildings and the three small hills on the horizon from which the town derived it's name.

The next day before school started we registered in the office with the registrar Mr. Perry Havens. I was given a list of books I needed to collect in the 'Book Room.' It actually was a Bible and Book Store which meant that I was to have paid for the books. Nobody said anything and I just picked

President L. E. Maxwell.

up the books, said thank you and went to my room. I don't know what I thought. It may seem that I was very naive. Maybe. I rather think it was just simple faith that God would provide though I was not even aware of thinking that.

That exercise being completed we went from classroom to classroom to meet our teachers for the various subjects. We were also assigned seats alphabetically by our last name. Each teacher gave a short introduction and prayer. Oh yes, the boys sat on one side of the aisle and the girls on the other. Never the twain did meet! The seating was the same in the dining room, boys and girls in separate sections and we were assigned our places at the tables. All the formalities took a good part of the day because there were long line-ups for everything. We were close to two thousand students.

Then there was time to do things in our own rooms like getting our books and things in place. Suddenly I remembered an envelope with a sheet of paper that Mother had given me just before I left home. As she handed it to me she said, "Child, write to us as soon as you arrive because we will be concerned." I knew I had enough time to write the letter before supper and I did. Then I wrote my parents' address on it and mine and sealed it. A stamp? I had none. I remember very clearly praying, "Dear Lord, you know my parents will be anxious to hear from me. I have no 3 cent stamp. But when you supply it, I will mail it." With that I put it on my book shelf above my table and forgot about it.

I should say right here that I did not possess a purse or a wallet. Why did I need one? I didn't because I had no money to put in it. I really did not have even one "red penny" as we used to say. Please believe me. It was no cause for concern to me. God, who saved my soul would provide. My Mother had given me a pen though. It probably was the only one in the house. She knew I needed a pen to write a letter with.

The next day classes started in earnest. It was wonderful! I thanked the Lord over and over again for bringing me to Bible School. After the first two classes I had a free period to go to my room. Right about that time it started to snow. Soon it was a blizzard as only the prairies can produce. I was sitting by my desk and felt a cold draft on my feet. None of the doors fitted too well, especially the ones to our rooms. There must have been an inch or more under our door.

The door outside swung open wide with a gust of wind as it must not have been latched properly. Then a second gust of wind blew it shut with a loud bang. Oh, it was so cold I raised my feet off the floor as I looked toward the bottom of the door. You know what? A three cent stamp blew under the door into our room! My roommate was in class. I took the stamp and went to each of the rooms on our floor and asked if anyone had just come from the Post Office after buying stamps and losing one. They all said they had not. Several asked me if I really thought they would venture into town in such a blizzard.

There I was left holding the stamp, so I walked back to my room not knowing what else to do. As I entered my room, my eyes fell on the letter on my shelf. Then with great emotion it dawned on me what had happened. I knelt by my chair still holding the stamp and said, "Lord, you did send a stamp. You DID send a stamp. Thank you, Lord. Thank you." I do not have the words to tell you how precious that experience was. I wept for joy. To think that He cared when I asked for a small stamp. It was the beginning of some understanding at least that God is a God of detail not just of the big things. I mailed the letter at once.

It was indeed so wonderful to be able to study God's Word under godly men and women. It seemed to me as if it was the first time in my life that I heard that the Holy Spirit was a Person. Oh, I knew about Him but thought His only function was to bring us to Christ. I did not know, or at least not understand, that He had an ongoing ministry in our lives. Sometimes when I knelt down to pray God's love and presence so flooded my soul I could hardly stand it.

Then there were the times when I really struggled over some new truth or a rule I was to obey. I wore long hair with a clip at the back of my neck to hold it together neatly as it hung way down my back. There came a day when I felt I should do it up in a roll. I did not want to. I do not remember anyone telling me to roll my hair up. But, reluctantly I acquired a long piece of wire from somewhere and bent it so I could catch my hair between the wires. Then I rolled it way up and bent the ends of the wire under to secure it.

A few days later one of the girls came to me and asked me why I rolled up my hair. I told her that I had not wanted to but I just felt I should. She then told me she had been struggling over something and when she saw me change my hair-do, it gave her the courage to do what she knew she should. So I had been an unwitting example. It made me realize that we are a witness in one way or another even if we are not aware of it.

A few weeks into the first school term, an announcement was made that all Bible School girls were to visit Mrs. Waldock's office to have their skirts measured. Ours were to be 12 inches from the floor, the high school girls 15 inches. Mrs. Waldock sat on her chair holding a yard stick. Well, I had thought mine were okay but no, one was 3 inches too short. There was no hem to let down so I had to put a frill on. I had no frill and no money to buy one. Here was my dilemma, I had to pray for money to buy a frill that I did not want.

Well, I prayed and some dear soul enclosed a dollar bill in her letter to me. It was obvious that the Lord had provided. On went the frill and now I matched a lot of the girls. I did not tell you this to make fun at the rules or of Mrs. Waldock. Those were the rules, I had known about them before I came, so I knew I must obey. I was glad I had obeyed for there are many rules in life we must obey. There is always someone in life we must obey and especially God, our Father.

Years later in India, when I had to make rules for some 160 girls in our boarding school there were some who balked at them. I was glad to relate my experiences. There must be rules otherwise everyone would do what was right in their own eyes. What chaos that would be!

I can also see the wisdom of having boys and girls sitting in separate sections. Too often young people who sense the call of God on their lives get side-tracked by one of the opposite sex. They get married and never fulfill what they felt was God's will. I have talked to quite a few who have regretted what they did. Not that God (nor I, for that matter) is against marriage. He just wants us to be in His will. Again, in India they do not only have boys and girls sit separately but they go to entirely separate schools. So I got good training and preparation for my life's ministry while at Prairie Bible.

As for putting my hair up in a roll, it fitted right in with the Indian women and girls. No one, but no one let their hair hang loose. In modern India, some girls do cut their hair or let it hang loose but years ago only an harlot would do that. So no training we get is wasted. Sooner or later, we will be thankful for it, if only for the fact that we learned to obey.

Now, is curiosity getting the best of you in regards to what I did about those text books I picked up? Yes, God provided. One day someone gave me an envelope saying it had been given to them by someone else to give to me. In the envelope was a note and $50.00 cash to go and pay for my textbooks. I never found out who did it but I thanked the Lord for it. Years later, I was able to pay for someone else's books. It gave me so much joy.

It was the custom at Prairie (that's how we liked to refer to it) for Mr. Maxwell to make announcements before we were dismissed from the supper table. Sometimes names of students were called out to go and see a teacher, or Mr. Maxwell, or the head of their work crew, or whatever.

On one such occasion my name was called and I was asked to go to the office of the registrar to see Mr. Havens. I had no idea what for. I quickly learned that on our arrival when we registered we were to have paid some room and board. I had given absolutely no thought to that when I registered. Mr. Havens was so very gracious and hardly knew how to ask this poor innocent girl if she had anything to pay for what was owing. I told him that I had no money. Then he broke out in a wide grin and said someone had sent money to pay for me till Christmas. I was ecstatic that God had provided and I could continue to study the Bible.

Come Christmas vacation, almost every student went home to their parents. I had no money so I knew I would be staying in the dorm. But two of my very good friends (sisters) Katherine and Margaret Thiessen who lived not far from Three Hills with their Mother invited me to spend Christmas with them. That was wonderful. I got to know and love their Mother very much. They gave me a very good time. I really appreciated it for it was my first Christmas ever away from home. Katherine and her Mother are with the Lord. Margaret went to Africa as a missionary, later married, is now widowed and lives in a care home in Linden, AB.

Probably about the middle of February 1942, I was once more called to see the registrar. This time I had a good idea what it was about, but I had no fear. After the exchange of greetings he again asked me if I intended to pay for my room and board. I gave him the same answer. Again he informed me that someone had paid for it till the end of term. I walked back as if on air for I was so thankful I would be able to stay.

Mrs. Thiessen and I going out to do the milking

I want to tell a bit more about our rooms. We did not have a sink or running water in our room. But we had a little wooden stand with an enamel washbasin on it. The stand was enclosed with a curtain and had a slop pail underneath that we emptied whenever it was full. That's where we took our bath when our roommate was out.

The bathroom or toilet was way down the end of the hall. There were several cubicles and in each was a commode with a big pail inside. Every evening while we were was at supper a crew of boys, whom we dubbed the Gold Crew, came and emptied the pails. That was their gratis work.

All of us students did gratis work for a certain amount of time every day. That kept our room and board down so that more could afford to attend. In fact there was no hired help. Students took care of the cows and the milking. Another crew of men did all the baking.

My first year I peeled potatoes, carrots, turnips, cut up cabbage or whatever. That was right after breakfast and just before classes. I think sometimes I must have come to class with carrot or potato peelings in my hair or hanging from my glasses.

Our Dean of Women was Miss Ruth King and she was very kind. Miss Eilleen Singleton was her assistant. The cooks in charge of the kitchen were Miss Cora Harris and Miss Edith Johnson. My second year I worked on the cooking crew so for 2 years they were my good bosses. The students I cooked with were Edith Milloy (Devitt), Gladys Beckett (Tuck) and Clara Lapohn (Walker). We learned a lot about cooking in large amounts in steam kettles. Once a week we had peanut butter for breakfast. They had quite an idea - we put it into a big kettle and poured lots of boiling water on it while we mixed it with a beater. It stretched it as well as making it healthier. We did not get as much fat. Every Friday we cut up lots of apples for apple and raisin salad and cooked mounds of macaroni and cheese. It was everyone's favourite.

Another favourite meal was Sunday lunch. For we had lots of delicious roast beef with the trimmings and apple pie for dessert. We cook crew girls as well as some extra help made all those pies on Saturday morning. I enjoyed all the meals.

But one thing that I did not like about mealtime was that I had to talk. I was so shy. I was shy as a young child and I never lost it. It was painful to try to make conversation, especially when I sat at the head of the table. It was so bad I'd sometimes get sick to my stomach when I thought of going down to a meal. I was glad when breakfast was over but then I feared lunch and supper.

Some of my teachers were Miss Miller, Mr. J. M. Murray, Mr. Ernie

Richardson, Miss Marjorie Reading and I have already mentioned Mr. Maxwell. I loved all my teachers and they taught us well. Since I did not have high school I had to take four years at Prairie. Miss Reading taught English and emphasized how important it was to talk and read clearly. She taught us to always read the introduction to a book first as well as the foreword. She also gave me a notebook and taught me how to take notes in classes and in church, even a few shorthand symbols so as to save time. Oh yes, Miss Anderson taught music. I remember we had to lie on a couch and learn how to breathe from the diaphragm.

Parent's auction sale. Oct. 19, 1942

Shortly after school opened in October, prayer groups were organized. Sheets of paper were put up on the bulletin board, one for each continent. They had lines below for us to sign up to pray for a certain continent for that term.

When I saw them, a battle began to rage within me. My brother Sam had gone to Africa as a missionary in 1939. I wanted to pray for one of the continents, but somehow I thought if I signed up for one then the Lord might think I wanted to go there as a missionary. Sam was two years older than I and I thought God might just call me next.

The lists stayed up for awhile, then one day at noon they announced that the lists were coming down that day. If we had not signed up we must do it right away. I was in turmoil. Finally, I timidly signed up under North America. Why North America? Well, when I was a child I used to think my parents were very old and would die soon. I wanted to be the one to take care of them when they could not do it anymore. So I reasoned that if I HAD to be a missionary and my parents got sick then I'd be close enough to be able to return home to care for them. Anyway, I learned a lot about different missions on our continent as I prayed.

Shortly before the end of my first term at Prairie, Miss King asked me to see her in her office. I was shocked when she asked if I would consider staying for the summer and work as a 'summer girl.' She explained that if I did, I would earn my room and board for my second year. That sounded very good and I said I would pray about it. I did pray and I sensed God leading me to accept that offer.

There were about six or seven more girls that were asked to stay. We worked hard side by side all summer and became good friends. I still correspond with several of them. Our first job was to scrub all the dorm rooms, both the Bible School and High School. Later on we made lots of sauerkraut for the winter. When the fruit season started we canned lots of peaches and pears.

The Church services continued in the summer. It gave us a chance to get to know the local families who lived in the area. We also got to know the staff members better for they stayed there all year. Some in their own homes and the single staff members lived in the dorms too. We were invited in turn to many of their homes for meals and that was a very special treat.

A big change or event took place in our family in 1942. In October my parents sold the farm and house. They had a huge sale to sell all the farm machinery, cattle, horses, and any furniture that they did not want to bring along. The rest was loaded into a boxcar with the family dog. My brother Edwin rode in the boxcar to keep an eye on the dog. I believe that had its advantage too for they did not have to buy a ticket for him. The rest of the family which by now was small rode in the coach. They moved to Mission, BC.

In one way I felt kind of sad that I could not be there to help them. I also knew it was the end of another chapter in my life for I would not be going back to the old farm anymore. Everything would be different from now on. However, I did go back to visit several times in later years.

I have mentioned several of my teachers at Prairie. One I forgot to mention was a lady by the name of Miss Heffner. She had not been well all my first year. So it was that she died that summer. I probably forgot to mention all the teachers and I feel bad because each had a definite input into my spiritual growth there at Prairie.

There were others who were good friends as well as good examples. There was Miss Ida Heyer, secretary to Mr. Maxwell. Miss Lillian Grasley, Miss Ida Harrison, head of the laundry department. Later Mrs. McLennan, Miss Helma Olson, and Marie Thiessen were on staff. Marie worked in the print shop. I thank God upon every remembrance of them. Most of them are with the Lord now.

Before I close this chapter, I want to tell you a bit about my roommate I mentioned earlier. I still will not give her name. She was very kind, she shared her chocolates with me or any treats she had even though I never had any to share with her. But I seemed to irk her with some things I did. I am not telling you this to put her in a bad light but to tell you how God used those experiences to help me grow. She had been brought up Roman Catholic and was the only one in her family to leave that church, as far as I know.

As I said before, we did not have many clothes, just what we needed. Mother had taught me to hang my clothes over the back of a chair when I took them off at night. I had to wear them again the next day. We did not have a new set for each day as we do now. That habit of mine bothered my roommate. She wanted me to fold them up and put them back in the cupboard with the clean set. I could not bring myself to do that so she told me I was not a Christian. That went on for a long time. If she had told me that two years prior, I would have believed her. But now I KNEW my salvation did not depend on how I felt or what anyone said or did to me.

I always knelt by my bed for my devotions. But after a while, because I had not changed my habit (in regards to clothes) she started to kick my feet every time I knelt down. I ignored it but it finally got to me. I started to see myself as a stumbling block to her and felt very guilty.

Probably after about three months of this I could not take it anymore. I got up off my knees at 10:00 p.m., put on my overshoes, coat and marched out of our room to go and see if one of my teachers had any advice for me. My roommate told me I would be reported by the night watchman for being out of my room at that hour. I did not meet him and was glad.

Our perents ready to go to town. 1940

I had to walk quite a way to the teacher's room. She was surprised when I knocked on her door. I told her how guilty I felt. She sat me down and told me the staff knew about my roommate. They had been praying for me, and for her too. Then she told me that the Lord was allowing this test for a purpose. I was to guard my heart very carefully against a bitter spirit toward her. She also said this would not be the first time anyone would say hurtful things to me. I could not control what others said and did but I could and must control my response. We both prayed and I went back to my room with a big burden lifted.

My roommate did not ask me where I had been and I did not tell her. But I am sure she could see I had cried even though I was now smiling. I do not remember if she ever said and did those things again or not.

Two years down the road I was given the job of floor supervisor - only we were called 'floor bosses.' I was quite surprised that there were other roommates who had difficulties. Now they came to see me for counsel. God had prepared me through my experience. One girl discovered that every time she went to brush her teeth, her toothbrush was already wet. So she bought another one. The new one was wet too. She finally ran out of money and that's when she came to me. Her roommate was using her toothbrush. Ugh! Enough of that!

CHAPTER 7

A Fire and Gods Provision

We summer girls were busy and it made the time go fast. I remember how good I felt that the students were returning to clean dormitories in October. I was assigned to the same room I had before. This time my roommate was my younger sister Rosa. We enjoyed the winter together.

My sister Rosa and I.

When my second school year began the same prayer charts were put up on the wall in the dining room. Would you believe I had as great a battle as I did the year before? It took me two weeks to make a decision as to what country I would pray for. I was tempted to sign up under North America again. But finally, I decided it would be Africa because my brother Sam was there.

I was still afraid that my signing up for a certain country might be mistaken by God as meaning that I wanted to go there. More likely the real reason was that if God made me go to Africa as a missionary, and my parents needed help I might be able to return home. Certainly between Sam and I we might be able to come up with enough money for my ticket. So I prayed for Africa for six months.

Meanwhile our parents were hale and hearty, living in BC. They picked a lot of berries and apples for their neighbours to earn some cash. Dad raised rabbits for a while. But when it came to selling them, he found it hard to let them go.

My parents standing by all that is left after the fire.

Then they bought around two thousand chicks (it could be more) and raised them. They sat and cleaned eggs by the hour and then took them to market. They were in the chicken business for nearly 9 years. I am sure they did not think of dying. I was worried in vain. On June 23, 1952, exactly 10 years after coming to BC, their house burned down while they went to town to shop. Since they had no house right there it was hard to keep looking after the chickens, so they must have sold them. None of us can remember exactly what happened.

The new house.

A couple by the name of Peter and Inez Bergen, friends of our parents, sold their house (on Cade Barr Road) to them for $800.00 if I remember correctly. News spread quickly about the fire and that our parents had no insurance. The men from Cedar Valley Mennonite Church gathered with shovels, backhoes, or whatever and dug a basement under the house all in one day. Our parents were able to move into the house the same day the other burned. I am unclear about it because I was in Three Hills. A good friend of our family and neighbour Harry Harms was right there helping too.

I forgot to tell you what caused the fire. The kitchen stove was fired by sawdust. There was a good sized sawdust hopper fastened to the side of the stove. Dad filled it with sawdust every day. It slowly filtered into the firebox regulated by a little trap door. The more fire you wanted the farther you opened the trapdoor. The suspicion was that there must have been a shell in one of the trees from which the sawdust came and when it entered the firebox it exploded. It was wonderful that our parents were not at home or they would most certainly have been killed. All they went to town for was milk. It was God's timing. Thankfully, they were also able to save the barn.

Now Dad had to find a way of supporting them. He struck upon quite a unique idea. He went to the produce stores and asked the managers if he could haul away their wooden boxes after they were emptied of fruit and vegetables. The managers were happy because it saved them the trouble.

Dad had a small pickup truck and brought it home full of boxes every day. Many times there would be lettuce, cabbage or various kinds of produce that did not sell left in the boxes. Mother removed the outer leaves or cut out the bad spots and so had enough good stuff left that they could eat. They even passed some of it on to their family. God continued to provide for our parents.

What did Dad do with the boxes? Glad you asked. He repaired them and took them to the Chinese vegetable farmers who were very glad to buy them. Then the farmers took those same boxes to the stores again and yes, Dad picked up those same boxes. And again he repaired them and so around and around the boxes went. It was a lot of work for Dad but in no time he had paid for the house. Again God provided.

In due time, they retired and did not have to work so hard. Dad had a good driving record. He never had an accident but when he was 86 years old he decided it was time to give it up. So he drove to the police station and handed in his driver's license. I believe he got some kind of citation from them. They gave him a permit to drive the car home and that was it. Bless his heart.

Now back to Prairie. There were many good musicians and singers. So about twice a year they would give us a wonderful treat by doing a concert. In those early years Prairie had a radio broadcast on Sunday morning over CFCN in Calgary. Dear Miss Anderson even got me to sing in a sextet on the air one summer. That's my only claim to fame!!

Some of us siblings on a HUGE stump near our home. June 27, 1943

Various Mission leaders came to Prairie to present the need of foreign missions to the student body. I was always deeply moved by the need. Among them was a colourful speaker named Rev. Silas Fox from India. A Rev. Davis represented the India Mission. That mission changed its name later. Then came Dr. T. J. Bach from the then Scandinavian Alliance Mission (SAM). It was later renamed TEAM which stands for The Evangelical Alliance Mission.

I was very much impressed by his godliness and great humility. He often said that we should live so close to Jesus that everyone we met would find it easier to love Jesus. Whether he talked to an older woman or a young girl he would call them 'girlie.' He had visited mission fields and told us stories we will never forget.

CHAPTER 8

Third year at Prairie

In the spring of 1943 both my sister Rosa and I were asked to be summer girls. We enjoyed the summer very much. When school started in the fall, Rosa was not well and had to return home. However, she returned two years later and went on to graduate in 1948. So Phyllis Duncan became my roommate in the same room above the dining room.

My gratis work that year and the following year was mail girl. Another girl by the name of Alice Wiebe worked with me. We went to the office and sorted the mail by dorms. Two men delivered to the men's dorms and staff houses. I enjoyed it very much because I got to know each girl in school.

You should have seen us at Christmas time when all the parcels started to come. Somehow the girls almost seemed to think the parcels were from us. I like chocolates and I got more chocolates during those two years than at any time in my life. The girls always shared with the mail girl. Good thing I did not know then that chocolates are not good for you. I could not have eaten them with a clear conscience.

Prairie was and is a missionary training school. Student graduates from the early years would come back to school and tell us about their experiences. Missions was always before us. In fact, the first time any of us went to the Tabernacle for Sunday Services we saw four lines on the wall behind the platform that read:

Because I tightly clutched my little earthly store,
Nor sent Thy messengers unto some distant shore?
Is there a soul who died, who died because of me?
Forever shut away from Heaven and from Thee?

I read that every Sunday for four years. So did the other students for as long as they attended there. We will never forget those words. I was back at Prairie in October of 1995 for our 50 Class Reunion and regraduation. We received a diploma for having served the Lord for 50 years. It was good to see those four lines were still up there. May we never forget the responsibility and privilege we have to give the gospel to those who have never heard.

Several times a year we had a day of fasting and prayer. Students would get up and ask God for forgiveness, or maybe a prayer of dedication to the Lord for service wherever or whatever that might be. On one such day I suddenly thought perhaps I should be a missionary too. Just as quickly I had reason for not being one. Was not I just a farm girl with no capabilities? I was not made like other students. I was very shy and had no education to speak of. I . . . I. . . I could not.

At that very moment Mr. Maxwell began to read a verse, Romans 9:20, "Nay but, O man, who art thou that repliest against God? Shall a thing formed say to him that formed it, 'Why hast thou made me thus?'" That hit me like a bolt of lightening. God knew what I was thinking and my mouth was stopped by that verse. However, I did not offer myself to God for His service that day, nor any day soon.

My sister Tillie and I in September 1942.

While I am on the subject of a fast day, I am reminded that my sister Tillie arrived at Prairie on one of those days to visit me. She arrived at noon just as we were dismissed for a break. She was hungry and ready to eat with me, only to discover there would be no meal served. Oh, she had food with her but it was a treat for me from home so she did not eat it. I do not remember how we solved that dilemma.

Among the treats she had brought were some smoked ooligans (very small fish). I am not sure I spelled it correctly. What's more I used to call them hooligans before someone kindly corrected me. One of my friends came into my room just then and helped herself to a fish. What almost made our stomaches turn was that she ate the whole thing, head, eyes, fins and innards. I guess she was hungry! Dear Norma Evans. Tillie and I still laugh about that whenever those fish are mentioned. They were really delicious though.

That school year finished in April as always. Our graduation exercises and spring conference were especially blessed. We were taught a new chorus which kept going through my mind. I will recite the words for you:

"Far above all, far above all
Jesus the crucified, far above all
Low at His footstool adoring I fall
God hath exalted H-I-M far above all."

My class motto.

CHAPTER 9

Working in Vancouver

The spring of 1944 I went home to BC. That is, I did not stay to work at Prairie for the summer. I felt I needed a watch and some other things for my final year. My dear friend Clara Lapohn from Prairie was going to BC too, to earn money for her final year.

We travelled together on the train at night. It was a beautiful moonlight night and I was intrigued by the scenery. The Rocky Mountains were so high and so beautiful with the moon shining on the snow covered peaks. I could hardly contain my joy. In fact, I could not. Passengers all around us were sleeping. I guess they had seen it before. But I thought this was too good for them to miss. I then did something I still don't understand how I had the courage, nay the nerve, to do because I was painfully shy. I got up and went and roused about a half dozen passengers and said, "Look at those mountains. And just think that God has exalted Jesus far above all that!" I remember I did not get any thank you's. They just closed their eyes again and slept some more.

You'd think I might have been embarrassed after all that. But strangely enough I was not. I just felt compelled to do it. Through the years as I have been reminded of that incident, I have stopped and prayed for those people. I believe the Lord prompted me to do such an unusual thing and maybe it caused one or another to think about Jesus Christ.

After I arrived at my parent's home I had a few good days rest. Then I contacted Clara and we went to a job seeker's office in Vancouver. Immediately we were each given several leads for women who were looking for girls to do day work for them. We were informed the going wage was $5.00 a day, streetcar fare and a sandwich.

But first, we had to find a room where we could stay. We found one at my sister Mary and her husband Tony Bojczuk's place, where we did not have to pay and that was wonderful. We then sat down and figured out how much we needed to earn. We needed fare back to school, room and board for the winter, a watch, books and so on. We counted the number of days of work we hopefully would have and how much we could spend on food. It turned out we would be able to buy a loaf of bread every other day and two tins of pork and beans and wieners. We heated a wiener each in with the beans. I must not forget to tell you that we always got our noon meal at the place we worked which helped an awful lot.

After about two months we stopped doing day work but I do not remember why. We went job hunting again and landed one at a Boys' Boarding home. There we washed pots and pans, washed the kitchen floor and probably prepared vegetables. The woman in charge really liked Clara from the first day. She did NOT like me no matter how hard I tried to please her. She just scolded and criticized me. One day I had enough so I walked up to her and gave her a big hug and told her I loved her. Again, I am surprised I did that because I was so shy. It made no difference in her but I felt better.

Pretty soon the school closed for the summer and we were without a job. Off to the job office again. It did not matter to us what we did just as long as we could work together. Next we got a job at a rake factory.

The next morning we trudged off to Powell Street to find the factory. We were within walking distance and to our benefit it saved car fare. I am not too sure if it was Powell or Cordova but one of those streets where we were a bit afraid to walk. We found it and the foreman, Mr. Fox greeted us. It was not a big factory, maybe only about 25 workers. We were given a pair of strong gloves, a pair of pliers and shown how to make metal rakes for grass. We pretty well wore out a pair of gloves almost every day. It was hard work and we stood on our feet all day.

But we were glad for any job and did it as best we could. We never told Mr. Fox or anyone that we were Christians. But I guess he found out because we did not use the language that he and the others did. So he began to tease us about it. Later on he jeered whenever he had to give us orders. He made fun of us in front of the other workers. This probably went on for two weeks.

One afternoon he came to us and asked if we would stay after work when we were finished. We said we would but had some misgivings about it. We thought perhaps he had enough of us Christians and was going to fire us. I thought if he did the Lord would have another job for us. When everybody was about to leave he reminded us again to be sure to stay behind.

When everybody was gone he took us to his office and asked us to sit down. Now that I think of it, he must have been the owner and manager. He asked us how does one become a Christian. We were only too glad to tell him but we thought he was just putting us on. Then one of us asked him if he would like to pray. He said that was okay, he just wanted to know how. Then he thanked us and excused us. As we walked home we did not know what to make of it but we prayed for him.

The next morning we came to work as usual. Some of the workers were standing outside. When we came closer we saw a piece of paper on the door that they were reading. It said, "Mr. Fox deceased during the night. Factory closed indefinitely." You can imagine what a shock that was. But Clara and I believe that he had a premonition that he was going to die. We also believe that he is in Heaven. It seems we had to be there for just those two weeks so he could ask how to be saved.

Neither Clara nor I can remember where we got a job next. But I know we were able to earn what we needed. The strange thing is I am still very fond of pork and beans!

It was good to be with Mother and Father off and on that summer. They were living in a different house and I had to get acquainted with BC. I helped a few times to clean eggs. I was surprised that they did it with sandpaper. Dad nailed some sandpaper on a rounded piece of wood and it worked very well. I asked why they did not wash them. They told me that the eggs wouldn't keep. Also they could not sell them if they did. Those that had to be washed were used up at home.

The chicken barn was close to 200 feet from the house. Dad brought a wire from the barn into the house and rigged it up to a switch. Chicken farmers were trying to get as many eggs as possible. About 3:00 a.m. Dad would get up and throw the switch which put all the bright lights on in the barn. The chickens were fooled into thinking it was morning and started scratching for food. If I remember correctly that caused the chickens to lay two eggs a day. Quite an idea, eh? Nowadays I guess the cruelty to animals groups would object and stage a protest.

P.B.I. staff picture in 1941-42.

CHAPTER 10

Final Year at Prairie

October of 1944 saw me on my way back to Three Hills. This time I went to the registrar's office right away to pay my room and board for six months. I wanted to be sure that was paid. I was also proudly wearing a watch.

A few days after school started those prayer group charts went up on the wall again. What country did I sign up for? Well, let me tell you first that during my Junior (third) year I had signed up to pray for South America. I guess the Lord had a bit more of my heart but I was still thinking that South America was not too far away. I might be able to go home, if I had to be a missionary to that country, should my parents get sick.

My final year, I decided to pray for India. I had not had a call to India but I felt I had to keep one step ahead of the Lord. Praying for India might satisfy the Lord so that he would not call me. So every day at noon a group of us, about thirty girls, gathered to pray for India.

One day during that prayer time, the leader named June, was telling us about the great need for missionaries in India. She went on at length about it. Then asked us a question, "Have you ever asked God if He would have you go to India as a missionary?" I said to myself, no I have not, I am afraid to. But I could not tell God no. So I told Him if He wanted me to be a missionary to India, I would go but that I would never go on any hunch of my own. He would have to make it VERY plain to me. The strange thing was after I prayed that prayer I completely forgot about it.

Clara and I had counted our money carefully so that all our needs would be met. There would be no extras, only what we had planned for. I, at least, thought I knew exactly what I would need. Just before Christmas exams the nib broke on my pen. You younger ones probably have never used a pen in which there was an ink bladder. There was a little lever on the barrel of the pen. We dipped the tip of the pen into an ink bottle and pumped that little lever up and down gently until the bladder was full. If one side of the nib broke off it would not write nor could it be filled.

This was an expense not budgeted for. What to do but ask the Lord! After all, had He not forgiven my sins and given me assurance? Nothing was too hard for the Lord after that so I asked Him for one dollar. I got it but from where I cannot remember now. I was in the habit of tithing and knew ten cents belonged to the Lord. So I got someone to give me change for the bill.

Downtown I went to buy a new fountain pen. The price was the same in all the stores, one dollar! What would I do? In the last store I told the owner, as I had the others, that I would be back. After I had gone out of the door, the owner followed and called me back. I went back and he said, "I have one pen, the same as what I showed you, but the box is all broken. I'll give it to you for ninety cents if you don't mind not having the box! Well, I did NOT need a box! Believe me, I had not told a single storekeeper or anyone else that I needed a pen and only had 90 cents. God had so graciously provided for me. All praise be to Him. He does what He says He will do and that is to provide our needs.

Being a senior at Prairie brought with it new responsibilities. One of which was that I was asked to teach a Sunday School class of students. I did not think I could do that but Mrs. Waldock had a teacher training class during the week and taught the next Sunday's lesson to all the Sunday School teachers. That was a blessed time and such a help.

Every year at Prairie was so wonderful and this my fourth year was no exception. It was hard to think of leaving and not coming back the following fall. Eventually, more of my family joined me at school. I mentioned Rosa (Rosie at the time) before. Then came Miriam, and brothers, Otto and Edwin. The boys were there to attend high school only. Prairie High School was not accredited at the time so they had to take government exams in order to qualify to study medicine.

Otto on my right, Edwin on my left.

There were two more expenditures before graduation which I had not reckoned with. One was a pair of white shoes and the other a white dress. As to the shoes, they were provided for by my brother Sam though he did not know I had been praying for money. Someone had enclosed a Canadian five dollar bill in a letter and he could not use it in Africa. Again I took it to the office to make change so I could tithe first. That left me $4.50 and off to town I went. The shoe store had just the right pair I needed for that exact amount. Thank you, Lord.

Now for the dress. One day when I came in from class there on my pillow was a piece of white cloth! I had done some sewing but I felt I could not sew well enough to make a graduation dress. It did not take long for me to share my joy with some close friends. Immediately one of them, Mary Toews (later Epp) offered to sew it for me. She did a good job but I do not know who gave me the material. Mary was very short so we, her friends, fondly called her 'Little Mary.' She was always cheerful so we might have called her Happy Mary.

We were seventy in our graduation class and because Jesus sent out seventy disciples at one time, it was almost a given that all of us would be missionaries. One of my friends asked me which country I was going to. When I told her none she said, "Then you come to China with me." Well, she did not get to go to China but became a Pastor's wife in Canada and served the Lord faithfully.

My parents came to Prairie for my graduation and that meant an awful lot to me. At conference time all of us students moved out of our rooms into class rooms. Conference guests moved into our rooms. Every conference Mr.

Maxwell would make an announcement and it was always the same. "When the sons of God come to conference, then cometh Satan also. Watch your precious possessions. They have a way of disappearing. A word to the wise is sufficient."

Before I leave the subject of Prairie I want to give some quotes of Mr. Maxwell's. One he most often used was, "It's the hardest thing in the world to keep balanced." He'd say it often just after he had given us two sides of a doctrine point. Another, "don't swallow hook, line and sinker when you hear something new. Test it first." I guess the best way is to just give his quotes line after line:

A man all wrapped up in himself makes a mighty small package
Suffering can make us or break us.
Keep short accounts with God.
Faith and life always go together: believe and behave.
Meet your issues, drive in a stake!
Don't let the world pour you into its mould.
Liberty is not license.
Cheer up, the worst is yet to come.
Cheer up, the worms will get you yet.
The greatest mission is submission.
You need a backbone instead of a wishbone.
When praying for missionaries he often prayed, 'Lord bless the women who are out there doing a man's job.'
After a woman missionary (usually a former student) had given a stirring report, he would say, 'Never man spake like this woman.'
Sometimes he talked about unspanked parents.
Every fall after new homesick and restless students arrived, he would speak on "unpack."
Aim at nothing and you'll be sure to hit it!
If you lay up treasures for a rainy day, God will see to it that you get them.
He said, "My Armenian friends say, 'watch that Maxwell, he's tainted with security.'
My Calvanist friends say, 'taint enough.'"
Keep on keeping on.

Well, those are just a few of his choice morsels of wisdom. I need to keep them handy where I can be reminded of them more often. The first one I gave about keeping balanced is one that his students refer to as 1 Maxwell 1:1. We bless his memory. He loved the Lord and taught us to love Him too. Rev. Leslie E. Maxwell went to be with the Lord on February 4, 1984 at the age of 88. His dear wife joined him in Heaven on December 3, 1992 at age 92. We all remember Mr. Maxwell as being a bundle of energy and he served the Lord with every bit of it. He was also a happy man who laughed a lot.

CHAPTER 11

Working with CSSM

When I left Prairie I did not know what lay ahead. I had no idea what God had planned for my life. But as for the summer I wanted to spend it working with children in Daily Vacation Bible School. Since I had been so much influenced by the Canadian Sunday School Mission (CSSM), I decided to join them. I applied and was accepted.

A VBS class, Martha Martens and I.

At that time we did not need to raise any money for travel or food. The only preparations we needed to make were to bring our bedding. They loaned each of us an air mattress, and we had instructions to take a quilt, fold it over and sew it up on two sides like a sleeping bag. They also loaned us a frying pan, thermos bottle, cup, plate, bowl, knife, fork, spoon and one pot to cook our food. We thought we were well supplied.

The day before we were to leave we all gathered in a church in Vancouver (or Surrey) for a testimony meeting and message of encouragement. We were sent out two by two. Miss Martha Martens (also from Prairie) and I were assigned to work together for the three months. The CSSM gave each of us bus or train fare to our first destination. We brought our own lunch for the trip. We went out trusting the Lord for our daily food and fare from one place to the next. If I remember correctly, the Mission sent us the fare to come back to Vancouver at the end of the summer.

We were assigned to work in the interior of BC. We had been given lessons to teach and some coloured paper to use for crafts. One place we were was Lake Arrowhead. I believe that was where we stayed with a lovely Christian family by the name of McQueen, who had about five children. I kept in contact with them even after they moved to one of the islands on the coast and until both Mr. and Mrs. McQueen died.

Another place was in a completely Finnish settlement. We stayed in one of the homes. They fed us well. It turned out that the Mission had made arrangements with a family in each area to house and feed us. These Finnish people taught us a few things about baths. One was the sauna bath and another was very much like the Japanese baths. In each VBS several children accepted the Lord Jesus and that was such a joy.

In one school we had a boy that gave us a lot of trouble. He constantly tried to disrupt class. One day he even managed to tip a bench over with about six children sitting on it. He was not mean just trying to keep the others from listening. We had a program for the parents in each school at the end of VBS. I was drilling the children on some of the things we had taught them. When I asked, "Who has sinned?" this little fellow raised his hand, stood up and said, "I have not." When he raised his hand I thought bless his heart he has listened to what we taught. But I was let down. However, we prayed for him for a long time. I often wonder where all those children are and if they followed through on their Christian walk.

I cannot remember the name of each place we were but another was Slocan City, BC. There was an Internment Camp for the Japanese people who had been moved inland from Vancouver during the war. Many of those people were professors, rich business men, doctors, lawyers and other professionals. I felt bad for the way they had been uprooted from their homes and businesses. Talking to several of the older women about their plight I told them how bad I felt and asked them for forgiveness on behalf of our government. I will never forget their most gracious responses. They said they understood why it had been done, it was war time. Here too, Martha and I saw children come to Jesus.

It was at Slocan City where we had the biggest attendance in the VBS and quite a few were saved. We thought perhaps it was because the Japanese were displaced that they willingly sent their children. As I said a few paragraphs back, my thoughts often go back to all those children we met and taught about Jesus. I hope that they have gone on with the Lord.

While in Slocan City, we met a couple, Barnett and Katherine Harrison, and their four little boys. This couple had been to Prairie too, so we had lots in common. They were holding VBS in the area as well during the summer holidays. They were both teaching in a school in Thrums, BC. They chose to go there because of the Doukhobors living in the area. They hoped to give the Gospel to them by living among them in the little village of Thrums.

I took time out right now to call Martha Martens and ask her what some of her memories were. She said we stayed in hotels a few times after long train trips. I asked her where we got the money from and she said it seemed the Lord always provided it just in time. But she said that the Mission did send us a small cheque a few times.

Martha also kept a diary in those days and from it she learned that we had four VBS's in Arrowhead. We stayed in homes where our hosts did not know the Lord. We both remember how we talked with them so earnestly about their need of a Saviour. Her diary tells us we held VBS in Galena Bay at Sixsmith (must be the name of the school), Gerough School and in Sicamous. We had very gracious hosts. In a couple of places we made our own meals right in the school where we lived in one of the back rooms. We were thankful for our air mattresses for we slept on the floor.

It was at the McQueen home we slept upstairs. It was very hot so we had the window open. In the middle of the night while we were sound asleep their huge tomcat jumped in off the roof and landed on my tummy. I screamed very, very loud and awakened everybody. We never had pets in our house so this cat really scared me. The children got a big kick out of that incident.

At the last school (can't remember the name) we had twenty-three children. The dates were approximately August 18 to 24. Here too, several children prayed to receive Jesus. Children so readily accept Jesus and that means they are spared a life of sin. On August 25 Martha and I boarded the train back to Vancouver. We were met by someone from CSSM and taken to a church where we gave reports of the summer's work. We also returned the borrowed items. So ended the summer of 1945. My heart was filled with joy because of what we had done in Jesus' name.

Brother Herb, in the Royal Navy. Taken behind Eaton's Store in Saskatoon. September 4, 1942 just before he left for Toronto to go overseas.

CHAPTER 12

An Unexpected Letter

On the journey home from the summer in the Columbia-Kootenay area, I had no idea what I was going to do that coming winter. But I do remember I was not concerned. Had not God forgiven my sins and let me know they were forgiven? Then, would He not continue to guide me? He did. I never cease to marvel at how many ways and means God uses to guide us and get us in the right place at the right time. My brother Sam often talks about God having a schedule for each of us and that it's wise to check with Him as to whether we are where He wants us.

Probably about two weeks after I arrived home I had a letter from the Harrisons whom we had met at Slocan City. I thought nothing of it. After the salutation he opened the letter with a verse of scripture. It was from Esther 4:14. Mr. Harrison took the first word of the verse and then skipped most of it till the last part. "For.....who knoweth whether thou art come to the kingdom for such a time as this." Let me digress a moment here to tell that my oldest brother Isaac got quite a (for want of a better word) "charge" out of that opening. For ever after, till his dying day, he ALWAYS started his letters to me with these three words "For who knoweth?" It was always a loving reminder as to how the course of my life changed through that letter.

The rest of the Harrison letter told me of their four little sons, David (about 6), Norman (5), Jimmy (3 1/2), and Johnny (a little over a year old), all of whom I had met. He went on to say that they had a hard time getting reliable help in the home to care for the youngest two boys while they were at school all day. Norman was actually too young for school but they took him along to make it easier for whoever took care of the younger two. A neighbour lady took care of them when she could but she had to be gone often.

The four Harrison brothers.

The Harrisons asked if I would be able to come and live in their home to care for the two youngest during the day and do all the housework till close of the school term next summer. It seems to me they sent money for the train ticket. I consulted with my parents and there did not seem to be anything to hinder me from going. The letter urged me to come just as soon as possible. I set a date and notified them so they could meet me at the Thrums train station upon my arrival.

I took the train that was called 'Kettle Valley', the same one I had taken in the spring. Again Mother packed a lovely lunch for me for the ten hour journey. All went well till about the half-way mark. Suddenly the train stopped. No one knew why. Eventually word trickled back to all the coaches that there had been a mud slide across the tracks. We waited. Then waited some more. It turned out we were delayed there a whole day.

Meanwhile the Harrisons had been at the station and finally went home when no trains came from either direction. They did not have to go far for the railroad track was just a few hundred yards from their house and quite a bit higher than their house.

I arrived the next morning just after they had gone to school. No one to meet me. But their neighbour who had the two boys saw me and came to my rescue. Harrisons had given her the house key so she let me in and left the boys with me. Here I was in a strange town and house, with two little boys till school closed in the late afternoon.By the way, the neighbour had been told to show me to my room.

When the Harrisons came home they gave me a very royal welcome. They had no idea what had delayed me but they had been praying for my safety. After supper they gave me a quick introduction to their schedule and my work. I was to be what we often call chief cook and bottle washer. I cleaned the house and washed all the clothes on a scrub board. As soon as we had snow I carried it in and melted it for washing clothes. There was an outhouse but of course it was too cold and too far to go. A big pail served very well. I carried it out in the morning.

Every time a train passed, it shook the whole house and it seemed they all came at night. Harrisons told me I would get used to it and never hear the trains. That seemed impossible because they kept me awake night after night. But it did not take long though and I never heard a one.

I was introduced to the four boys as Auntie Annie. That was very kind of them. I fell in love with them from the first. They were also told not to go to my room unless I invited them and they were very good about that. They were very obedient. Kay Harrison had made each of the boys a little sailor suit which they wore to church. We called them the four sailor boys. Mrs. Harrison had navy wool on hand and asked if I would knit them each a sleeveless sweater. I had never knitted before but I learned. They actually turned out very well with a bit of blue, red and white trim at the neck and arm holes.

Harrisons did not have a car so we went everywhere by bus or train. Not very far from Thrums was a town called Castlegar. Missionaries Fred and Madeline Woodrow lived there. They were independent of any mission if I remember correctly. They were there primarily to get the Gospel to the Doukhobors. However, they had rented a hall in town where they conducted Sunday services.

They invited Harrisons and me to attend and help in teaching Sunday School. Mr. Harrison also took turns at preaching. So, every Sunday morning saw us up early to catch the bus for Castlegar. We always got there on time for a cup of coffee which dear Madeline provided so graciously. We had to climb a short but very steep embankment to get to the road. On one of my early Sundays there, snow had fallen and it was cold. Mr. Harrison carried little

Johnny. It was very slippery and that seemed funny to Johnny. He started to giggle. That made Mr. Harrison laugh. The more he laughed the more he slid. By that time we were all laughing. We almost missed the bus. That was one of many fun things to remember.

My Sunday School class was the little ones. Sometimes I had four or five little pupils, but very often I had only two little boys. Yes, you guessed it, our own David and Norman. They were very attentive.

David married Ruth and went as missionaries to Hong Kong, Singapore and Taiwan. Right now they are in Korea.

Norman married Betty in Victoria, on Vancouver Island and sent me an invitation. I was home on furlough at the time but I really did not have money to make the trip by bus and boat. So I acknowledged the invitation and said I was very sorry but I could not come.

Well, the night before the wedding, Norm's Mother called me and said Norm was very disappointed. She said he had told her that Auntie Annie led him to the Lord and he so much wanted me to be present at his wedding. I had not known that.

All of a sudden I had money (probably someone helped me out). So the next morning my sister Hulda and her husband took me to the Airport and I went by plane, no less. It was a beautiful sunny day and the wedding was in a garden.

I asked Norm when it was I had led him to the Lord. It was then he told me that it was in one of those very early Sunday School classes in Castlegar when only he and David were in class. I had taught the story of Joseph. I had no idea what went on in his little heart. It showed again that the Holy Spirit does the work. It was a great encouragement to me. Thank you Norman, for sharing that with me at a time when I needed to hear it.

Norm and Betty went to Ethiopia with S.I.M. as missionaries. They returned home later because of poor health. In 1985 they moved to Toronto where Norm became assistant to the Canadian Director of SIM. In September of 1989 Norm came to Abbotsford to represent SIM at the funeral service for Rev. Albert Brant. Al and Evelyn were also missionaries in Ethiopia. After the service Norm came and gave me a hug and thanked me again for being instrumental in his conversion. It was then I learned that it was through Albert's influence that Norm and Betty went to Ethiopia. So the Lord uses different events and different people to influence people for Himself. Sometimes we are not even aware of what's happening. Let's be ready to fit into God's schedule at all times, to be a channel through whom the Holy Spirit can work.

My time at the Harrisons was a very blessed and happy one. It was an harmonious home where Christ was honoured. I never heard an unkind word in the home and have only happy memories.

We got to know our neighbours quite well. At their special festival times they would share some of their excellent cooking with us. They were very good bread bakers and also cooked the real Russian borsht. Everything had either cream or butter in it, often both. I loved their food.

The women most often were quite heavy. The men were more inclined to be on the thin side. It did not take long to find out why the women were heavier. In the spring the gardens needed to be cultivated. Then I saw a woman hitch herself to the front of the plow while her husband walked behind to guide it. It turned out to be quite a common sight in small villages.

We got to know a young Doukhobor couple by the name of George and Lillian Osachoff. They had a wee daughter named Lenna. They became Christians through the Woodrows I believe. They came to the church services in the hall on Sundays and helped teach Sunday School too. I enjoyed getting to know them. They later moved to the Vancouver area and are probably still there.

I had not known what the Lord had for me when I finished Bible School. Then when my summer with CSSM came to a close I did not know what I would do. I knew my time at the Harrisons would be finished at the end of school in June but again I did not know what was next. The Woodrows had hinted that perhaps I would come and help them in their work. Nothing was definite. I had no guidance.

It was now probably early February 1946. The Harrisons and David and Norman had gone to school. Jimmy and Johnny were playing outside. I was tidying up the house for the day. The floors were covered with linoleum and I used a corn broom to sweep the floors. On this particular morning, I was sweeping up as usual when I noticed a piece of paper on the floor. It was a bit too big for the usual scraps of paper. It was printed on both sides but there was scribbling on it. I realized it was my mail, a letter from the leader of our class at PBI, in other words a letter to us as alumnus. I looked around a bit more and found the envelope for it, addressed to me, also on the floor. The four boys had never been into my mail before. Evidently they had that time. I believe the Lord allowed it to happen for a specific reason. I still have that very piece of paper.

There I stood, sort of leaning on the broom with one hand and holding the paper in the other while I read its contents. It was a story about Ida Scudder. She related how her grandfather Dr. John Scudder might have been one of New York's most prominent physicians had he not read of India's (then) 600 million calling from their superstition and poverty. He left his lucrative practice and took his good sized family to India. One by one they came back to America to be educated. Seven of his children heard the call of God and went back to India as doctors and several of them died there from fever or whatever. One of his sons was her father who was in India right then with her mother. Ida had been born in India.

Yes, they were in India and she was holding a letter in her hand from them. Her father told young Ida that her Mother was very sick and that he did not have time to stay with her all the time. Would Ida come to India and help care for her mother, her father asked.

Ida did not know what to do."It is enough," said Ida, as she sat in Northfield with the summons in her hand. Why should all the Scudders be buried in India, she asked herself. She would go gladly to be with her mother while she was ill. As soon as she was well, she'd come back and live her life as other girls were living theirs.

So Ida took passage to India to be with her mother but only for a short while.

One evening while her mother was sleeping, Ida sat in another room reading. As the dusk of the twilight was deepening into the darkness of the night, a knock sounded at the door. A man stood before her. He was a high class Mohammedan, tall, slender and white robed. He bowed low and then spoke, "My young wife is ill, ill to the death. Will the gracious lady come to attend to her?"

Ida knew nothing of medicine, but she answered eagerly, "My father is a medical man. He will come to see your wife." The man drew himself up quite proudly and said, "No man has ever looked on the face of my wife. We are high born. I would rather a thousand times that she would die than that a man should look upon her face." Silently, he turned and went into the darkness.

Ida sat down again and thought. She was in India now, in India, with this pitiable child wife, who might be dying even as she sat there and thought of her. She was soon startled by a second knock.

"My wife," began this man as had the other, "is very sick. She is giving me much trouble. After all the pain I've taken, she may die unless the memsahib comes to help her."

"I am not a doctor", she explained. My father is a doctor. He will - -," but the man interrupted her with a proud uplifting of his turbaned head, as he said, "I am a high caste man. No man dare look upon the face of my wife." Even as he spoke he turned and disappeared into the darkness. Ida's thoughts went with him back to the girl. Perhaps she was dying even now. Something clutched at the heart of the American girl over there in India and choked her throat as she sat there, helpless and unhelping.

It was terrible that two calls should come in such rapid succession on the same night. As she shuddered at the thought, a third knock sounded. A third man stood before her. His voice was eager as he said, "My wife is very ill. They told me I could find help here from a wonderful foreign doctor who had done remarkable things. At last, there was a call for her father! "Oh yes, I will send my father," she answered gladly. The man straightened himself. "Not a man. You must come."

In vain did Ida plead that her father would come, but, sadly and alone the man departed. She sat down again. Were all the suffering child-wives in India calling for HER that night?

The night passed. The day dawned. Ida walked out into the street. As she passed a gateway she heard wailing and loud lamenting. It chilled her heart. She knew that the life of one of the child-wives had passed into Eternity with the passing of the night. She went on. At another house, the beating of the drums, the shrieks and the moans told her that a second wife had died.

She wanted to turn and go back to her parents home, but a relentlessness drew her on until she stood beside the crude bier which was to carry away the poor little body of the third wife. The skilled touch of a physician might have saved her. As she walked on she seemed to hear a call which came from the lips of the Man who hung upon a cross. The Cross seemed to be transplanted until it stood on India's soil. And the voice of Him upon it said, not "go ye," but, "I have died for you, Come and follow me."

After Ida's mother got well, Ida Scudder went back to New York and entered the Women's Medical College. She had heard the call of the women of India but above all the call of her Saviour. When she finished training she too went to India as so many Scudders had before her. I was taken to her place where she had a home in the Nilgiri Hills of South India. She was 80 at the time. She had not seen the need for Scudders to go to India and be buried there. But she did go there and yes, she died and was buried there too.

When I finished reading that article the Lord spoke to my heart. I was like Ida, I wanted to spend my life the way I wanted to, that is, to stay at home and take care of my parents.

Right there the Lord seemed to say to me, "Annie, do you remember that back there at Prairie one day during India prayer meeting you bowed your head and told me you would be willing to go to India if I called you? So, this is it. I want you to go to India as a missionary." At that instant, I remembered that prayer. I put the broom away and went to my bedroom.

I got down on my knees by my bed and with tears of surrender I told the Lord I would go. I also told Him that I knew that He could take care of my parents. While still on my knees I took my Bible and turned to Galatians where I had my devotions earlier that day. Now I was directed to Galatians 1:15, 16. "But when it pleased God, who separated me from my mother's womb, and called me by His grace, To reveal His Son in me, that I might preach Him among the heathen; immediately I conferred not with flesh and blood: (now part of vs. 17). Neither went I up to Jerusalem......but I went..." That is I determined to go straight ahead from that moment forward, to India.

That call was not to be mistaken. When the Harrisons came from school and supper was over I told them that I was on my way to India. It came as a shock to them but they stood with me. That night when they tucked their boys into bed and before they prayed with them, they told them that Auntie Annie was going to go to India as a missionary. The boys got very serious and said that if that was the case then they would not scare her anymore with bugs and worms. Then they prayed for me because they knew there would be many bugs in India. They kept their word and never again put any "gift" worms in my hand. We all remember those, "close your eyes, open your hand" tricks, don't we?

The next move was to apply to a Mission Board to send me. But which would it be? I prayed much and the more I thought of it, my mind went back to Prairie days. Of all the mission representatives that visited our school, Dr. T. J. Bach made the biggest impression on me. He at that time represented the Scandinavian Alliance Mission (SAM). His humility and love for the Lord I will never forget. As I thought of several missions that worked in India, more and more it was impressed upon me that I should apply to SAM. So I wasted no time doing just that. SAM several years later became TEAM which stands for The Evangelical Alliance Mission.

I continued working at the Harrisons while I waited for my application to be processed. I guess I thought I would have an answer back in a month. I did not realize that they contacted all the references I had given.

Once school was out, the Harrisons did not need me. Fred Woodrows then contacted me and gave me an invitation to come and live with them and work among the Doukhobors. I readily accepted that as the Lord's leading.

They had a missionary with them already and that was Clara Lapohn. I knew her well from Prairie days.

Clara had applied to China Inland Mission to go to China. So both she and I were waiting for our acceptance. The Woodrows had a nice little cottage in the back yard where we slept but we ate with the Woodrows.

The Harrison family in 1956.

I want to say a bit more about the Harrisons. When school closed they also moved to Castlegar. Mr. Harrison built a house there and they tried to get teaching jobs. I do not remember if they got jobs or not but it was not very long before they got a call to go to Two Rivers Bible Institute in Alberta. Mr. Harrison was one of the teachers there. During my first furlough I visited them at TRBI. It was so good to see them again and especially "my" four little angels. I was amazed at how much they had grown.

During that visit the Harrisons gave me a $5.00 gift. That was a lot those days and especially since they hardly got any salary. David gave me 48 cents, Jimmy 14 cents, and Johnny 12 cents. I don't know where Norman was! But that does not matter. I want to backtrack a bit and tell you that after my acceptance with TEAM and before I left on deputation work for the first time, the Harrison boys gave me a gift. They each came with their little savings bank and asked me to cup my hands while they emptied all they had into my hands. Then we counted it together and it totalled $1.47. How I rejoiced over the love they expressed by giving me all they had. That was the FIRST gift of money I received towards India. Tears come to my eyes even now when I think of it.

When I left the Harrisons they gave me the blanket I had slept under to take to India. Take it I did and used it till it was almost in shreds. Then I gave it to an Indian woman and she sewed an old sari on each side to make a warm blanket for her family.

Also before I left the Harrisons the four boys gave me a gift that I still have. It travelled to India and back with me and is now on my guest room wall. It's a little wooden plaque with a robin sitting on a branch with its beak wide open. There are six words on it from Isaiah 50:9, "..the Lord God will help me." In India it hung over my bed and usually those were the first words I saw when I awakened in the morning. What a glorious promise!

By now you have noted that the Harrison family means a lot to me. Mr. and Mrs. Harrison have been with the Lord for quite a few years. I still keep in contact with the boys as much as I can, when I have their correct addresses.

Now back to the Woodrows and Clara Lapohn (later Mrs. Tom Walker). It did not take long before Clara got word from her mission that her application was refused for health reasons. It came as a great shock and disappointment to her and to all of us. But their loss was our gain and later Tom's. For Clara served with Tom for many years in various pastorates, after a few more years in Castlegar. They are retired now of course. Clara and I worked together very well and we have fond memories of our days there.

The Woodrows, as I said before, were independent of a supporting mission board. They had raised support and people were faithful though they never got full support. Fred's dear Mother was one of their supporters and somehow she often scrounged up an extra dollar to send to her son. It was very good training for me. You must know that I had no income of my own (nor did Clara) and the Woodrows invited us to live and work with them on the condition that we all live on whatever money came in.

When there was money we ate, when there was none we sat down together and asked the Lord for food for supper. I remember one such day when there was no money. We had prayed and Fred went to the Post Office three times that day to see if the mail brought any money. Blessed be the Lord, on the third trip, there was a letter from dear Mother Woodrow with a one dollar bill enclosed. On the way home he stopped at the store and bought a couple loaves of bread and some ground hamburger meat. We had a lovely feast. There were quite a few times the same thing happened. We never went hungry. We lived from hand to mouth but it was from God's hand to our mouths. There is nothing wrong with that. It was very precious to see how God provided.

Mother Woodrow lived in Vancouver, BC and she had quite a family to care for. I don't remember if they were foster children, I rather think it was private, for single mothers or others that needed a place for their children where they would be loved and cared for. She always had about eight boys and girls. As soon as school finished in June, she would bring her little tribe to the Woodrows. Then Clara and I moved into the Woodrow's living room and slept on the couch. Mother Woodrow and children moved into the cabin. It was so good to be around Mother Woodrow. She was cheerful and had an easy way of managing her little brood. She loved them all into the Kingdom as far as I know.

When Mother Woodrow brought her children, Clara and I planned a VBS program just for them. The Woodrows had a beautiful backyard and garden where we had the classes. I have some pictures of those classes. Madeline and her mother-in-law sat on a bench on the side to listen in.

Clara Lapohn and I with the Woodrow clan at VBS.

Now a little about the Woodrows. I have not told you that they had two daughters Beverley and Elaine. Madeline played the piano beautifully and taught both of the girls to play. They must have been about eight and nine when

Madeline told us a secret, she was pregnant. In due time another daughter, Gwendolyn was born. Clara and I loved to babysit this sweet baby once in a while. She gave us some bad scares though. Once she held her breath till she turned blue. We prayed, we shook her, finally in desperation, one of us poked our finger into her mouth and realized she had nearly swallowed her tongue. When we pulled it out she breathed again. We told her parents when they came home and Madeline said she had done that before but forgot to tell us. She finally grew out of that stage and everyone was greatly relieved.

Elaine (back left), Beverley (right), Fred and Madeline Woodrow with wee Gwen (front).

I just stopped and called Fred Woodrow who is now living in Three Hills, Alberta. He lives by himself and does all his own cooking and cleaning. His dear wife and our friend Madeline went to be with the Lord quite a few years ago. I asked him how he came to go to the Castlegar area to work with the Doukhobors. He told me that when he was still single he and Fred Jarvis were working with CSSM or rather BC CSSM. They asked to go to that area and after spending the whole summer there felt burdened to go back as resident missionaries. Both got married and both couples went back. I think the Jarvis's worked near Trail, BC. The Woodrows lived in Castlegar until the Doukhobors all moved elsewhere. Castlegar is now a big city, taking in Kinaird and Utishenya towns. Businesses from Trail have moved there and it's a thriving place.

Clara Lapohn and I in Russian outfits.

Clara and I enjoying a joke.

Clara and I with our Doukhobor friends.

Clara and I with our separate classes outside

Watermelon picnic.

The Woodrows were very faithful in witnessing and many were saved, especially in the VBS's. Fred says he still gets letters from people that were saved as children in their classes years ago. They tell him how they may have wavered for a few years are now living for the Lord. Quite a few of them attended Prairie when they grew up.

Clara and I had many VBS programs. Often we lived right in the Russian homes. Clara was a bit more chubby than I and they used to say that Clara would make a good Russian wife but I would not. They were always glad to dress us up in their garb, usually all white, and take our pictures. Maybe I'll sneak in a picture or two of us in their dress.

When the place was farther away we lived in the school house. We knew that sometimes the Doukhobors would protest against the school system (government) by burning them down. Mr. Woodrow had warned us about that. He said they would never burn it with us inside. If we heard any suspicious noises during the night we were to make our presence known by quickly lighting the lantern and holding it up in the windows.

Would you know, one night we were awakened by the noise of tin cans. We got so scared. We shook so much we could hardly light the lantern. When we did and held it up to the window the rattling stopped and we knew what we feared was true. We did not think we could go back to our mattresses but we read Psalm 91 by light of the lantern. Then we put it back in the window and committed ourselves to the Lord. The Lord gave us His peace and we did go back to sleep with His protection.

In some districts the Doukhobor homes were scattered quite far, in other areas they lived in large community houses. This meant we had to walk far to visit all the homes. Some days we walked 15 miles in that hilly country. What a joy it was to be able to pray with the children as many accepted Jesus as Saviour during our meetings in schools and outdoors.

Once in a while we attended their church services. They did a lot of singing. They had good voices and sang in parts. Someone would preach but we did not get most of what was said. They served Communion. No, I think they just had the elements there on the table, a jug of water, a loaf of bread and a dish with salt. I do not remember what they represented. We did learn some Russian though, at least the most common words and phrases. We also learned some Russian hymns and choruses that the Christians sang.

The Doukhobors were quite a radical sect of Russians. The grave of their leader Peter Verigan was about a mile or so from Thrums. Every so often someone would try to dig up his body and move it. I don't think they ever succeeded. It was kind of scary for us when we lived in Thrums.

These people were very fond of watermelon. Every summer when they were ripe they would gather in a huge park to eat them and roll cookies. Everyone came from far and near. There were probably a thousand or more. The Woodrows, Clara and I would go too in order to pass out tracts. They protested again there, this time by taking off all their clothes, men and women alike. It was against the government. Certain ones, four or five, came ready to suddenly take a pin out of their skirt, blouse and hair which made clothes fall to the ground as they walked away.

It was very embarrassing. The police had been invited to watch the protest. They came prepared to arrest the Doukhobors and herd them to police cars to take them to jail. Then they protested in jail by going on hunger strikes. Similar to nowadays, isn't it? We ourselves found the Russians and Doukhobors very friendly and kind. When Clara and I lived in the schools the women would send all kinds of delicious food to us with their children.

The Woodrows were concerned about the souls right in Castlegar too, so they arranged for Clara and I to visit every single home. We would tell them about Jesus and leave them a tract. We also invited them to the services that were held every Sunday in the hall. I guess our reception was the same as in any other town. I should say that the townspeople were not Doukhobors.

The summer came and went and still no word from TEAM as to whether I had been accepted or not. But in the first couple of days in October 1946 the long awaited letter came. It stated that I was tentatively accepted pending my appearing before the board. They gave me the dates of the TEAM conference which would be held in Moody Church in Chicago around October 20. I was invited to attend and appear before the board. I was very happy. Now I had to make quick preparations to leave. When all was ready I said my very sad good byes and took the train to Chicago. Clara stayed on and she soon had another co-worker.

CHAPTER 13

Missionary Candidate and Deputation

My train arrived in Chicago very early on Sunday morning. Rev. J. F. Swanson from the mission office was there to meet me. He took me to Moody Bible Institute where I had some breakfast. I had travelled several days and nights and was very tired. But Mr. Swanson had pointed out Moody Church to me before he left and told me to plan on attending the service there that morning. I attended because it was within walking distance.

Monday morning Mission conference began right in the Institute where I was staying. It was wonderful to meet all the staff and many missionaries that were on furlough. I was scheduled to meet the mission board on Thursday. In the meantime I sat in on every conference session. They discussed various topics in each session throughout the day. Here is a sampling, problems on the mission field, problems between missionaries and missionaries, problems between nationals and missionaries and others.

That scared me and I thought, 'I don't want to add to those problems maybe I'd better not go.' But I was so shy, what was I to do? So I prayed, "Lord, please send Brother Bach to me after the meeting, so I can tell him." Would you know, as soon as the meeting was dismissed Brother Bach came straight to the back row where I was standing. He put his hand on my shoulder and asked, "What is it girlie?" How is that for a quick answer to my prayer?

I told him that the subjects they had discussed scared me and I'd rather not go to the field. I asked if he would please give back my application form before the board met on Thursday. He smiled, prayed for me and asked me to come to the board room after lunch to tell them what I had told him. I told him I did not want to take their time, that I just wanted my papers back but he got me to promise that I would come.

After lunch I made my way upstairs and knocked on the door. Brother Bach came to the door and invited me in. As I entered all the men stood and that rather scared this little country girl. I was motioned to a chair and asked to sit down. I refused. I just stood there and held out my hands for the papers. After I repeated my request once or twice more, he asked me again to please sit down. When I did he said, now will you please tell these brethren what you told me this noon? I then told them how the discussions had scared me and that I certainly did not want to go to India to be a hindrance. I also said that I did not want to appear before them on Thursday so could they please return my application forms to me now and I'd go home.

Brother Bach then said, "Will you trust these men to make that decision?" I finally said yes. Then he called three of the men to join him and they laid hands on me and prayed for me. After those wonderful prayers of dedication

I had a peace about it that the Lord's will would be done. The conference continued all day each day and I really enjoyed it. In between they had Bible Study, prayer meetings, testimonies, and messages.

Thursday came and so did the 2 o'clock board meeting. I had thought they might ask me lots of questions about doctrine but they did not because that was on my papers. Now I, along with the other candidates, was asked to give a brief testimony. All missionaries were invited to attend this meeting and it was indeed very precious. Missionaries on furlough gave testimonies too. At the end of the board meeting the candidates were told that the mission would notify each of us by letter whether we were accepted for service or not.

As the conference went on I was again convinced by the Holy Spirit that the Lord indeed had called me to be a missionary. Also that when He calls He enables. Now I was hoping and praying that I would be accepted. We had a session that taught us deputation was not begging for support but rather a wonderful opportunity to be a blessing. To see souls saved and see how the Lord would provide support without our asking people.

I went back to Castlegar to await my letter from the board. It came quite soon and I was very thankful. Along with my acceptance letter came a list of contact people where I might be able to give my testimony. I wrote to all of them, probably 20 names, and if I remember correctly none of them answered but I was not deterred by that.

Mr. Woodrow drew a map of India on a big flour sack which he got from his wife Madeline. I had a very small suitcase which held all the clothes I owned that were good enough to take. They were a brown suit, two blouses and one or two dresses. The mission had sent me a box of literature to take and some books to sell. I decided I would go to Manitoba first to some of our Hoeppner relatives I had never met. They might let me speak and perhaps one would lead to another, I thought. That's just what happened.

DEPUTATION

So off I went by train probably about the middle of November to Isaac Hoeppners just outside of Morden. My mother is related to Mr. Hoeppner somehow, maybe third cousins. I called them Uncle and Aunt. Uncle Isaac said he did not know just how we were related but that we could always make it a closer relation. He and Auntie treated me like a daughter. That was not for want of their own children for they had seventeen or eighteen. I spent about three months in and out of their home that winter, yes and Christmas too. I spoke in their church where Uncle Isaac was the pastor.

They got me opportunities to speak in all the towns in that area. Often it was so cold and hard to heat the church for just one meeting during the week. So they took to announcing the meetings to be held in schools since they were being heated anyway. In many of those meetings I was asked to speak in Low German. It sounded strange to me to talk that language in church. In a few places I was requested to speak in German. Well, I could read it and understand it all but we never spoke it. I said I could not. They insisted I try. So try I did, but after a few minutes they said please use the Low German.

You may wonder what I spoke on. I had not been to India nor did I have slides but I did get a few statistics about India's population figures and religions. Then, I told my life story, something of my upbringing, my struggles with assurance of salvation(now you know that story too) and my call to India. All this often took an hour and a half. When I think of it now that was a l-o-n-g speech. No one objected for they did not have as many missionaries then as we do now. They also had more time in winter. I remember that the Hoeppner children (where I was staying) did the chores as quickly as possible and then came to every meeting I spoke at. Bless their hearts! I told them that they had already heard my story but they said they wanted to hear it over and over again.

It was wonderful to hear that here and there someone was saved while I was speaking. I had not realized till then that there are a lot of people who lack assurance. One Sunday morning in Morden I was speaking in Glencross Church to an older Sunday School Class usually taught by Mrs. Katherine Brown. I had prepared a lesson but when I got up I felt I should tell again briefly how I was saved. All of a sudden a dear older lady spoke up in Low German and said to me, “Then I am saved too. God be praised!” Whenever she had doubts her husband had read scripture and prayed with her and she rejoiced again, but he had died and she had no one that could help her.

How I rejoiced when someone realized, like I had, that we cannot trust our feelings only God’s Word. Then there were those that the Lord spoke to about being a missionary when I spoke. Some told me then and some told me years later. What an encouragement that is, no matter when they tell you.

After my Manitoba speaking tour I went to Saskatchewan. I’ll mention a few places. To Brotherfield Church, Salem Church, Waldheim, Hepburn Bible School, Dalmeny, Langham, Kinistino, Beatty and Melfort where my brother Herb (and his family) was the pastor. Also Carlea Bible School. Then back to Manitoba for about two months. I spent quite a bit of time at my cousin Bill Jantz and his wife Tenie. I also spoke at Winnipeg Bible Institute where Rev. Wesley Affleck was the principal.

One evening I spoke at one of the churches in Winnipeg. I don’t remember which one but I had a terrible time. I seemed to say words backwards and lost my thread of thought. When I asked if there was anyone that wanted to be saved, I started to cry. I think it was because I was nervous. No one came to see me later, so I rushed out and took the streetcar back to Bill and Tenie. I went straight to my room, threw myself on the bed and sobbed. I told the Lord that I had made such a mess and I wondered if anyone got anything out of it.

In a few minutes, Tenie called upstairs and said a woman had followed me to their place and wanted to talk to me. She sent her upstairs. This lady told me that she had come to the meeting as a last resort. She was a woman living in deep sin and wanted to be free. Nothing I said at the meeting had touched her except my tears. She had told herself that everybody was happy, no one cried like she did so often. So when she saw my tears she thought maybe I could help her. She felt I had cried for her. She accepted the Lord that evening as we knelt by the bed. I was so touched when I realized that the Lord used my nervous cry to touch her broken heart.

At all of the meetings people very graciously gave me an offering. As I look at some of the amounts, they seem like very little in comparison to later years.

However at the time it was a lot. Sometimes it was $2.00, $15.95, $5.00, $12.36. Individuals often gave me $1.00. I know they really could not afford even that. I received enough to go from place to place. Many times, of course someone would take me free by car. Many dear relatives and friends gave me items for my outfit for India. Some gave bed sheets, pillow cases, dress material, tooth brushes, hand cream and blankets. In that way most of my outfit was provided. When I had a box full I'd mail it home to my parents because I could not carry it all.

I must tell you that when I was in Saskatchewan doing deputation meetings I visited my dear Aunt Tena Heppner. She was the widow of my mother's brother Anton. They had seven children, two of them were married but she still had five at home. She did not have very much and it was cold with lots of snow. She had just ordered a parcel from Eatons and it came while I was there. She opened it to find a flannelette sheet, two towels, and some flannelette yardage to make nightgowns for her children. She at once passed the sheet and towels to me and said they were for India. Then she cut two yards of flannelette and also gave that to me. I protested with tears in my eyes but she would not take any of it back. She said she had no money so she wanted to give what she had. Bless her heart. Many, probably all of the people gave so sacrificially. I often asked the Lord to bless them for it and meet their needs. I am sure He did.

Aunt Tena did not have much to serve at mealtimes. She used to resort to a meal that I liked very much. She had bread but nothing to put on it so she made a sauce with some cream, sugar and vanilla to dip the bread in. I have tried many times to make it but it never tasted like Aunt Tena's. Her daughter Nettie Hildebrandt, and her brother Cornie and wife Mary were here last spring and we talked about it. They too remember how good it was when their Mother made it.

My daily travel needs were met as were my clothes. I never told anyone that I needed support and no one ever asked me. But I felt that was not up to me. Had not God forgiven my sins and let me know they were forgiven? Nothing else was too hard for Him I knew.

TEAM missionaries Art and Helen Dalke were in charge of the Canadian office in Moose Jaw. They had informed me that they were taking a group of candidates to Toronto to Peoples' Church to attend their annual spring missionary conference. Dr. Oswald Smith asked for TEAM missionaries their church could support. So I took the Great Northern Train from Winnipeg to Hallock, Minnesota on April 27, 1947. There I met the Dalkes, Roy Martens (married Adelina), Margaret Hartt (married later), and Pauline Gibbs (married Peter Hanks and went to India and Nepal).

That made six in the car as we travelled to Toronto via Minneapolis, Chicago, and Detroit. We arrived on May 1 and some of us gave our testimonies that first night of the conference and all of us spoke several times during the next four days. You know what happened? The church took on some support for all the candidates except for me. That still did not concern me.

On May 5, our group left Toronto for Pontiac, Michigan to attend our TEAM annual conference. When the conference ended the six of us started on our way home via Chicago. They dropped me off at my cousin Bill's again.

Then I did more deputation at Plum Coulee, Rosenfeld, Altona, Rosefarm, Horndean, Lowe Farm, Sperling and Homewood.

I had a couple of experiences where I was turned away because I was not with a Mennonite Mission and because I was a woman. That did not deter me. One preacher allowed his two huge dogs loose around me. I was so scared I prayed. Then his wife came and called the dogs off. It was during a bad snowstorm. I got off the bus on the road and had a long driveway to walk up. She gave me something hot to eat and drink then had me lie down on the couch in the living room to get warmed up. I heard her scold him in the kitchen for his attitude. He had called off the congregational meeting because I was a woman but bless her heart she called a women's meeting instead. I am glad I do not remember the name or the town. I never held it against him.

In one church they had announced that I would speak in the evening service. I went to the church prepared to speak but just before the meeting the pastor told me he would give me one minute. I heard later that he had discovered that I was with a "Faith Mission" and not with their denomination. Just before the offering was taken the pastor announced that "contrary to what was said this morning, the offering will not go to Annie Goertz. It will go to our church instead." I gave my one minute testimony and asked the Lord to use it. As I left the church, there were several at the door who shook hands with me, assured me of their prayers and gave me money. All told I was given $75.00. That was more than I had received anywhere else up to that time I think.

At one place I was asked to go about 50 miles to speak at a Sunday evening service. It was a stormy night, lots of snow but my Aunt was brave and drove me out there. We were a bit late because of the weather but we were ushered right to the front pew. A man was speaking and we thought he was filling in till I got there. Then another man (maybe the pastor) spoke. When he finished a deacon went forward and said he would make the conclusion. He did and dismissed the service with a prayer. I saw some whispering because some (I guess most) were wondering what had happened.

My aunt and I had to spend the night and went back to Winnipeg the next morning. I stayed with Bill and Tenie till June 22. That day Mr. Halsey Warman (TEAM missionary on furlough) came to our house with a check for $50.00 from two brothers who had arranged that meeting. They had intended to give that in the collection for me but since I did not speak they kept it till later. They told Halsey it was not for India but for me to use personally for anything I needed.

Well, that money was a very definite answer to my prayer. I had heard of a course taught by Wycliffe Translators at Caronport from June 23 to September 5. It cost $50.00 for room and board for the entire period. I had been given money for India or my passage but I was very conscientious and felt I could not use it for this course. I had asked the Lord to send me that amount with no strings attached. Here it was! Praise the Lord! He rules and overrules what happens to us.

June 22 was a crucial day. If the money did not come it meant I could not go to Caronport. Well, I took the train that night to Moose Jaw and from there I went to Caronport. Classes started the next day. I realized right away this would be a great benefit to me in learning an Indian language.

Time went very fast. Mr. and Mrs. George Cowan were in charge. We were very busy because I did not write in my diary even once during that time.

A month or two prior to my going to Caronport, Mr. Vernon Mortenson (TEAM China missionary) had asked me if I had any support pledged. I told him I had none. He told me people will be quicker to pledge when they hear that a candidate has a departure date but no support. So he set a date in October 1947.

Exactly halfway through the course, I had a phone call from Mr. Mortensen from Chicago telling me that a church in Port Huron, Michigan wanted me to come at once and candidate for possible support.

I went to see Mr. Cowan and told him of the call. He asked me if I felt I was benefiting from the course and I told him I was. Then he asked me how I happened to come there.I told him how I had prayed for the fifty dollars and how God provided.Then he said he thought that if God only wanted me there for half of the time He would have only given me $25.00. We prayed and I agreed with George. He felt there was nothing wrong with me going right after I finished. So I called Mr. Mortenson and said I would come as soon after September 5 as possible. He notified the church for me.

Next I contacted the Church myself and we set an arrival date of September 18. That was later than expected but there was business to be taken care of at the mission office in Chicago first.

Well, the day arrived and my train was late. I learned that Port Huron is connected to Sarnia, Ontario, Canada by the Blue Water Bridge. I was scheduled to give my testimony at their prayer meeting. Pastor Don Allbaugh (wife Lois) and Monty (wife Marie) Solliday met me and took me to Solliday's for supper. We had to eat fast and yet we wanted to get acquainted a bit before the service.

I spent the night with the Sollidays and their son Craig gave me his bedroom and he went upstairs to sleep. What caught my attention was that he opened a small door on the living room wall (above the couch) where some stairs lead up to his bed in what I guess was an attic.

We went to the church and after an introduction I gave a short testimony. I stayed there through Sunday and spoke again in both services. After the congregation had heard me three times and I had been in the homes of Cal and Laura Recor, the Davidsons, the Schleichers, and the Halls they felt they were ready for a vote as to whether they would give me some support or not.

When it was time to vote, Marie Solliday took me out to the nursery while they decided what to do. After what seemed like a long time, they called us back in to the sanctuary. I did not blame them for taking their time. After all, we had never seen each other before. Then questions were to be asked but no one wanted to go first. Finally Howard Hall got up and asked, "How old are you, Annie?" The ladies boo-hooed him (in fun) and then I said, "I'm twenty-eight." Next someone asked how much support was needed. I replied it was $550.00 for one year.

Someone else asked what I would do if they could not keep their pledge. I said I would not do anything. If for one reason or another they could not come up with it all, the Lord would have some other way to provide for me. I knew the Lord would not let me starve to death. It seemed like a huge amount to them, and to me! And it was in those days. They had never done anything like this and it was new to me too. They had never seen a missionary before, as far as I knew.

They decided they would take on all of my support. I guess they thought that was what was required of them. I was overjoyed for I had not expected to get it all from one source. But the Lord was in it and that is what was decided. Their one request was that I write them one letter a month to let them know how they could pray. I readily agreed to that.

While I was visiting their homes I asked how they ever heard about me and my need for support. Theirs was a main line denominational church which belonged to a Synod. A member of their church named Mrs. North was the first to become a Christian. She had a concern for others and invited a friend to her home for Bible Study. That friend became a Christian and invited another. On it went till there must have been about sixteen in the class. I hope I remember this correctly.

Howard and Frances Hall.

Now Mrs. North had a concern for the whole church. She and some others met with the church board to ask if they might move the class to church and have it on Sunday as a Sunday School Class to invite others. They were given permission. I believe it was about that time the Halls who had been attending another church started coming to this church. I wonder if I can recall the correct name of this church because it has changed names several times. I believe it was Ross Memorial Congregational Church, at that time. Now it is called Ross Bible Church.

After the Halls joined, a few others came from nearby churches. More people got saved and then they were able to have more Sunday School Classes. Eventually, there was a majority of born again people in the church so they felt constrained to ask the synod if they could call their own pastor instead of having one assigned. It was granted and they wrote to Bob Jones University to ask for a pastor.

The University recommended Don Allbaugh and his wife Lois, and this was to be their first pastorate. This couple loved the Lord very much and wanted to see souls saved. Pastor Don preached salvation messages and many walked the isle to accept Jesus. When most were saved he began to preach Missions to them. After a while the congregation asked him to find a missionary for them to support.

He suggested they get the addresses of a few mission boards to see if they had someone to send. Several did not respond because evidently Ross Church was not the right denomination. Two boards responded.

One wrote a very short letter, not particularly informative. TEAM was the other mission they had contacted. I may be prejudiced, but my mission sent them a two page letter at once. One page explained how to support a missionary, the other page told them that I had a departure date and no support. It also told them a bit about me.

Now that is probably when someone at Ross called the Chicago office and said, "Send Annie Goertz as soon as possible." And that was the day when Mr. Mortenson called me at Caronport. Now isn't that an amazing story to God's faithfulness? I got all of my support from one church! Little did it matter that I had travelled for nine months in Canada and had not received any support. The Lord knew all along what He was going to do. I was, and am, so glad that I had left it all with the Lord. Oh, there was a little lacking on my passage money but Ross Church took that on too.

Annie in 1947

Isaac, Mother, Father, Joe.

CHAPTER 14

Bon Voyage!

Now that I had all my support it was time to make preparations for my departure to India. Someone drove me from Port Huron to Chicago on September 22. I was very thankful. The driver was the son of one of the Ross Church members. He was Roman Catholic and not too friendly towards Protestants so here was his chance to ask me many questions. Several times he remarked how different I was. I knew his Mom was really praying for us.

He dropped me off at the Mission Office that was in Chicago at the time. It is now in Wheaton, Illinois. I talked to Mr. Mortenson and he set my departure date for anytime after October 22, based on availability.

Left to right: Otto, Martha, Annie, Mother, Dad. Annie leaving home for the first term.

On September 24 I was taken to the train station to go to Moose Jaw to see the Dalkes. While there I did some shopping. I also had two teeth filled and cleaned for $5.00! Oh for those days, eh?

My next stop was Castlegar to say my final good byes to the Woodrows and Clara. I went to Trail to have my picture taken because Ross Church wanted an 8x10 picture. I also got one for my parents which cost me $7.50. On September 30 I took the train for Mission, BC to my parents home. But before I left the Woodrows they gave me a beautiful thirty-two piece dinner set in the Hollyhock pattern. That served me until I retired.

So I had from October 1 to 11 at home. I did a lot of packing, visiting, and had my injections. I spoke in Dad and Mother's church too. I had not been home for two years so there was a lot to catch up on. October 11 came all too soon which meant good byes. We all had to be up early. Before we left for Vancouver Railway Station, my parents had Bible reading and prayer with me. They gave me Psalm 23 which often was a comfort to me. My parents took my baggage in their small truck. Otto took sister Martha and me in his car. I bought my ticket for New York for $57.80.

There was the bonding of baggage and other things to do in order to take it across the border without paying duty. It was hard knowing that this was my last day with my family for seven years to come.

ALL ABOARD!

Those were the words we heard at 5:00 p.m. I said good bye with tears as did my family. I heard later that Mother had felt so bad when she saw the train take me away alone that she grabbed one of the huge posts on the railway platform and wept very hard. I stood and waved and wept until I could not see them anymore. Before I knew it the men from US customs and immigration came to interview me in the coach. When they saw me crying they hardly asked me anything.

I slept a lot as the train chugged along. I arrived in Chicago at 9:00 in the morning. There I kept busy with letters and a bit more shopping for a typewriter and a camera. I was to sail from New York on October 22 so I was all ready to go to New York on the 20th. We started carrying down my luggage from the third floor at Mission Headquarters when someone from the first floor called up to me saying, "Your sailing has been cancelled for the 22nd. Do not go to New York."

So back to my room I went. Now I had time on my hands. I helped some in the office and really appreciated getting to know everybody. My sailing date was set again for November 12. I wanted to stop at Ross Church in Port Huron to see them again so I left Chicago on November 1. I became a member of that church and they had a commissioning service for me.

Now time was getting short and I left for New York on November 3. There I had to see to getting my baggage out of bond which seemed impossible. We had TEAM missionaries there and I was able to see New York some.

November 12 came and I went to the docks. Halsey and Ruth Warman and their three children were returning to India which is why I went on this particular ship. The mission did not want me to go by myself. The name of our ship was, THE QUEEN MARY. I was all excited! But there was one problem that did not go away. We could not get my luggage freed. A man from Neptune Shipping did all he could but finally I had to board

I'm standing beside the Warman family aboard the Queen Mary.

without it. He very kindly presented me with a beautiful corsage. I went into my cabin to put my small carry on bag down then back up on deck.

The Queen Mary.

The Queen Mary was to pull away at 5:00 p.m. The Neptune man ran from place to place to see about my baggage. Then just about 15 minutes before we pulled away he cupped his hands over his mouth to make his voice carry and shouted, "Miss Goertz, your luggage is on, Praise the Lord!" Yes, indeed I did praise Him! Slowly, ever so slowly we moved. We stood and watched until we could not see the Statue of Liberty anymore and then we went to our cabins. My cabin was D56. There were four in our cabin, Gwen Gardener and Frances Stevenson were both with The United Church. Edith Clare Walden was with Christian Missionary Society. On my bed was a big box of chocolates that my mission had ordered and placed there. How thoughtful!

Peering out of a Port Hole.

November 13. REALLY India bound! 'The Queen Mary is such a huge ship,' is what I entered in my diary. Over two thousand passengers on board, eight hundred of them in tourist class (my class). What a bad storm all night! I got up to get ready for breakfast and I did not know what was wrong with me. I threw up. I had no idea that meant being seasick. So I was brave and went to breakfast. I no sooner got into the dining room when I knew I could not eat. I called to one of the waiters, "I'm going to be sick, where do I go?" In no uncertain tone he said, "For goodness sake, not in here."

I went back to my cabin and stayed in bed all that day and most of the journey for that matter. I was very disappointed for I had not expected to be sick. As soon as I lifted my head off my pillow I was sick. My cabin mates were all fine except Frances who was sick for a couple days then she got her sea legs. Mrs. Warman was very sick too.

I became acquainted with Miss Luella Burley, a nurse with the Christian & Missionary Alliance. She used to come to see me and bring me tomato juice. Nothing stayed down though. I begged for ice cream but she and the others kept telling me it would make it worse. Finally, the day before we docked in Southampton, England, Luella brought me some. Well, it stayed down and soon I was able to get up for a bit.

On November 14 I wrote, "Still rolling, pitching and tossing. I was so thrilled about the Queen Mary but I have changed my mind. I am so sick. To add to it, Halsey keeps telling his wife Ruth and me that it is all in our head."

November 15, tried to get up but no go.

Sunday, November 16 I was up for an hour but not able to eat.

November 17 I had ice cream again and in a short time I was able to get up.

Tuesday, November 18. Feel much better. Wrote to my parents and a few postcards to mail in England. At 1:30 p.m. docked at Southampton. What a mad rush! We (tourist class) were not allowed to disembark till 5:00 p.m. My roommates, Mrs. Warman and children took the train to London to the China Inland Mission (CIM) Home. Mr. Warman and I stayed to take delivery of our baggage and turn it over to the American Express Company. We finally got that done. It was so cold and dark. We got something to eat and took a train to London too at 9:00 p.m. Arrived in London at midnight and took a taxi to the CIM home.

I stayed at the Men's Training School but I do not remember where the Warmans stayed. My hostess was wonderful. She had placed hot water bottles in my bed and as soon as I arrived she brought me a tray of hot food. I really appreciated that because there was no heating in my room. I ate with the Warmans in the main CIM dining room after that.

November 19, 1947. In London. The Warmans and I went downtown to see Westminster Abbey. I've noted in my diary that everything looks grey, old and bombed out. I was disappointed for I did not realize how much damage had been done during the war.

November 20 a red letter day. Princess Elizabeth married the Duke of Edenborough! We heard the ceremony on the radio and it was very interesting. After lunch we went downtown to stand on the side of a street where the bridal couple would pass in their carriage on the way to Waterloo Station for their honeymoon. We stood at Whitehall for one and a half hours before they came. Then just at the crucial moment everybody in front of us waved flags and we could not see. However, I did get one glimpse so I could say I saw them.

November 21. Another exciting day. We took a special boat train for Southampton. There at 11:00 a.m. we boarded the S.S. Strathmore for our trip to India. We had lunch on the ship. Then stood on deck and watched the tugboats push us away from harbor at 5:30 p.m. It was most interesting.

Saturday November 22. What a rough journey and I was so seasick again. I decided to stay on deck to see if the fresh air might help. Was all wrapped up in steamer robes for it was very cold. My cabin had twelve bunks beds but only eleven of us. It was cabin D241. My cabin mates were Edith Walden,

Frances Steveson, Gwen Gardener, Luella Burley, Dorcas Tyers, Ruth Thermond, Ruth Christopherson, Miriam Corey, Mrs. G.A. Sword. We were all missionaries headed for India or Burma. Luella (I told you about her before) was a great help to me. She got me prepared for India as much as she could. She also told me that I would meet missionaries that were not born again. I was very thankful she had warned me, for I did meet quite a few.

On Sunday the ocean was calm and I was so thankful. Some of us missionaries had a Bible study in the afternoon. On Monday the weather was good too and we saw land once in a while. All we saw was a flock of sea gulls following us for food that was thrown overboard. At 6:30 p.m. we passed the Rock of Gibraltar. It was very pretty with all the lights. Later passed Tangiers.

November 25. Smooth during day but rough at night. I washed my hair with the salt water and how sticky it was! So Dorcas washed it for me again with some water softener.

Wednesday, November 26. Wrote a letter to my parents to be mailed in Malta tomorrow. We are sailing along the coast of Africa in the Mediterranean Sea. We see quite a few ships.

November 27. Docked at Malta at 8:00 a.m. We got off the ship and to land in small launches. We sailed again at 3:00 p.m. I twisted my foot on deck a few days ago and it is still painful.

November 28. Calm waters. I am reading, "Behind the Ranges" and it is a real blessing to me. In devotions I read about Paul's shipwreck at Malta from Acts 27.

November 29. My brother Jake's birthday. Docked at Port Said at 7:30 p.m. We were not allowed off the ship nor were we allowed to barter with the bumboats either. I guess they were called that because they begged as well.

November 30. We left Port Said at 4:30 a.m. while we were asleep. When we awakened we were in the Suez Canal. How narrow! For the most part all looks dry and bleak. Passed Suez City just before supper. Read Exodus 14 and part of chapter 15. I've been reminded of Joseph when I see the Egyptians in their long robes. Still in the Canal, it is 87 miles long.

December 1. We are changing to lighter clothes. It is very warm. Our beds were stripped of woolen blankets and replaced with lighter ones. The crew changed to white clothes from Navy or black. Doctor says I tore ligaments in my ankle. Gave infra-red light.

Hold everything while I back track. I meant to tell you what the fares were on the ships. Fare on S.S. Queen Mary from New York to Southampton, England was $265.98. From Southampton to Bombay on the S.S. Strathmore was $165.00. Wouldn't it be nice to go on a cruise now with those kinds of fares?

December 2. I've noted that it is very hot on the Red Sea. I got infra-red for my ankle again. I finished reading the book by James Fraser titled, "Behind the Ranges." Then I started reading, "Papa was a Preacher." It was my turn to teach at the children's meeting. Told the story of Joseph using flannel graph. Our cabin had an onion sandwich party at 11:00 p.m. Crazy?

December 3. Still very hot on Red Sea. Arrived at ADEN at 5:00 p.m. and no one allowed ashore. It is 986 miles from Suez to Aden.

December 4. Had last infra-red. Filled out customs declaration in preparation for Bombay.

December 5. We were given tours of the ships bridge, engine room and refrigeration room. Very interesting. We set our clocks ahead half an hour every night.

December 6. Brother Otto's birthday. Paid the Doctor $5.00 for infrared.

Sunday, December 7. Warm day. I took a picture of the sunset. The last one on my family and Canada. The sunrise tomorrow will be on my future in India. Did some packing. Got tips ready.

Our whole family taken the day of our parent's 60th wedding anniversary. 1964

CHAPTER 15

Arrival in India, Language Study

Monday, December 8. ARRIVED IN BOMBAY, INDIA at 8:30 a.m. What a thrill! Luella and I stood on deck right in front to see the tugs pull us (this reminds me of the angels that will carry us to Heaven after our earthly voyage). Doesn't seem possible that I'm really here! There was a building right across from where we docked and I was surprised to see one of our missionaries Norma Tharaldsen waving to me. After a bit the field Chairman Mr. Don Hillis (wife Doris) joined Norma. Low and behold at 9:00 a.m. Elizabeth Parker's ship docked. She had left 2 months before I did. They had serious engine trouble and thus were delayed. We got off the boat to try to locate our baggage but it was nowhere. So we went back on the ship and had our lunch.

Don Hillis came onto the ship to meet me. When he located my cabin he greeted me and his first question after that was, "Did you save any apples from the ship for us?" I did not know that it was the custom for missionaries to save their fruit the last few days on ship for the missionaries. At that time there were no apples available up country. The next thing he said was, "Annie let's pray." So we knelt and he prayed, "Dear Lord, thank you so much for Annie. Thank you for bringing her out to help us." Of course he asked for the Lord's guidance and blessing upon me too. I was very touched and encouraged by his prayer.

Eventually, after standing in line a l-o-n-g time we got my baggage. They could not open my wooden boxes so let me go after they looked in my carry on suitcases. How I thanked the Lord. Some salt was leaking out of one of my boxes, the coolie licked it and spit it out. I had to laugh. Norma had come to meet Elizabeth and they left by train to go to Dondaiche to do language study there.

Don took me to the Frykenbergs (who were not TEAM missionaries) where we had tea. I had left my baggage with American Express for them to ship to Amalner where I would study language. After tea Don and I went to a Youth for Christ meeting where he spoke. We took the train that evening at 8:45 for Navapur where the Hillises and Jane McNally were stationed. I was to stay there for the time being to get acquainted I guess. Don had brought me a bedding roll as well and we slept on board seats. He took the upper berth and I the lower. Every time the train stopped at a station during the night, I heard shouting. I did not know what was happening. People talked very loud and I thought they were quarrelling. I asked Don and he said those were cheha (tea), bananas and samosa vendors. I was so surprised at how the women responded with a smile when I smiled. A smile is the same in any language.

December 9. We arrived in Navapur at 11:00 a.m. Everybody I see salutes and says, "Salaam" (peace be to you). That is the Christian's greeting. The Hindus say namaste or namaskar. Doris and Jane showed me around the compound including the boy's school and boarding. Later they went to town and I went along - we went through two creeks. We had bananas, they were so sweet and juicy, hence that entry! I was to eat many of those during my stay in India. It was hot during day but cold at night. There's no heating in the houses. I was afraid to go to sleep because I saw a few lizards in the room. I had no mosquito net. During the night the lizards ran up and down the screening on the verandah and I was sure they were snakes. I was terrified and kept my head covered all night. I do not think I got any sleep at all.

The next day Doris gave me my first dose of anti-malaria medicine called Paludrine. Unfortunately the damage had already been done. I had been bitten by a mosquito or two and about two weeks later came down with malaria. More about that later.

December 11. Sister Hulda's birthday. I did some ironing with a gas iron for Doris and me. After lunch Doris, Jane and I walked to a village three miles away to see a sick boy. Also had a women's meeting there. Doris sold a few pills. On the way home we stopped at another village for a meeting. People gave us eggs, six in all, to take home. That interested me. We had to cross a stream, Doris took her shoes and socks off and walked through. I still had a bandage on my ankle so Jane and I piled up some rocks and we walked on those. The water was too dirty for me to walk through!!! To bed at nine, I'm very tired from walking I wrote.

The next day Doris took me to Chinchpada Hospital Compound. She wanted to introduce me to the missionaries there, Dr. Karl Klokke and his wife Esther and Marie Christensen. On Sunday, December 14, I gave my testimony through interpretation and I got all mixed up. Had communion too and that was precious. The day after I arrived in Navapur a telegram had come from the Amalner missionaries, "Send Goertz." So after lunch that day Jane and I took the train to Amalner. I felt the trip was very dirty and it was HOT.

Don Hulin (language student) was at the station on his bike to meet us. We took a tonga (two wheeled cart drawn by a horse) to their bungalow. Church service was about to begin so we washed up quickly. But I had to go to the bathroom and I could not see a toilet anywhere. I saw some boxes but those did not look like what I was to use. In desperation I opened one lid, then the other and they each had a shiny white enamel pot in them. That could not be it. But, there was some toilet paper between the two. That was my clue that this must be it. Those boxes turned out to be commodes which the sweeper would come and empty twice a day.

I gave a short testimony at church by interpretation again. The Christians sang a song of welcome for me. Oh yes, when we arrived from the station there was a huge welcome banner up on the roof of the bungalow. Then Don Hulin went up on the roof and played, "From Greenland's Icy Mountain" on his trumpet. It sounded heavenly to me and meant a lot. I slept in Mildred Sawyer's room out in the back of the compound. I saw a lizard right away so I asked for a net to keep the lizards, skeeters and rats off of me. I had a good sleep.

The next day Jane, Doris Fraser and I walked to town. I bought a sun hel-

Taken shortly after arriving in Amalner.

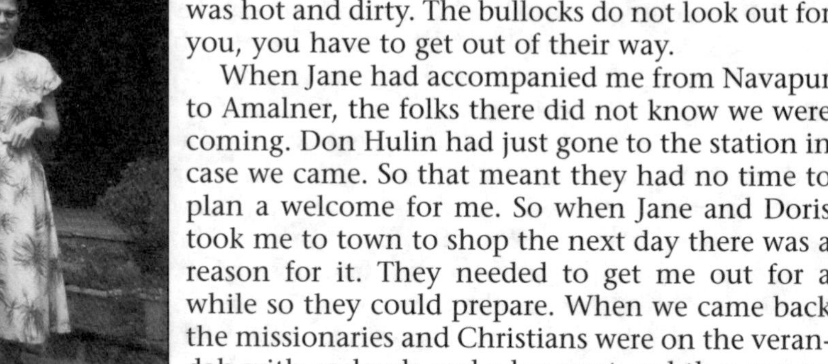

met, sandals (we call them chappals), some bars of soap and some notebooks for language study. It was hot and dirty. The bullocks do not look out for you, you have to get out of their way.

When Jane had accompanied me from Navapur to Amalner, the folks there did not know we were coming. Don Hulin had just gone to the station in case we came. So that meant they had no time to plan a welcome for me. So when Jane and Doris took me to town to shop the next day there was a reason for it. They needed to get me out for a while so they could prepare. When we came back the missionaries and Christians were on the verandah with garlands and a bouquet and they sang a welcome song for me.

Then we went inside where the table was set with the best dishes they had for a lovely dinner. The food was better than I had expected. But when it came to the cake it was different. They did not have enough flour because of rationing so they made it out of jowari flour (the grain looks quite a bit like popcorn). The cake held together until they started to cut it, then it all crumbled in a heap! The flour was too coarse for cakes. It tasted good anyway.

I am washing clothes with a 'stamper.'

Our breakfast was pretty well the same every morning. It consisted of one slice of toast each (rationing), a boiled egg, peanut butter (homemade), jam, a banana and tea. I did not enjoy the peanut butter as much after I saw how it was made. The peanuts, which are plentiful in India, were roasted. Then the cook (an Indian man) would take a pot of them to the kitchen floor. Here was a big, flat, heavy stone with another heavy round stone used as a rolling pin. He put a few hand fulls of peanuts on the stone and started to crush them with the round stone. It was a tedious job. After the oil began to come out, it got softer and spread on the stone. He held the flat stone steady with his toes. Did you guess it?

Moses and I washed my clothes on a scrub board for many years.

The TEAM missionary family at annual conference in 1968.

Yes, it came to his toes and got on them, too! He just wiped it off his toes and pushed it back on the little pile. He did that over and over until the consistency was nice and smooth. Then into a jar it would go. It tasted good too. You can get used to almost anything I guess.

After I had seen that peanut butter factory(?) I decided there must be a more sanitary way of making it. I kept my eyes open for a meat grinder. Probably about twenty years later I was able to purchase one from a missionary going home to retire. Then in case you are interested, my cook Moses would put the peanuts through the grinder exactly seven times and it came out very smooth.

It was now December 16 and I remembered it was my oldest brother Isaac's birthday. I learned that we sent our clothes, bedding and laundry to the dhobi (washerman). In order to get our own clothes back each piece had to be marked with name tape. The only place we could get those tapes was to order them from Montgomery Ward in the United States. So that's what I did that day. By the way, the dhobi carried our bundle of clothes off on his head. He boiled the clothes in ash water and that took all the colours out of course. Most of us got some kind of itch. So my roommate and I washed ours in a tub with a 'stamper.' It looked like a funnel with a long handle. We'd push it up and down until the clothes were clean. Most missionaries started to have their clothes washed at home for the same reason.

CHAPTER 16

My Time in Amalner

Still December 16. I had been in India eight days. This had given me time to get used to the climate and food. Now it was time to buckle down to language study. A language pandit was hired to teach me. His name was Mr. Hiwale and it meant winter or cold season. He taught me the first lesson. There were about ten other missionaries studying Marathi. Amalner used to be the official language school for our mission. However, right after the close of the war we had many new missionaries come out so a second one was opened in Dondaiche. The days that followed I spent mostly writing letters and studying Marathi. Mr. Hiwale taught me a few simple words and phrases first, then started on the alphabet. One day he told me that the next day he would teach me a very difficult letter. It was a backwards 'T.' You put your tongue back and blow out air. That's about the best way I can explain it. So, I made the sound and he sounded a bit disappointed as he said the missionaries must have told me how to do it. I told him they had not but that I had taken a course in Linguistics in Canada which helped me. That course did help me an awful lot.

A sign in Marathi of Acts 16:31.

I needed an English/Marathi dictionary and one vice versa. They were not available in our small town so I ordered from a Christian book shop in Poona. I imagine I ordered a Marathi Bible and a hymn book at the same time.

On December 24 everyone gathered outside for a love feast. We all sat on rugs on the ground. We had rice which was good, the chapattis were very good too. The curry was made with mutton in it, which was goat's meat. We were eating with our fingers for my first time I think and I found the curry very spicy. My thoughtful senior missionary had given me a banana to eat when it got too hot. She sat next to me. Well, I could not get the meat between my fingers for it was too slippery. When I did manage, I gagged for I thought I was eating the entrails. It most likely was so. The missionary quietly told me it was a "no no" to gag on the food that the Christians had prepared so graciously. I managed to eat a little but I probably went to bed hungry.

That night at midnight the young people rang the church gong for 20 minutes. They came around to sing carols just after we had fallen asleep and it sounded like angels singing. I'll never forget how wonderful it was to be awakened by such singing.

Rev. Chapde helping his wife Hira Bai wash clothes.

Christmas Day after breakfast we opened our gifts. We had drawn names. I was so new and did not know what to buy. Indeed what was there to buy in that little town? Mildred gave me a napkin ring. I gave her a bar of ivory soap and a package of chewing gum I had brought from home. She was most gracious but that surely was not a very exciting gift to give her. I guess I am too practical.

At 9:00 a.m. we all went to church for the service. Rev. Chopde gave the message as he was the pastor of our church. Of course I did not understand anything. In the afternoon the children gave a lovely program on Jesus' birth. The little ones were so cute. Indian people are born actors I think.

December 27. My baggage arrived from Bombay. I opened some of the boxes. The first one I opened was a mess. I had put in some tins of jam, you know the ones with lids that you can open and close again. Well, all that bouncing had opened all three tins. Can you picture the flies, worms, and stench? And my disappointment?

The India field annual conference used to be held in Amalner between Christmas and New Years. But just before I arrived, they had a polio outbreak in Amalner. One of the Indian children on the compound got it and so did little one year old David Hulin (his parents were Don and Beulah). Beulah had to massage his limbs for a long time each day. Because of the polio, the conference was switched to Dharangaon (a station about 20 miles away).

It began on December 30 and we took the train at 5:00 p.m. We had our supper there and the first meeting that evening. Don Hillis spoke but first he welcomed the new missionaries (about nine of us) with these words, "God sent you, India needs you, we thank God for you." I was assigned along with six other missionaries and children to sleep in one of the three classrooms. The walls were brick and whitewashed, the floor was of dirt and varnished with cow dung. It was dry so did not smell. The bathroom for all of us who were sleeping in the classrooms was a small tent right outside in front. The toilets inside the tent were a row of commodes, which by now, I was used to. We had brought our own mosquito nets and slept on army folding cots.

December 31. The morning and evening sessions were devotional with a lot of prayer especially in the morning. That evening we had a watch night service. Mr. Frykenberg was our speaker from a Baptist Mission in Bombay. There had been a lot of riots and stampeding in India after it gained independence on August 15, just months before I arrived. Mr. Frykenberg said that night that a little bag of salt opened and scattered along the road would stop any furious animals in stampede. They're hungry for salt and will stop at the smell of it. So we, as good salt, should stop riots in India by our presence.

JANUARY 1, 1948

Still in Dharangaon at conference. This was the day I got a splitting headache after lunch. The next day my head was still bad but I attended the meetings. On the third I vomited. Mrs.Martha Thomas gave me sulphadiazine. My temperature was 101 degrees. Dr. Klokke came to see me and said it could be malaria, dengue fever or just a tummy upset. He could not tell without some tests. I was in bed all the next day. On the fifth, I was able to be up but not well. It was the last day of conference.

Maybe some of you may think I am going into too much detail but I am writing this for my family and know they would like to know first impressions and experiences. Maybe some prospective missionary will read it and find it helpful. Later on I won't go into as much detail, but this is proving a real blessing to me to relive my life. I can recall the emotions and circumstances so vividly and thank God for how He was so near and got me through.

January 6. After breakfast we were taken by jeep to the station where we took the train back to Amalner which was home now. Zoe Anne Alford had been living in the bungalow with Doris Fraser but she went somewhere else after conference. So now I moved from Millie's room into Doris' room. Doris was from near Chicago and nearly finished her language study.

Dr. Klokke gave typhoid injections to all the mishes but since I was not well he asked me to go to Parola when I fully recovered to get my shot from Richard Thomas. He and his wife Martha ran a clinic. I went by bus and it was fun trying to make people understand where I was going since I did not know Marathi. How happy I was when I saw Thomas' cook there with a note to get in the tonga and go back with him to the bungalow.

They were so very busy but Dick gave me my typhoid injection. I stayed in the house and read magazines most of the day. Later Martha asked me to help her in the clinic. I have no idea what I did, maybe counting pills, or something like that. I spent two days with them and then back home on Monday, January 12. I had brought mosquito netting from home and that day I made it up and used it from then on.

The same day I had a letter from my brother Herb (two years younger than I) and his family telling me they had been accepted with TEAM to go to Portugal. I was so happy. He and his wife spent one term there.

On Sundays I went into town with Doris to teach Sunday School to some children. She did not speak much Marathi and I none. But we managed somehow. It made me feel helpless and useless because I could not converse with them.

I asked the missionaries, Ray and Gertrude Rutan (they were house parents to the language students) if the people walking past the bungalow every day or riding in their ox carts were Christians. They said no. Most likely not a single Christian walked past us. There were two or three Christian families living down by the Railway station but I had met them by now and knew them. This made me feel very, very sad. Here I was, knowing Jesus and the gospel, but could not give it to them because I could not speak their language. Then I thought of how I had to study for two years before I would be much good to anyone.

It almost drove me to despair. To think that hundreds and thousands were passing our place and all going to a Christless grave sooner or later. It seemed there was nothing I could do. Some nights the burden of those souls so overcame me that I could not sleep. I got up and quietly slipped outside where I could cry and pray. In the morning I'd study Marathi with renewed vigour.

The desk the rat jumped on.

On January 19 Roy and Adelina Martens arrived in Bombay. They were with TEAM and were coming here for language study. Bill and Joan Reid were here studying too. January 23. Doris and I caught a rat on our window sill in Rutan's trap. The night before a rat gave us so much trouble. I heard a noise and then bump, something bounced onto my mosquito net. I was so glad I was under the net. Upon inspection I saw he had chewed on the nosepiece on my glasses. The irregular edge made a sore on my nose the next day. We just got back into bed when he came back again. We got up and tried to kill him with sticks. He was quicker than we were and jumped from chair to desk to dresser. Then he sat up and looked at us. We finally managed to hit him and that slowed him down enough so we could kill him.

Remember I set sail for India on November 12? Well, my sister Martha was married to Art Douglas on November 15, while I was at sea. On January 25 I had my first letter from her and it looked strange to see her signature as Martha Douglas. The same day I had a letter from my sister Rosa and in it she told me she felt God had called her to South America. She was planning to apply to TEAM. She did apply and was accepted but later ill health stopped her from going.

One day a woman, whom Gertrude had hired to help with housework, was sweeping our stone floor. She gave testimony of how glad she was that she was a Christian. Now she could go to the villages to camp with the Rutans and give her testimony to the village women. Doris and I were blessed by her testimony. Doris and I prayed together that God would help us never lose the vision of giving the gospel to the lost. We also prayed that we would never get used to sin and seeing the lost. I asked myself if I really believed that people around me were lost and going to Hell. Yes, I did and I do.

About that time, some of us went to the station to see Einer and Audrey Berthelsen who were going through on the train. They had come from Chinchpada where their first baby Judy was born. We were anxious to see baby Judy. She was sleeping on a pillow. The Berthelsens had two more daughters and soon after that Audrey went to be with the Lord. Einer married Mary Holgerson later. On the way back from the station I stopped in a shop and bought my first sari, a pink one. A sari is about five or six yards long with pretty borders on it.

January 30. My diary starts out saying I studied hard all day. Then in the evening it ends by entering shocking sad news, "MAHATMA GANDHI WAS SHOT TO DEATH TODAY." I remember what a shock it was. All stores, schools and market places were closed the next day, as India mourned its great leader.

One of our Christian men was down by the river (which flowed past our place) and heard a man say that Christ and Mahatma Gandhi were alike in many ways. Christ died on Friday, so did Gandhi. Christ died for a cause, so did Gandhi. Christ rose the third day, so would Gandhi. Then he ended by saying, now Gandhi is my Christ. Because of the heat, Gandhi was cremated that same evening, as they do all their dead. We heard that many stayed at that cremation site for three days to witness Gandhi's resurrection. But of course, he did not rise again. I should say that only Hindus cremate their dead, except little children. Moslems bury theirs.

February 2. My brother Herb's birthday. People still in mourning, shops closed, and many riots. Word had it that a Brahmin shot Gandhi. So because of that a Brahmin College teacher in our town was badly beaten up by his students near the railway station. Rumours abounded that as Pakistan was for Moslems, so India should be for Hindus. With Independence gained not that many months back we wondered what might happen. In India no one talks of India by that name. It's usually Hindustan which means, the place of the Hindus. Nowadays they call their country Bharat.

The next day Doris rode her bike out to Amalgaon camp to take the mail to Rutans. She had to carry it through two streams and had a puncture. Little David Reid fell out of a tree and broke his arm. Some of our students left for language school in the hills.

February 12 was the twelfth and final day of mourning after Gandhi was killed. They mourn for twelve days and then have a ceremonial cleansing bath.

February 26 was the day that Doris and I started our long journey to language school in Mahableshwar. It was too hot on the plains for new missionaries to stay. The next day we arrived in Poona where we got our bus. It was a 75 mile trip from there which was so winding and almost straight up a mountain. We were very tired but so thankful for God's care over us. In Mahab we set up our own housekeeping and filled our lamps with kerosene as there was no electricity.

We attended classes with many other missionaries from various missions. Then we also had our private tutoring classes with a pandit. This school was of great help to me and to everyone. Mr. Satralkar and Mr. Desai were my pandits. They were both Brahmins. I was on Lesson 17 in Amalner but in Mahab the students were on Lesson 25. So my pandits helped me catch up. It meant I had to study every minute possible.

There was quite a large Union Church in Mahab and it was good to attend an English speaking service. It felt so good to wear our dress clothes and hats again. Six of us missionaries had rented a house in Mahab which made it cheaper for all of us. Einer and Audrey Berthelsen with wee Judy, Charles and Virginia Hayward, Doris and I. We took turns doing the housekeeping. Before long Virginia and Charles went down the hill to a hospital in Wai to have their first baby. Thomas was born on March 22 and weighed a little over 9lbs. He was healthy but he was born with harelip. It made everyone sad. He had

The little cloths they put on sticks at New Year's hanging above the buildings.

several surgeries and they turned out good.

April 10 was the Indian New Year's Day. They count it from the time a certain ruler started to reign and that was about 162 years at that time. They celebrate our New Year too. Early in the morning they bring out long bamboo sticks which have a sari tied at the top to represent hope for enough clothes for the coming year. At the tip of the stick they put a brass upside down vessel to represent hope for enough food. Then they hang a garland of coloured sugar candy over all of that.

One day a snake charmer came and wanted his cobra to dance for us. He asked for Rupees two. We said no but he tried to tempt us by bringing the snake's head out of the basket just a wee bit. I got scared and ran screaming from there. A little while later a man came with two monkeys, a big one dressed in a sweater and pants with a wee baby. He had them do all kinds of tricks. They were good so gave him 3 annas.

Oh, I forgot to tell you what money we used. First there was the rupee. Sixteen annas made one rupee and twelve pice made one anna. The annas had holes in the middle. Many years later it was changed to a different system with only rupees and pay (pronounced pie). One hundred pay make one rupee. It's much simpler. The change was hard for the poor people and vendors. They used to count the knuckles on their fingers to do their arithmetic. Now I think they use little pebbles.

As far as weights and measures go, they used to have pounds and ounces but it was changed to the metric system of kilograms, litres and kilometres.

One day about nineteen of us hiked to Dhobi Water Falls. We had a time of devotions and singing and it was blessed. Down below us the dhobis washermen were whacking away at the rocks with their clothes,(maybe our clothes). On the way back we stopped at Aram Hotel (which means rest) to have a meal. It was so spicy I could hardly eat anything. That's where I got a bit more of my education. We were eating with our fingers and I was informed that one never touches food with the left hand. The left hand is unclean.

One day while in Mahab I took the bus down to Panchgani to visit Mrs. Warman and the children. I had not seen them since the Queen Mary. I had been told that on a certain date the rains begin in Mahab. They are called the Monsoons. When it begins to rain it does not stop for three months. Everyone makes sure they are down on the plains in time because the buses cannot drive down those 75 miles in the mud. I was told when the fog starts to blow in that is a sign the monsoons will follow soon. On May 20 the fog began. The school quickly had exams for the missionaries except me because I had not covered enough material yet. Everybody made their way down the hill. Some stay there all year long like shopkeepers, Anglo-Indians and a few missionaries who have a ministry there, and who have no need to go down.

The Berthelsens, Doris and I left Mahab on June 1. The buses were crowded and the trains too. We got there a bit late so the train started to move before Doris could get on. She had to crawl through the window. That's something I have done a few times since too.

We spent a day in Bombay and got home on June 4. Everything was covered with dust. Paulus swept down the walls and floors. We were very tired but it was too hot to sleep. We took our cots out on the verandah where it was a bit cooler. I had to take a lot of salt pills.

June 15. My brother Edwin's birthday. It was getting a bit cooler as we had some rain. On June 17, I turned twenty-nine. The missionaries had a lovely dinner for me and gave me a lovely gift. Our pandit gave his resignation so we don't know what we will do. Found another rat in our room when we went to get ready for bed. The next day I had a touch of malaria.

Doris and I slept on one end of the verandah and the Reids at the other. It was a huge verandah. Early one morning we heard a commotion from the Reid side. Joan had the baby in bed and was nursing him. She was hot and wiped the perspiration from her brow with her hand. Then she put her arm down beside her and felt a rope lying there. She raised up to look and realized it was a 31 inch snake. She called Bill and when he saw it was a snake he grabbed her and the baby to pull them off the cot. He killed it and that's the commotion we heard. She was under a net so we don't know when it crawled up beside her. We knew God had protected her and the baby.

A few days later I wrote that we killed two scorpions on the door before we went in from the verandah. We also caught and threw five lizards out of our room. That was almost a daily occurrence. A few days later I was awakened by nibbling at my finger. I swatted around in the dark and finally was able to turn my flashlight on in the excitement. There sat a rat at the foot of my bed. We chased him into the bathroom. We were going to kill it in the morning but he got out through a hole in the tiles. The next night he came back again. And the next day, as I was studying from my looseleaf notebook I saw scorpion legs trying to wriggle out from between the pages. That was scarey. It would have stung me if I had not seen it. A scorpion sting is most painful and lasts for days.

While I am on the scorpion subject I will tell you that whenever anyone got stung I tried to kill the pain with everything I could think of. I'd put soda paste on, peroxide, Dettol, vinegar, salt, mustard mixture and perfume but nothing helped. The children cried all night for three nights. Quite a few years later I read somewhere that putting bicycle inner tube cement on the bite would stop the pain within minutes and it did. After that I always kept a tube of cement with my medicines and used it often.

My cook leaned against the wall one day and was stung on his back close to his heart. Then I had to run fast for the cement. I have only been stung once and it was a baby scorpion. It was sitting on my sandal and when I slipped my foot in it got me. It was terribly painful. I was quick to put cement on. It really worked miraculously.

For July 4, I wrote that we sang, "America" and "Star Spangled Banner" before meals. I was the only Canadian living with all of those Americans. In church that morning a lizard ran up my leg. Doris and I went to teach Sunday

Miss Tara Chopde teaching me the language.

School in town as we did every Sunday. I had covered my helmet with plastic to keep the rain off. The children felt it. Then they tore off a piece of my Kleenex and said it looked like paper. I had a zipper on the side of my dress and somehow those children saw it. They managed to open it to look inside before I realized what was happening! When I was ready to take my bath that night I grabbed my nighty off the hook behind the door and when I laid it down out crawled a big scorpion! It seemed everything happened to me that day.

I said we lost our pandit and we had to study on our own for a few weeks. Then we got the pastor's daughter Tara Bai Chopde to teach us and she did a good job. God provided for us again.

The missionaries were great and invited me to their stations so I could get to see and learn more about the overall work. So we went to Dharangaon where we had the conference for a weekend. Bob and Jean Couture, Zoe Anne Alford and Hilda Dalke worked there. Before we went to bed I heard chi chi chi every now and then. I asked what that noise was and they said tsustundri which means blind mice. There was no net on my bed so I did not sleep at all for fear of blind mice and rats. The next night they kindly provided a net.

The next day I went home and soon had a headache, backache and fever of 102.2 degrees. That malaria lasted several days. I got it very often during my years in India. There were two more birthdays in my family, Tillie's on July 15 and Martha's on July 16. I've noted in my diary that I had constant headaches ever since returning from Mahab. Dr. Klokke said to rest for one hour every afternoon.

For the next month or so I did not make many entries in my diary except that I visited one more station. The main entries were that we continued to have rats in our room. So we got some cement and water and mixed it. Then we climbed up a ladder and closed the holes that were on the wall near the ceiling. It was the wall between Reid's bathroom and ours the rats used as a thoroughfare.

We knew there was still a rat in our room but how to catch it? We put a cracker on the desk as bait, then tied a string around the cracker. The other end we tied to a fly swatter. We knew if the rat tugged at the cracker the swatter would fall off, we'd hear it and be able to kill it. It worked as planned. Kill it we did!

Ray and Gertrude Rutan left Amalner, probably to go on furlough. On August 27 Oscar and Dora Meberg arrived to be our houseparents.

I did not make any entries again until September 3 which was a Hindu Festival called Porla. It's the day they don't work the bullocks but worship them instead. We as Christians dared not hitch up our bullocks either for fear of causing problems. They spread beautiful blankets on the bullocks (oxen), painted the horns a very bright red, made big colourful paper headdresses for them and fed them lots of sugar candy. They often gauge a man's wealth by how many bullocks he has. They make their living with the bullock, which is why they give it a lot of honour and worship it that one day. The next day they were not treated that good. It's hard to get fodder and water for them so the animals are usually quite skinny.

It was about this time I had been trying out my Marathi on the people. The Christians on the compound were used to 'missionary Marathi' and they sort of understood what I was trying to say. But when I travelled on the train those women did not expect me to speak their language because I was a foreigner, a tourist as far as they knew.

One day I was trying to converse with the women on the train. They motioned with their hands and said, "We don't speak English." I was not ready to give up so quickly so I tried again. Same response. Then I said slowly, "Listen! Listen! I am not speaking English, I am trying to speak your language." Wonder of wonders, they understood and said to each other that I was speaking their language. That heartened me.

However, when I got home, I began to think that I should be speaking better than I was by now. It suddenly made me very discouraged, so much so that tears came to my eyes. I looked at my textbooks and the Marathi Bible and wondered if I would ever learn the language. Whenever I had a burden, I was in the habit of cupping my hands in front of me and verbalize my burden or problem into my hands as it were. Then I held my hands up to God and told Him that I was giving it to Him because there was nothing I could do about it. I did not feel any different as I did it but I did it as an act of the will. I knew that He would take ANYTHING that I gave Him.

So here was my language problem. This time I put all the books on my bed and knelt beside it. It was such a big problem. Suddenly I burst into tears and said, "Lord, just look at these books," as I pointed them out to Him. "I will never learn this language, then what good will I be to You or the people? Let me go home. There I can lead people to the Lord in three languages. None of those do me any good here!" I sobbed before the Lord. He saw me. He heard me. He cared. He spoke to my heart (not my ears), "Annie, I know Marathi, I will teach you." I am crying now as I write this. I remember it so well.

How precious of the Lord to respond to me in that way. He does not always, or even often, do that. But He cares just as much and wants us to trust Him, no matter what. Well, I dried my tears and said thanks to God. I gathered my books and took them back to my desk where I continued my studies. I never forgot that He would teach me and He did. Praise God! I never told anyone about that till years later.

October 10. My brother Isaac is getting married to Alma Neufeld in Main Centre, SK on her twentieth birthday. Isaac is forty-three. The Lord blessed them with twelve lovely children. I, of course, was not able to be at the wedding. In fact, I was able to attend only four of my siblings' weddings.

The Marathi language has three genders, and EVERY SINGLE THING is one of those three. It's very much like German or Low German in that regard. Also in Marathi the verb is at the end of the sentence like in German. The 'R's have to be rolled and that was okay for I was born with that gift on my tongue. I had never realized that not everybody could roll the 'R's. One of the students could not do it and the pronunciation did not come out right. We went for a walk and I was to teach her. So I rolled my 'R's for her as she peered into my mouth to see what the tongue did to make that sound. She tried and tried and ended up crying. Poor dear. So, knowing other languages was definitely a plus for me.

But those genders. And there are four 'T's, each one changes by placing your tongue in a different position and also by aspirating. There are four 'D's too, two 'P's, two 'B's, two 'N's, two 'K's and so on. Often only one letter made the difference between one word and another, especially by aspirating a letter that should not be.

One evening the cook (in Amalner) and I were making supper together. I was mixing up some dressing for salad and had a little milk left over. I knew it would spoil by morning since we had no fridge. So I told the cook to use the milk in some cocoa because it would spoil by morning. He smiled and said I had said it would get scared by morning, "gaberun gele". I used the wrong tense too. He said I should have said, "kerab ho oon zail." As it is written it does not look alike but when someone says it fast it sounds so much the same. That was not the only time I goofed, but we had a good laugh each time and it did not discourage me. You have to be able to laugh at yourself not just at others.

I believe it was that same evening I made way too much potato salad. Usually we ate that amount but this time I could see there was going to be some left. We could not afford to throw it away so I announced to all the students, "Eat. If we don't finish it, you will get it fried for breakfast." They laughed. But I managed to save it from spoiling by keeping it open on the veranda overnight. It was the cold season. In the morning I rinsed off some of the dressing and fry it I did, for breakfast! You must believe me, they were angels, they all ate it cheerfully. At least so it seemed. Maybe they thought if they didn't they'd get it for lunch!! I think they were glad when Dora Meberg came back after the weekend away.

We misunderstand even in English, don't we? One morning Don Hulin told me at the breakfast table what their wee Davie (the one with polio) had prayed before they came to the table. He prayed, "We thank Thee for the fellowship and for all the boats." So Daddy had explained that fellowship was not a boat. Sweet, isn't it?

Again in between our study, Doris and I were invited to Raver by the Warmans. The trains were crowded as always. We usually travelled third class. There was second and first as well. On the way back we tried to get into third class again. Some men behind us thought we were tourists and that we could not understand them. They said, "You go into first, you are rich." With that he gave me a very hard kick in my lower back. I almost fainted it hurt so much then and for several months. It could have been very serious because of my spina bifida condition.

We had to change trains and then we got into the women's compartment. We noticed the women gave us lots of space even though it was crowded. They seemed very scared to have us there. After a few minutes we felt the train slowing and it stopped. Some men were riding on the running boards. They thought we were men so stopped the train and got the police to remove us.

We did not know what was happening. The police came and when he saw us he said, "They are not men. They are foreign women!" So we were allowed to stay.

Later we figured it out. We were wearing sun helmets (which they had seen only British men wear). We both wore glasses and were reading the newspaper. At that time very few women could read. One of us reached up for something and with that the bracelets (glass bangles) that we wore on our wrist came into view. They had been covered by our long sleeved sweater. Bracelets are a sign that you are a woman. Alas, now that their fears were alleviated, they moved closer to us. In fact, we hardly had enough space to sit after that.

India has a lot of festivals connected with Hinduism. I told you about two already, Pola and New Years Day. Now I'll tell you about another one called Horli. That's one when everyone was uneasy. Men and/or boys would try to get a hold of wood to burn. If they could not, they might steal furniture like cots or chairs. So folks would keep everything inside so they could not get at it.

Another was Karli (there actually is not an 'R' in it but a back 'L' that sounds like an 'R'. Karli stands for the black goddess of death. It's scarey for them because they need to try to appease her.

During the first part of October is the festival of Dasra when they worship the goddess Lakshmi. She's the goddess of wealth. All the merchants bring their account books out and worship them.

A few weeks after that is Divali, the festival of lights. It's a very pretty sight. They put little oil lamps all around the outside of the house or passageway and even in the house. Usually they make real tiny shallow saucer-like dishes of clay. They pour cooking oil in them and a loose string which they light. Of course all of these celebrations call for special food and lots of it. Then there is another feast when they worship the goddess Durga. I can't recall now what it's all about.

Then there's the Ganpatti feast. In short, the story of it's origin goes something like this. A couple got married and right away the young man named Shiwaji, was called into the army. So she continued to live in their house. One day as she took a bath she noticed a lot of dirt coming off. The more she washed, the more dirt fell on the ground, in fact so much so that a baby boy was formed. She was overjoyed and picked him up and cared for him.

Shiwaji was released from the army and came home unannounced. The little boy was now four years old and playing out in front of the house. When Shiwaji saw him he got upset, or rather was jealous that a man (meaning male) was staying with his wife. He pulled out his sword and cut off the boy's head. Then he went in to greet his wife. She asked him if he had seen their son outside. He said yes. But quickly ran out to see what had come of the boy. He was going to put the head back on but it had rolled down the hill.

He felt terrible, ran down the hill to see if he could find it. He could not so began to pray. Then he decided he'd cut off the head of the first living creature he'd come across. Well, he met an elephant so he cut off it's head and carried it home. He put it on his son's torso. But because this boy looked so different, people came to see him and started to worship him. Sometimes the god is called Elephant god. On that festival they make clay replicas of the god and worship them. When they are finished worshipping them they take them in long processions and dump them in the river. I have forgotten what that is supposed to mean. They have millions of gods and goddesses but I have just mentioned a few of the main ones.

The Christians do not take part in those festivals except some nominal ones do. They do have something to offset that. They call it the Home Festival. They clean the whole house. First they move everything out while they put a fresh coat of manure varnish on the walls and floors. They polish all their brass vessels till they look like mirrors.

If they have a rough shelf or two, to display the vessels on, they like to cover them with something. So I would give them my newspapers. They cut them into beautiful patterns and it looked really nice, as nice as anything you could buy here at home.

We usually celebrated for several days. The congregation would go to two homes each evening until every home had been visited. They came to my home too. First to see how nice, clean and decorated it was. Second, to sing some hymns, hear the pastor read a scripture portion and pray for the home. Third, if the people could afford it, they might serve sweet tea, or maybe a banana each. Some did not serve anything and that was perfectly alright. The main thing was to look at the homes and pray for the family. It meant a lot to everyone.

Most homes did not have electricity, so they put out little oil lamps all over the house so we could see for our inspection!

November 2. My sister Mary's birthday. Some of the language students finished their studies and were assigned work in other places. That day, Roy and Adelina Martens and Elizabeth Parker moved to Amalner to continue language study. The Martens had only been there for half a day when a telegram came saying that Roy's mother had passed away after surgery. That was sad news. We enjoyed them and their wee daughter Charlotte. Charlotte would sit in her high chair at the table. When we were finished the hostess would say we were all excused. Charlotte would get so excited, clap her hands and say, "Cue me, cue me." That meant excuse me, excuse me.

The missionaries so graciously taught their children (MK's as we called them) to address the other missionaries as auntie and uncle. That was really nice and for years those children seemed more like nephews and nieces to us than our own because we saw them more often. Some of them still address us that way, bless their hearts. Just today I had a letter from Stan and Annamaria Goertzen in Italy and they call me Auntie Annie. Stan was a baby when his parents Henry and Marion were missionaries in India. They later transferred to Trinidad.

It's been good over the years to watch the M.K.'s grow up and grow in the Lord. Quite a few, like Stan, have become missionaries too. TEAM had its own school for the missionary children. Several times the teachers, who also were missionaries, had the children give a play on the life of some missionary during our annual field conference. One I remember very well was on the life of David Livingston in Africa.

One of the scenes was where David Livingston was in a tent by himself kneeling on the ground beside his army cot and praying for Africa. That moved me very much. That night I knelt by my bed and dedicated myself afresh to the Lord and India.

We think of India as being a Hindu country and it is mostly that. But that was not always so. For many hundreds of years it was almost all Christian. Then people's hearts got cold and they forsook the Lord like we are doing in America. India became Hindu again. Hundreds of years later it turned to Christianity only to revert back to Hinduism again. History has it that the Apostle Thomas went to South India and preached the gospel. There are many people or churches there who still call their denomination The Marthomites or the church of St. Thomas because of him. So India has had the light of the gospel. I pray she may again turn to the true and living God.

Often when we gave the gospel to anyone, be it on a bus or train, most would nod their heads and say that what we were telling them was true. They admitted they did not get peace nor forgiveness of sin when they offered something to their gods and prayed. Some even had tears in their eyes. But then they said, "it's not for us, not for me, we have to stay with what we have been taught." It was so sad to hear one after another say that through the years.

Now back to my language study. I kept at it so much that I began to have trouble sleeping. Tears came easily especially when I had a lot of malaria, bacillary and Amoebic dysentaries. So I was advised to go to our mission hospital in Chinchpada to see our Dr. Klokke. He gave me medicine for my ailments but said I needed to get away from the books more. He showed me a bird book he and Esther had, gave me the address and advised me to order it. Then I was to get out some each day and look for birds and identify them. I got Doris to go with me and that proved beneficial to my health as well as being very interesting. One time he gave me some plants to take home to plant, weed and water.

Dora Meberg gave out medicine in Amalner to the compound people and any others that happened to hear about it. A baby boy close to a year old was quite sick and she went out regularly to give him some medicine and take his temperature. One afternoon she was busy and asked if I would go and take his temp. I did and came back alarmed because it was 108 degrees. She said that could not be, he would die if it was that high. So she went out to check and sure enough it was that high. And the baby did die that night. That poor mother and father had three of their children die within one year. We felt so bad for them.

I continued with my studies and was thankful to be making progress.

The Mebergs had baby Teddy. Once in a while they would both go to town and asked me to look in on sleeping Teddy. I tiptoed into their room and leaned over the crib so I could look through the mosquito net. Just as I was trying to be so quiet a squirrel ran up my leg but I thought it was a snake. I screamed something horrible and it almost stopped Teddy's heart and mine. Then he screamed. I picked him up to comfort him and just about that time his parents returned. Mr. Meberg told me that the poor squirrel thought I was a tree!?

By this time Doris had finished her language study and was working as secretary to Mr. Meberg who was our field chairman. The end of December 1948 brought the annual conference to Amalner again. Remember the year before it had to be moved to Dharangaon because of polio? Our TEAM General Director, Dr. David Johnson from Chicago came out and was our speaker.

I believe it was at that same conference that we had a wedding. I don't remember who the missionaries were. Everyone tried to help make it as nice as possible. The bride had a long gown and there was no way they could allow her to drag it along the ground outside or in the church. She was provided with a long, white cloth to walk on. It looked lovely. When we went to bed that night none of us had any sheets on our beds. Yes, they really did strip our beds as a last minute resort. I guess they did not have time to ask anyone. But it was fine and we all had a good laugh about it.

I have not said anything about letters from home. I was able to keep in touch with my parents and family. Remember I had been so afraid that my parents might get sick and need me? Well, they kept very healthy and worked very hard. My first Christmas in India they sent me a little parcel with a pair of pink socks and a broach. I may have requested those. Cotton socks wore out fast. I see in my diary that I started darning my socks almost as soon as I got there. I walked a lot and that wore holes in cotton socks.

The year 1949 passed quite uneventful as I remember. My diaries are missing for that year with some others. I cannot figure out what happened to them because I faithfully wrote in them every day. The Halls saved all of my letters and gave them to me. Jesse and Toini Wingard and Harvey and Dawn Strauss saved some too. I really appreciate that because that helps to fill in the missing information. Early in January of that year I sent my passport to New Delhi for renewal and it only cost $2.00 US. What is it now? I think it's $50.00 or more.

I wrote my first Marathi exam in February 1949 and passed. How I thanked God for that. I had been told to take my full time for study and would not need to write the second one until December 1949. All of a sudden a change in personnel in Dharangaon meant I would be needed there. So would I take it in October instead. That meant some scrambling but I made the trip to Poona and wrote it. Again I passed and was so thankful. Oh how free I felt! No more formal study for me. But by no means did it mean I knew the language. Learning it in a book is different than speaking it. You can imagine I'd often run back to my books. Marathi is the fifth hardest language in the world to learn we were told.

Talking about the language and how discouraged I became after I had been studying it for six months or so got me thinking just now. Namely, how come that at other times I always said if God can forgive my sins and let me know they are forgiven, then nothing is too hard for Him? Why did I not think of it in the same way in regards to the language. I think my experience so far had been mostly trusting the Lord for money. Now He wanted me to learn to trust Him in other areas and remember that nothing is too hard for Him in any area.

In our family the boys all had Peter as their second name. We girls did not have any and that was fine by me and by all of us girls. Imagine my surprise when I was required to have a second name in India. Not ordinarily but on any bank accounts and on all government forms and documents. I could not choose one. It had to be my Dad's name Peter, just like my brothers.

I objected at first and said women don't take a man's name. Nothing would change that rule! I asked for the reason behind it. I was informed that a girl always takes her father's name for a second one until she gets married. She then takes her husband's name. That made sense to me because it did to them. So after that when asked my name I volunteered, Annie Peter Goertz.

I said earlier that a river ran past our house in Amalner. When the monsoons started, the first rain sometimes was like a cloudburst. It would just come down 'in sheets' like we say and flood the river. We called it a flash flood. The ground was so dry that the river would overflow it's banks. In no time the water came up to our yard and flooded it with maybe a foot of water. It really seemed like more than that but I am not sure now. Anyway, the snakes would be drowned out of their hiding places and could be seen swimming in our yard. Gave me the shivers. All kinds of debris was washed up on our yard. After the rain stopped, the water receded just as fast because it soaked into the ground.

We had a flood like that several times. One time one of our men went down to the river to see what it looked like because the bridge was very low. Everybody knew that if you were caught on the bridge there was no time to escape. Sure enough, he saw that a bullock cart had been on the bridge. The rushing water swept it off and somehow the man was hanging onto the upside down cart. The bullocks were swimming. The missionary asked him if there had been anyone else on the cart with him. He said, "yes my wife, but she has been washed away down river. But don't worry about her, I can get another, just help me rescue my bullocks."

It made the missionary mad and after the water subsided he went down stream and there he found the body on the shore. I am sure that not all of the men would have felt that way if his wife was drowned, but this one did. Most of us were not able to sleep that night for thinking of that poor woman. Another soul had gone to a Christless Eternity.

When I first made application to TEAM they sent me some general information forms to fill out. One asked why I applied to them, the story of my conversion, and how I was called to India. It also asked if I was accepted with the mission to go to India, what did I hope to do in India. Well, I knew nothing about the work our mission was doing in India except that I had seen somewhere in their magazine that they had an orphanage. That struck a warm spot in my heart.

So the first thing that came to mind was that I would write down orphanage work. But then I thought, no, I do not want to choose my area of ministry I will leave that to the Lord. Instead, I knelt down by my bed with the form in front of me and pointed to that line and said, "Lord, will you please fill in that blank?" I mailed it to the mission.

After several months I was accepted, as I have already told you. Soon after that, the current issue of the mission magazine called "THE BROADCASTER" was sent to me. I was anxious to go through it so as to get better acquainted with the Mission. The first thing I came across was the minutes of the Board of Directors. They have long since stopped that custom because the mission got bigger and it would take way too much room.

My eyes got real big as I read about my acceptance, though that in itself was not such a surprise for I expected it to be there and I was real happy about that. When I read the next sentence it said, "And she has been accepted to work in the orphanage in Dharangaon." I was shocked, God must have put that in that blank for I certainly did not, but I rejoiced.

That was not the last of that! When I arrived on the field I was asked why I had felt that I knew enough about the work so as to be able to say where I wanted to go. Stationing the new missionaries was done by the field council!! Well, nothing serious came out of that for I explained from A to Z (like mother used to say) my side of the story. Also, that I was indeed very happy to have them station me where I was most needed when the time came.

So it was ironic when I was suddenly encouraged to take my second language exam earlier than scheduled because I was urgently needed in the orphanage in Dharangaon! God's ways are so wonderful when we allow Him to lead us. He can bring it all to pass so naturally. We do not have to break down doors in order to do what we feel He wants us to do.

He will show us His way if we are willing to do it. Why would He reveal His will when He knows we won't do it? He wants nothing more than for us to know His will and do it. Why would He keep it a secret from us? Does not make sense, does it? We may not know His will WHEN we think we should but He has to have us and the circumstances all lined up perfectly in His timing. He is rarely early in supplying our need or in revealing His will, but HE IS NEVER TOO LATE! Praise The Lord!

Before I tell about my move from Amalner, I want to mention a few more things that took place there. From that very first Sunday in Amalner, I was always amazed at all the various kinds of footwear that were left outside the church door on the steps or veranda. If you were one of the later ones to arrive, you had to be careful not to fall over them. Oh, they were placed neatly but so close together. I was surprised each one managed to step back into his/her own shoes or chappals after the meeting. Some were new, some all worn out and I often wondered how many miles each pair had walked. No one had a car and none came by bus.

Another thing I noticed very soon was that no one ever places his Bible on the floor. If you could not hold it in your hand or on your lap you put something else down on the floor first. It might be a hankie or even your songbook. Most put a paper cover on the Bible too, to protect the Bible. Remember how we used to make paper covers for our textbooks in grade school? Most Marathi Bibles are about three inches thick because poorer quality of paper had to be used so that the people could afford to buy them. Some lovely leather bound ones were available at much higher prices.

I told you earlier that I was glad I had learned to obey the rules at Prairie, and of course, I learned that first at home. Well, I told you that when I first went to Amalner for language study that Ray and Gertrude Rutan were in charge. Gertrude mostly took charge of us students and Ray was our field treasurer. So most of Ray's work was in his office with the typewriter. The windows were always open because of the heat so anyone walking by heard him clicking away at the typewriter. To the nationals, using a typewriter was associated only with work. It was true too, that on Sunday he did not use it.

We students studied hard all week but never on Sunday. Sunday was the day we wrote letters to our families, supporters and friends. That was the day we took our typewriters out because it was faster and we could make copies if needed. Now can you imagine what was going on in the minds of the local Christians?

Giving out Bibles and New Testaments in church to school girls for memorizing Scripture.

You've got it! One day Ray asked us students to stay at the table for a few minutes after lunch. He told us that the Indian pastor, (a very fine Godly man) had come to tell him that the students using the typewriter on Sunday was (in their minds) associated with work. Would he please ask us to refrain from doing that. Sunday was for rest, not work. We should be examples.

I think I must have hung my head. The others may have too. That would work hardship for us. It meant we had to write letters by hand on Sunday. If there was typing to be done we had to make time for it somehow during the week and take away from study time. It was hard at first, and I thought we should explain to them that there was a difference between Ray's typing and ours.

Then I realized that this was an occasion to remember that I had come to help not hinder. Before I came I was very willing to learn their customs and abide by them, except where it might be against Scripture. I had not expected something like this though! But here was my opportunity to submit to the authority of the local church and do it willingly and cheerfully. Then it did not bother me anymore. But it was not a once for all victory. There was always something new that came up, some new custom or culture to get used to. It was not one-sided for they had to get used to our culture too.

For example, our way is, "to jump right in with both feet" and tell people right off what we came for or came to talk over. The Indian people would come over and sit and talk about this and that. They have lots of time to broach the subject. Then after a cup of tea and having "talked around the world" they will hint at something. But you still don't know what is on their heart. Eventually, they will come out with it. I really came to appreciate that. One is not quite so apt to hurt someone.

In Amalner we had no fridge so eggs had to be placed in a pan of water. First though, our drinking water was boiled and then poured into an earthen vessel. These vessels were quite large and held one or two pails full, some even more. The vessels were made of a mixture of earth and horse manure. It was shaped by a potter and sun dried for awhile. Then they were placed in a kiln where they were baked until they were nice and hard. They were not strong though, if you bumped it too hard it would crumble or crack. It held the water but it was also porous and that worked like a cooling system. As the water seeped out slowly the air would strike it and cool it nicely.

This pot was placed on a tall metal stand with three legs and two rings. The water pot was placed into the top ring. The bottom ring was smaller and on that ring we placed a shallow earthen pot. As the water seeped out of the top one it ran into the one below. We could not waste that water so that's where we put the eggs.

I could hardly drink water the first week or so. But the missionaries explained to me that the vessels were baked so long, they were sterile. The 'mardka' earthen pot had a big belly on it with a narrow opening. We kept an old soup ladle in it to dip water with. Because the water was boiled it formed a slimy film on the inside of the pot, which had to be washed carefully every few days. The milkman brought us fresh milk every morning which had to be boiled up to three times a day and then cooled in water.

First Orphan Reunion in 1976. Story on page 228

CHAPTER 17

Move to Dharangaon

As soon as I had written my language exam and knew I had passed I started to pack up my stuff. And on November 28, 1949 I moved to Dharangaon. I cannot remember how I got my 'stuff' over there but probably I hired a small lorry. Lorry is British for truck. It was only 22 miles by road and 45 minutes by train.

Dharangaon was an older Mission station than Amalner, though it was started by another Mission. It was started during the great famine in that area around 1900. Two young ladies from the United States had studied the language at an Alliance Mission station another 20 miles or so from there. They then hired a bullock cart and went in a different direction each day to scout out the land and find a suitable place to start an orphanage. They settled on Dharangaon. Dharangaon had been a hot spot when the British were ruling India. Many officers and soldiers made it their headquarters. The whole town had a stone wall around it with a huge gate which is still there. I walked through that gate every single time I went to town. Much of the wall has crumpled of course.

A British cemetery is in that town and I often read the names of the officers on the tombstones. Most of them died of cholera or typhoid fever. Their wives and children's names were there too. None of them lived very long. Disease took them to an early grave. A two storey building was pointed out to me where one of the officers took his life. No one had lived in it since and it too was crumbling. The population of the town was around 36,000.

Those two ladies took in quite a few babies that were found beside their dead parents. Sickness hit them too and one died after a few years. The one that was left wrote to a couple back home and asked them to come and help her. Come they did but his wife died almost right away. What could he do but marry the other lady? This couple's name was Scarf.

They worked hard and built a church and proper rooms for the orphans. After one or two men were saved they trained them as evangelists. Small houses were built for them too. Eventually they decided to start a school for the children and yes, even the girls would be allowed to attend. So far there were no girls in the town school.

The work was going good and then something happened around 1928 or so. The Scarfs and children were supported completely by one couple in California. This couple were both killed instantly in a car accident and alas they had not made out a Will! The money stopped and the Scarfs did not know what to do. After quite a while someone finally wrote to them and told them that the couple had died. It was then that the Scarfs went to Amalner and told our mission (TEAM)that they were starving. They told them they could have the mission station as is. They had only to promise to support them till they died, as well as care for the orphans as long as any of them lived. That's how that Mission, whose name was Peniel, merged with our Mission. I saw the Scarfs' names on the tombstones in the British cemetery as well. Incidentally, that's where I would have been buried had I died in India.

When I came to Dharangaon there were still three or four of those first orphans alive. I helped care for them till they too went to be with the Lord. Thoma Bai was one of them and she had been blind since she was a small child if I remember correctly. There was another cemetery for the local Christians which the municipal office named the Christian Cemetery. It was about a mile out of town and in between two fields. We had to check often because sometimes the farmers would plough over the graves. There had been a fence around it but the posts and wire were removed. The British Cemetery was not very big and enclosed by a very high and thick stone wall.

While I tell you about this cemetery would be a good time to tell how we made use of it many years later. My cook Moses, who had served me so faithfully for many years had no house of his own. He lived in quarters that I rented for him. I knew he would have no work after I retired in 1984 and therefore no place to live. He was blind in one eye and was completely deaf in both ears. He was getting old too according to Indian standards which was about 55. He had a wife and a married son at home but the son was sick and could not work at the time.

I wanted to try to build him a small house, more likely a hut, before I retired but I had no money. First I would need to buy a plot. I tried to have the Mission give him a few metres off in one corner of the compound, but that would not work. If it was done for one there would be others asking. That was so true. Then I went from one shet (rich merchant) to another to plead for a wee piece of their land. I had been praying a lot about it, so surely one of them would be moved by the Lord to part with a bit of land. They smiled very graciously and said nothing. Well, silence is an answer too.

I was not about to give up but kept going back to them all. One day one of them said, " You have a place to build a house for Moses, just build it!" I asked where. He told me that the British Cemetery belongs to our Mission and there is a rule on the books that entitles every cemetery to have a caretaker live on the grounds. He then informed me all I needed to do was make application to the Municipal Office. So I did at once and I believe it took only three or four days before I had written permission in my hands. Let me tell you that nothing ever, before or after, was as easy and fast as that. Anyone who has ever lived there will verify that.

When a few of the retired missionaries at home and some on the field heard of it they sent some money to have the little house built. Praise The Lord!!

I told you I moved to Dharangaon and immediately launched into giving you two pages of background or history of that mission station.

The work in Dharangaon was divided up among three lady missionaries. The running and maintenance of the station along with the evangelistic work in town and the surrounding areas was under the supervision of a lady from Sweden named Miss Augusta Swanson. The Christian Girl's School and Hostel

Augusta Swanson and I.

was under Miss Gladys Henriksen's charge. We affectionately called her Glady. She was from Chicago, Illinois. The Baby Home was in the care of Miss Catherine Iobst from Pennsylvania. Katie was due for furlough the first part of February so I had about two months to learn from her.

Augusta arrived in India probably about the mid 1920's. She left her parents in Sweden at age 16 to make a life in the United States. She had trouble with her right hip but no one knew what it was. Her Dad did not want her to go because that hip was bigger than the other and he said she would be quarantined or sent back home. The Mother said for him not to worry for she would make a little pillow for the left hip so they would look the same!!!

Augusta arrived in New York and found a job as a homemaker for a rich family. Her hip got worse and one night it burst open and was very painful. She had to go to the doctor who diagnosed it as TB of the hip bone. She was in a TB Sanitarium for about two years. During that time some Christians visited her and gave her a Bible. She was not interested in Christianity but she was so lonely lying on that open veranda month after month so she welcomed their visits. She began to read the Bible and soon she realized her lost state without Christ and accepted Him as her Saviour.

She kept reading and it interested her that Jesus had healed so many people while He was on earth. One day she said, "Dear Lord, if you will heal me, I will be a missionary as long as I live." I believe she was healed instantly and was discharged from the Sanitarium. She then enrolled at Moody Bible Institute in Chicago. The Lord provided for her miraculously. Her hip remained big though and she walked with a stoop but it did not stop her from roughing it in tents while camping in the villages of India. She travelled by oxcart from village to village with an Evangelist, a Bible Woman, and a man to care for the oxen. They carried three tents with them. Augusta became a very dear friend and I learned a lot from her.

Augusta and Glady were my senior missionaries. Glady arrived in India in 1934. She was a very loving person. Both she and Augusta were women of prayer. Augusta went to be with the Lord on September17, 1987 at age 96 in Colorado. Glady went to be with the Lord on May 21, 1999 at age 92 in Chicago.

Sometimes when someone came to the door and they wondered if they should give him money, they would each talk in their mother tongue.

So I learned a bit of Swedish and Norwegian by listening to them but I did

Orphans playing in the sand.

not know which was which. The word for money was penger. I remember some other expressions but I will not flaunt my ignorance by spelling them wrong.

I have been trying to remember just which babies were in the Baby Home when I came. I had it all logged in my diaries but sadly some are missing. I was robbed once and it may be one or two were taken. I will name the ones I remember that were there to immediately win my heart.

Sushila Airao was born September 1, 1948 and was brought to the Baby Home on November 17. She is married to a teacher. Philip Mukunda Karle was born August 3, 1948 and brought September 26. He never got married and is a wanderer. I have not heard of his whereabouts for several years now. My heart is heavy because he has just disappeared. Stephen Pundit was born April 11, 1949 and was brought July 11. He is married and is a State Bus driver. Premanand Patil born August 24, 1942. He was going to school but still staying in the Baby Home when I came. He has his own machine shop and is married. Ramesh Swarge was born in Dharangaon on November 23, 1949. His mother Vasti was widowed about two months before. She was one of our orphans and had been married to an evangelist who died of typhoid fever. Vivek Anand Valvi born July 4, 1946 and brought as a wee baby. By the way, he was adopted by a Christian family at age 3 but it did not work out so he came back to us and we were very glad. We wanted him to be loved and cared for. Sadly though Vivek died young in 1997 and left a wife and three children.

You may wonder why I name these children. You do not know them and no doubt will never meet any of them. This is my story and these children and others that I will yet name are a big part of my life. I often refer to them as my children (please pray for each one as you read their names). More correctly perhaps I should say 'our' children. For quite a few missionaries had a part in taking some of the babies into the Baby Home and caring for them. In a sense, they became the Mission's children for it was the mission that paid for everything they needed.

At the same time we were encouraged to get supporters for them from North America. That was wonderful, for those individuals and Sunday School classes really took them into their hearts and prayed for them. If any of you who were their supporters read this, I want to thank you again for your faithfulness in sending support for them and for praying. God has and will reward you. You will meet them in Heaven.

Another reason for my including each orphan child's name in this book is because there is NO FAMILY register anywhere on earth where their names are entered. Writing that sentence makes tears come to my eyes, for it is the truth. They do not know who their parents are and in most cases we do not either. Three that decided to look for them were even more thankful that they had been brought to us because their parents worshipped idols with no knowledge of Jesus.

Still another reason for giving their names, is that some of them read English and if at all possible I want to get a copy of this book to those. It will be heart warming for them to see their names in print in Mai's book (Mai means mother or older sister).

Often a baby was brought to us by a grandmother, grandfather, uncle, aunt or sister because the Mother had suddenly died, or both parents died of typhoid. We believed them and accepted the baby, later to discover the story was not true. However, we always accepted them because if we did not we knew the baby would not live for one or two reasons.

When the children started to school (on our compound) they were transferred to the hostel under Gladys' care. That made room for more babies. This had been practised for many years. That meant there were older orphan girls living in the hostel along with those who came from their parent's homes in distant villages. These children were mostly pastor's, evangelist's and teacher's daughters. I should explain that in the Baby Home we had both boys and girls but in the Hostel we had only girls. When the boys started school they were transferred to our Boy's Mission Hostels either in Navapur or in Pimpalner. That was always heart breaking for me because I knew it would be more difficult for them to be with older boys. That proved to be too true. They were sometimes mistreated by the boys because they had no parents to defend them. The missionaries in charge there did not realize most of the time that this was going on until later or they would surely have stopped it.

I always had two young Indian girls (akkas) living in the Baby Home with the children. There were anywhere from ten to twelve children in the home, one time we had fifteen but not for very long. I spent a good part of my day with them. The very tiny babies, or the sick ones I'd bring into my bedroom. I also kept every new baby in my room until I was able to assess their health. One time I had three little babies in their hanging cradles in my room because they cried so much at night and the akkas did not get their sleep. They were two and three months old.

About an hour after I got to sleep one cried, so I changed and fed him. He fell asleep and I got back into bed only to hear the next one cry so I changed and fed. Then the third one cried so I changed and fed him. Back to bed with a sigh of relief only to hear the first one's call again. It seemed unending every night. I had a rocker in my room so I'd sit and feed them. Sometimes I prayed for sleep and sometimes I just cried. I felt I had to keep them quiet because my colleagues needed their sleep too. After about two months of this I decided I had to do something.

Augusta and Glady both went to a mela (out door rally) in another district. They would be gone for several days so I was going to get the babies to sleep through the night. Before that I had placed the three cradles in a row beside my bed and tied an old belt from my dresses to each cradle. Then I tied them together at the other end and I held that knot in my hand. I rocked all three cradles at one time. That was a load!

But now I took the baskets off the rocker part and placed each basket in a different room for the night. I fed each baby near midnight, put on plenty of diapers and put them in their baskets, (by now they were about six months old) then I went to bed.

True to habit they started to cry but I felt I had to let them cry.

They cried for several hours. So did I! I felt so mean, I can't tell you how hard that was. The next night they cried less and so did I. The third night they slept right through and so did I. The fourth night Augusta and Glady were back so I brought the baskets back into my room. At breakfast they both said, "You must have taken the babies back to the Baby Home. We never heard them cry." When I told them what I had done they called me a meanie. But they knew it was the right thing to do because both of them had had their turn in the Baby home a few years before ever I came.

When I arrived in Dharangaon I was given a daily Bible Class of girls to teach. I wondered how that would go. I still had to learn a lot in conversing in Marathi. But I was given a curriculum and went to work preparing my lesson for each day. My two dictionaries, English/Marathi and Marathi/English were a big help. I believe my language picked up faster because of that and having to speak to the little children. I never forgot that God had told me He would help me learn Marathi and I thanked Him for every improvement I noticed. Many in my homeland were praying for me.

On Sunday the girls all marched to church in their good clothes and their hair in braids with colourful ribbons. They sat on the floor on huge rugs near the platform. Next sat the Baby Home children with their akkas. I sat on a chair beside them. Glady sat on a chair near the school girls. Augusta and the other adults sat on wooden benches behind all of us. The men on one side and the women on the other.

We had quite an elaborate bell system worked out for all the different things that took place in one day or during the week. Nobody had a watch except we three ladies. I will try to explain by way of dots. A huge flat piece of heavy iron which hung from a tree served as our bell or gong. Another piece of iron was used to beat the gong. The children all knew what the various beats meant. There actually was a very lovely brass bell in the church tower. It was rung by pulling a rope. Often the rope was broken so the gong served well:

For meal time: •••••••••••••••••••••
For school: • • • • • • • • • • •
For Church: •• •• •• •• •• •• ••

I observed how Glady took care of the girls in the Hostel though she had a matron who lived with them. I also took note of how she counselled them, both the orphan girls and the others who came from their villages. She got one of the orphan girls married shortly after I came and I watched the whole process.

But the first thing I learned from her was how to prepare for and celebrate

Christmas. Remember I moved there the end of November so it was time to begin preparations right away. She asked me to accompany her to town to buy yards and yards of cloth for dresses. Then one Saturday was set apart when she called a tailor to come and take measurements of all the orphan girls. That was very exciting for them.

The next thing was to scout around on bazaar day to find little toys for each one. Very little was available but we managed to buy each one something. Then we bought lots of ribbon to match the colour of their clothes. They might also get a bar of toilet soap, some earrings, and a balloon. Glady had dear sisters who loved to send parcels and they might send enough hankies for each one to have one.

They always got peanuts (they are grown there) and sweets (candies). There were no paper or plastic bags available in the market to fill with goodies. So I was delegated to sew paper bags from newspaper, on the sewing machine which did the trick.

When all the clothes were made up they had to be wrapped. But we had no wrapping paper! Again, newspaper filled the bill very adequately. We tied it up with coloured pieces of wool. Then underneath the wool we slipped an old Christmas card of ours. They could not read the English on it and we wrote their names in Marathi. We put up an old synthetic Christmas Tree that someone had brought out years before and decorated it. It really looked nice.

Then all the parcels were put around the tree and you would have agreed that it was beautiful! Those colourful cards really made them look so Christmassy (is that a word?). The goodie bags were open so we could not put them around the tree since they would spill. We used our large galvanized tub, in which we scrubbed our clothes and it was just perfect.

On Christmas Eve we had our celebrations. The girls all went home to their villages for a month of holidays but before they left they were given a sweet lime and a Christmas card to take home. You could not have given them anything better, they were so happy they could pin up that card on their wall at home. We were very careful to give them only the cards that had Nativity scenes and things on them.

At 6:00 p.m. the three of us invited the orphan girls to our living room and you should have heard their, "Oh's" and "Ah's." The tree was so pretty with the colourful presents underneath. We had lit lots of small candles and placed them around the room. I must say it was pretty. Christmas comes during the coldest season of the year when night temperatures go down to about 50 degrees Fahrenheit. That does not seem cold to you but when no homes are heated it is cold. So we would bring some of the large rugs from the church to spread on our cold stone floor.

Then Glady would sit in her favourite white wicker chair right beside the tree and emcee the celebration. Let me digress a bit here and tell you that after Glady retired I took over the School and Hostel. I tried to do things very much the same as she had, at least at first. When I called the orphans in for our Christmas Eve celebration I carried on the age old custom. After we started to sing, one of the orphan girls stopped singing and came to ask me to get up for a minute. When I did she switched my chair. I had been sitting in a different chair. I had to sit in that white wicker chair like Henriksen Mai always had.

After that I made sure I sat in the correct chair. I fondly recall our own family customs. Therefore I was and am, glad that the missionaries had established customs for the orphans that they too, wanted to hold to. That made it HOME. I am quite sure that Glady did not even realize that the children had taken note of such details. She just sat where she was comfortable. Father, please bless our children today in India and care for them in their own homes and families. Amen.

Now back to the story. First we sang carols then Glady read the Christmas story from the Bible and prayed. She often emphasized that we must make sure we have room in our hearts and lives for Jesus. Then it was time to give out the presents. I can still see them hugging the present and waiting till everyone had theirs. There probably were around thirty which included the Baby Home children. When the last one had their gift they all opened them together. They even folded the newspaper carefully to take to their room to put into their tin suitcases as a bottom liner. Nothing was wasted. When everyone had quieted down the candy bags were given out.

Finally, about 8:30 or 9:00 p.m. they were tired. So they gathered up their precious gifts and with many "upkarmante Mai" (thank you Mai) went home. Not before they wished us all a happy Christmas.

Then we would quickly straighten out the rugs, replace the candles and bring in more candy bags since we made enough for everyone. We called the local Christians and workers, including the pastor's family. The four teachers had all gone home for Christmas. We sang carols, Gladys read the Bible and prayed. We did not have gifts for them just candy. It was such a happy time for them and us.

They went home about 10:30 or 11:00 p.m. They thanked us and wished us a happy Christmas. We responded, "to you too" in Marathi. After all had gone, we sat down to our Christmas Eve celebration exactly at midnight! We had not had supper for we were too busy with last minute preparations. Instead we had high tea at 4:00 p.m. Now we opened our gifts, sang English carols and had coffee and some delicacies that Augusta had prepared. I was so thirsty and drank one cup of coffee after another until I think I drank five cups. I have never had that much coffee before or since. Augusta kept saying, "Annie, you will not sleep." I told her a couple of times that coffee had never kept me awake and it wouldn't now. Well, it did. I really did not sleep at all! And I was so tired. It's funny how at Christmas when I have coffee with some goodies I always think of that first Christmas in India 1949. It brings back wonderful memories.

It was shortly after Christmas that I had the joy of taking in a child for the first time. It was Suvarta Aaron Govande, a girlie just past her third birthday. Her father was an evangelist with our mission. Her Mother had TB but since they lived in a village, no one seemed to take note of it. Eventually, the mother could not get up anymore so she just kept her child beside her all the time. The Mother died but not before she had passed her TB on to her wee child.

The person that brought Suvarta to me did not say anything about the Mother having had TB. She got good food in the Baby Home, Cod Liver Oil, Vitamins and fresh air. So the TB became encapsulated in her lungs and did not manifest itself for about three years. Then the children got whooping cough and Suvarta got it too. That coughing loosened the disease and it travelled from her lung to her brain.

Holding two of my babies.

That was so sad for she began to get seizures often. They lasted so long. Often I feared for her life. Somehow we discovered that she had TB. She got treatment and has been fine since. However, it did leave one leg and hand paralyzed. Suvarta means, "good news." I arranged her marriage years later and she and her hubby have two lovely sons. I'll tell more about that wedding later.

Suvarta had been exposing other children to TB before we knew she had it. Then I realized some girls were showing symptoms of it. So I had to take groups of girls 20 miles on the train to Jalgaon to the Civil Hospital to get their chests screened. Sadly two or three had it and I sent them to our TB Hospital in nearby Parola where they were treated and are now fine. We thank the Lord that more did not get it. I think in all I took about sixty girls for screening and stood right there while the Doctor explained to me what he saw. I did not have a lead apron on like he did. Praise God nothing happened to me as a result of all that exposure to the x-ray. I did not know the danger of x-ray at the time.

Suvarta was born on May 15, 1946 and is now 54 years old.

CHAPTER 18

General, In Dharangaon

The month of January 1950 gave me opportunity to really get into the Baby Home routine. We had our own medical clinic complete with various medicines. Also a hair cutting/clipper set, for I cut the children's hair. It was a little easier to cut the girl's hair than the boy's! When I think back now, it looked as if I had placed a bowl on the boy's head and cut around the edge. I hope I got better as time went on.

About once in two months I cut all of their finger and toe nails. That was quite a job for ten children it meant one hundred of each finger and toe nails! It took quite a while that's why I mention it. It was always a fun time.

Our clinic cupboards also held forceps to pull teeth. At first I pulled mostly baby teeth. Later when the Baby Home was closed and I worked in the Hostel and school I pulled bigger teeth. With my left hand I steadied their head against my chest and with the other hand I pulled. I used to tell them that I put love on the forceps and it did not hurt as much. The nerve of me!! It seemed to work though!

As soon as the tooth came out they held out their hand for it. Everybody admired it. Some just put them into their pocket to go into their suitcase later. Others ran outside and tried to throw the tooth over the house. Of course, they did not succeed but I asked them why they did it. They said that if you do not do that another tooth would not come in it's place.

I explained to them how wonderfully God had made our bodies. Wounds heal, blood clots, broken bones knit together again, and just as surely as one tooth comes out the one underneath wiggles it's way out. Also that the second tooth is bigger. I told them that throwing a tooth over the hut or house is superstition and that we as Christians must not believe in that.

The dentist's office was always open on Thursday, market day! Lo and behold, when I pulled teeth the next time, some of the girls from the previous time were there. As soon as I pulled a tooth, they surrounded the girl and explained to her that she must not throw it over the house, "because we are Christians." It was so rewarding to see and hear that.

Catherine Iobst left early in February and now I was alone with all those precious children. How I prayed for wisdom and patience in my every dealing with each one. In fact, I asked the Lord to help me never to say anything to any of the little ones that I did not want them to remember the rest of their lives. I mean no hurting words. Just as they remember the good, they remember the unkind too. I think back to my Mother. I do not remember her ever saying anything to me that hurt. I wanted so much to be like Mother. Even though I was alone now, I was very glad to have Glady because she gave me guidance and advice anytime I asked.

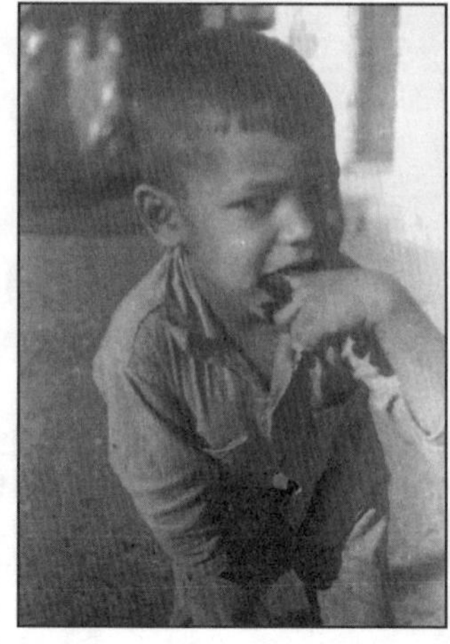
Prakash brushing his teeth.

Going back to Katie, people had fun with her surname. One time when she was on vacation someone came from the post office with a telegram addressed to, Catherine at 10B Street. Another time they called her, 'Miss I upset.' I can't laugh though, I got it too! I was most often called Gorts, or Miss George. One pastor used to call me Guts (with a bit different pronunciation) and in Marathi it means, "it thickened." My coworker always got a big laugh out of that.

On February 22, 1950 a sweet three month old baby boy was brought to the Home. He had no name but because he was such a happy baby I called him Prakash, which means light. Now I had to find a father's name and surname for him. We knew he came from the fishermen's caste. So I went to our Pastor Rev. Sojwal and asked him if he knew what names were prevalent among them. He suggested Satyavan Sharungpani. So that's what it was.

Prakash was well and grew to be an obedient boy. Sometimes I needed someone to relay a message to someone else, maybe to the akkas. I could always rely on him to repeat the message just as I had given it. When he was school age he was sent to the Boys' Boarding in Navapur. The boys took their baths right by the well, as it was down the hill away from other houses.

Prakash got all soaped up and then was asked by another boy to help him hoist the pail of water from above the open well. You see it was an open well and the water was pulled up with a pail tied to a rope. They had to reach over the well a bit which was dangerous. The pail was heavy and he was only about nine years old by then. He slipped because of the soap on his feet and fell into the well. He cracked his head severely on the side of the well because it got narrower and died instantly. That was very sad.

I was in the Hills on vacation when word got to me about it. I felt as if I should go right back but that would do no good. There was nothing I could do. He was buried within a few hours because it was the hot season. My comfort was that Prakash was in Heaven because I knew he had accepted Jesus into his heart. It was very hard on his orphan brothers. They missed his cheerful presence.

The well Prakash fell into and died.

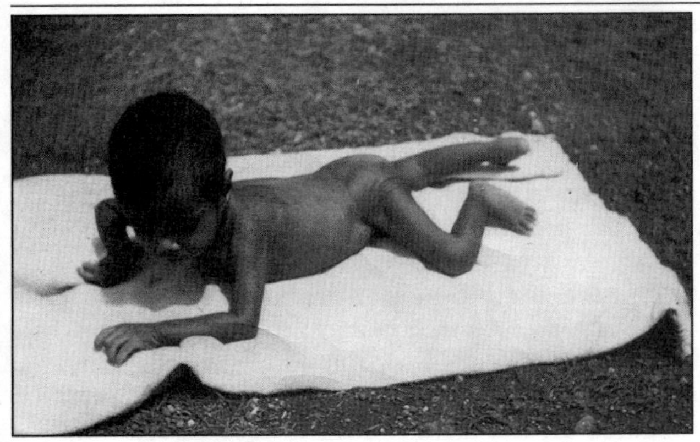

Prabhaker the day he was brought to us.

The next child, another boy, to be brought to us was Prabhaker Rama Muka. He was seven months old. He loved to play in the sand and gravel in front of the Home like the others. Sadly, he ate a lot of it and several times he almost died. He outgrew that and became a lovely fat child. He never got married.

A poor sketch of the swing.

We had a special fund called Work Support. We were able to buy things for our ministry with that which we could not have had otherwise. I had wanted to have a swing made for the children but there was nothing in the fund for me because I was so new in the ministry. Someone from home (sorry I do not remember who) wrote and asked if there was anything I needed for the children. Immediately, I thought of a swing.

We really needed a different kind of swing, one that would hold all the children. So I hired a carpenter and gave him the dimensions, six or seven feet long by about four feet wide. A very sturdy frame was made from big poles of wood and set in cement in the ground. A set of two metal poles were hung from the pole overhead by a large iron ring. The metal poles were separated at the bottom end in this ^ shape and each end was fastened to another large ring at each corner of the board. I'll try to make a little sketch.

One aspect we had not given special thought to was the distance of the swing from the ground. Now I realized it had to be low enough so that if they should fall off, as they most certainly would, they would not break a limb. It also had to be high enough so that their little heads would not be squashed as the rest kept swinging. They were too young to be able to stop a loaded swing if someone fell off. We got it figured out just right for no serious accidents ever happened. And you know, that swing lasted for 45 years!

That reminds me I planted two lemon trees my first year in Dharangaon. Both of them yielded enough to supply all of us. When I went back to Dharangaon in 1993 the headmaster took me over to those trees. The white ants had eaten them so there was just a bit of a stump left. He had wanted to dig them up and throw them away but he wanted my permission. He knew I had planted them. Bless his heart. That was Mr. Diwanji T. Valvi (wife Sarah).

When I told you about going to Rev. Sojwal to get a name for our little baby, I did not mention his wife was Anna Bai (Bai means woman). They were a Godly couple. She was the Hostel Matron for many, many years. In fact, she was the first one and knew all the history of Dharangaon, some of which I have already given. I believe she was one of the earliest orphans taken by Peniel Mission. The Sojwals had no children so they adopted a baby named Madhukar. Madhukar became the president of one of the Christian Colleges in Poona.

One of our orphans Kamal Khare, used to help Anna Bai in her home quite a bit. She milked the water buffalos, scoured pots and pans all the while attending our school. She really became like a second adopted child to them. They were very good to her. When Anna Bai was old and very frail, Kamal Bai took her into her home and cared for her until she died. Rev. Sojwal had died long before. Kamal too had been married and now was alone with her two little daughters Sheilza & Shamla. Kamal was very enterprising for she took teacher's training and taught till about 4 years ago.

Kamal had her 68th birthday in 1999 and her health was not good at all. About 4 years ago while walking to town an ox attacked her from behind and mauled her till she was almost killed. She never recovered from that. Her daughter and son-in-law were living with her in order to care for her. Her son-in-law died in January 1999 of liver complications, leaving his wife Shamla and two young children. That was bad enough but then in September 1999, her daughter Shamla got burned while making tea and died ten days later. Now there are two little orphans ages six and eight. Sorrow upon sorrow! Kamal cannot care for them so the other grandparents have taken them but they too are old so they all need prayer.

Anna Bai used to tell us of the "olden days." One day I asked her just how the mission happened to build where it did. It was a good mile or more from the big gate I talked about. She told me how those first two ladies had lived in a small rented house with a few babies they had brought with them from Jalgaon. They wanted a bigger place so they could take in more children but the municipality would not sell them any land.

However, these ladies were not to be deterred easily and they applied for land over and over and over again. What's more, the people did not want Christians in town. When they came out of their house people would throw rotten eggs and tomatoes at them. They always responded in love. Quite often they were told to just leave. Dharangaon, as then, is still a very staunch Hindu town. I can only think of three people from the town that became Christians. All three have passed away.

After about a year of repeatedly asking for land the town office got tired of them. They offered them the former Hindu Burning Grounds out of town. For some reason they had moved it to another area. They had offered the land free to farmers but no takers. All were afraid the spirits of the dead might be roaming there looking for their bodies. Well, these ladies were not afraid and at once accepted the offer. Now the men did not know what to do because they really did not want Christians in town but they did not go back on their offer. Praise the Lord, these ladies walked out of the office that day with the title deed in their hands, and it was a GIFT!

I was so blessed by that story. Those ladies really had to endure a lot of persecution, probably more than Anna Bai knew about. Someday they will see the hundreds of girls in Heaven that have come to Jesus as a result of what they started so many years ago in Dharangaon.

You know about our Christmas, now Palm Sunday. On Palm Sunday some of the workers would go early to look for Palm trees along the road, but of course, there were none. So they brought back an oxcart full of branches off any tree. We were close to two hundred people and each one needed a branch.

After each person had one we lined up and with the pastor leading us we marched around the church seven times while we sang, "Hosanna! Hosanna!" I never asked why we did that, and seven times at that! I must admit the first time I joined them I was almost scared the church would implode. After the last round was completed we all dropped our branches on a pile outside and entered the church for the service.

On Good Friday we had a three hour service. A few years later the service was shortened because it was too hot. A week or two in advance the church panch (board) met and decided who would speak. The custom every year was that seven different people would each speak on one of the seven last words that Jesus spoke while on the cross. It really was a great blessing as we all took our turn.

On Easter morning everyone got up long before daylight for the sunrise service. Just as the sun sets almost instantly in the evening so it rises just as suddenly in the morning. We (mostly children) had about a mile to walk down the road to a little knoll. So we had to hurry if we wanted to see the sun rise. The children got so excited and shouted when the sun suddenly burst over that little hill. The Pastor then led us in a song that would be equivalent to our "He Lives." Then we all went back and had breakfast in our respective homes.

Shortly after breakfast we had our Easter service in church. When there were people wanting to be baptized it was done on Easter Sunday. There was no river close by so we baptized in a small tank made of slabs of stone sunk in the ground. This had originally been made to soak the bricks while we had a school built. It looked as if it would be good for baptisms so we just left it there. It was not deep so the candidates had to kneel down so they could be immersed. The water was carried in by pail by the older girls.

Our worker's children and orphans were baptized there. But every now and again some of the girls that were saved in our hostel wanted to be baptized there too. Maybe there was no church in their village, or for whatever reason they chose to have it done where they were saved. But, our pastor never baptized a minor before he had written permission from the girl's parents. The church could have been in deep trouble if he had.

Mother's Day came next and the pastor always gave a good message on the role of mothers. I do not remember exactly how that day was celebrated when Augusta and Glady were still there. But after they left I lived alone. So I will tell you what was done then. The summer holidays were on so only the orphan girls were at home. The girls got up early to prepare vegetables, potatoes and whatever we were going to have for lunch. I often ate with them during the holidays because it made it more like a family.

After church, I gave the girls some money from their accounts that they kept with me and they went to town to buy me a gift. I really did not want gifts because they had so little money. At the same time I was the only Mother they knew so I let them have that joy. I also had to teach them customs that they in turn would teach their children. If I did not, who would? I loved them and I had to teach them to love me. So Mother's Day was always a happy and emotional time. You taught your children how to hug you, how to kiss you, and how to say, "I love you." It was my joy, privilege and responsibility to teach those things to the orphan children as well. They have reciprocated that love to me above and beyond what I could have imagined. How I thank God for 'my' family in India.

Now back to Mother's Day again, I forgot to say that when the girls left for town, I did something too. I donned an apron in the hostel kitchen and did the cooking. The stove was an open fire on the floor. It was not difficult for they had cut all the onions, garlic, potatoes and ground the spices. They were gone for a couple of hours anyway, so when they returned dinner was ready, rice and all.

That has to be one of the very, very special times I had with "my" girls. This little custom always seemed to draw us closer each time. What rejoices my heart so is that they now celebrate Mother's Day the same way in their homes. Just a few months ago I had letters from some of the girls telling me what their children had done for them on Mother's Day. They also told me that they celebrate Christmas with their husband and children like we did at home.

On March 12, 1950 a man from a village not far from our hospital in Chinchpada brought his infant son to the doctor and asked if he would take him. The reason being the Mother died two weeks before and he was unable to care for him. The child was 10 months old. His birth date was given as May 28, 1949. He was fat, healthy and happy and the nurses loved caring for him. He crawled around on the hospital floors.

The doctor was concerned that he would get sick from crawling on the germ ridden floors, so they notified me to come and get him. On March 18 I went by train to bring him home. I went prepared with milk bottles, some clothes, blanket and diapers. His name was Sadanand Ramchand Khumbhar. Sadanand means "always happy" and that certainly suited him.

We took the midnight train from Chinchpada and had a very frightening experience. We were barely 15 minutes out of the station when the train stopped. The baby and I were the only ones in that compartment. I had noticed that some women had stuffed bags and bags of stuff under my bench and the one facing me then left. I thought nothing of it.

Evidently the bags contained contraband of some kind. As soon as the train stopped about five men jumped on and took all the bags and threw them out of the train. They wasted no time and in so doing they knocked the baby bottle out of my hand. That scared the baby and he screamed and I felt like it too. They had no intentions of harming us but I did not know that. They jumped off and I quickly locked all the doors. How I thanked God that we were safe and I wondered who in the homeland might have been praying for me.

In retrospect, I think those men were hired by the Railway because there were certain grains and woods that were not to be transported from one area to another. The hospital was in West Khandesh and I lived in East Khandesh. It was the government that issued those orders. Years later West Khandesh was renamed Dhulia Dt. and East Khandesh was named Jalgaon Dt. Some of you will remember East Khandesh as my first address.

When Sadanand started school in Navapur he was told that his last name Khumbhar was the name of his caste. Khumbhar is a profession that means Potter. After he was married he went to the village where he came from and found his father. His surname was actually Sanyasi so he changed his name to that. By profession Sadanand is a tailor and has made several beautiful dresses for me. He has a lovely wife Leela and three children.

In those early years, the 1940's through the 1960's there was really no proper food for a baby to survive on when a mother died. They could not afford to buy milk so instead gave them tea. There was not enough milk in that so the baby starved to death. Hindu people did not want their children to become Christians so often they just kept them at home until they died. Others waited till the last minute before they brought them. As a result they brought me quite a few babies who died either that same day or the day after, no matter what I tried. That was very hard as you can imagine.

While Glady was still there she was so kind and washed the little bodies and prepared them for burial. After she left I did it. Sometimes, I had a cardboard box to bury them in or a small wooden box in which I had bought laundry soap. The babies that we had only for a few hours or days had a service outside in the shade with a few people and two men would carry the body to the cemetery and bury it. It was a comfort to know they were with Jesus. Our own men dug the grave and it was difficult in the stony ground.

When adults died we bought five yards of black cloth and wrapped the body in it. Then the men put it on the oxcart and took it to the cemetery. An adult required a bigger hole so the men would sometimes start digging before the person was actually gone. That sounds very crude and cruel but that was life in a very hot climate where every hour you keep the body above the ground is too long.

During my time in Dharangaon, two of our Pastors died. Rev. Sojwal and Rev. D. S. Ramteke though many years apart. Their families did not have money to make a coffin. So the mission hired a carpenter who made the coffin right there on the compound. In the first case, Glady was able to send someone quickly on the bus to Amalner to ask the missionary there to come and take the funeral. The second one died when I had company. Rev. Einer and Mary Berthelsen happened to be visiting and I was so glad because there was no one else to call.

After the funeral we all walked to the cemetery behind the oxcart 'hearse.' This was strange to all our Hindu, Jain and Moslem neighbours because none of their women ever go to the burial or burning grounds. Moslems and Jains bury their dead whereas the Hindus burn them.

When someone dies, the family members and relatives will not eat or drink until the body has been cared for. Sometimes that means almost a whole day, depending on circumstances, without a drop of water in that heat. I often wondered how they survived.

The Hindus are afraid that the spirit of the deceased will linger near the house after the body has been removed. So the women grab a towel or any piece of clothing and walk behind the body and "shoo" the spirit away so that it will follow the body. If they don't they fear the spirit will try to get back in the house. That cloth had to be washed right away. That night they closed the doors and shutters very tight. If the wind should rattle the door they are terribly frightened. It was really hard to see all that.

When funeral processions go down the street they have someone go ahead beating a drum. I have heard two reasons for the drums, if it is so or not, I do not know. One is to warn people to get out of the way because no one wants to get too close. They carry the body with the face uncovered, sometimes the corpse is in a sitting position. The second reason is so that the spirit will be able to hear where the body is and follow.

A few times I have been on the street when a funeral procession came by. I stepped aside of course to let them pass. The women chasing the spirit had gone back home. But people living in homes nearby would pour water on the road behind the procession. A funeral procession makes everything nearby unclean. The water cleanses the road. One time, I stepped onto the road a little too quickly and almost got doused with water. Women on the second storey had heard the drum and threw water out of their window on to the road without looking to see if anyone was walking below. The clean water would not hurt anyone, in fact it would purify that person?

Talking about being purified reminds me of an experience I had while riding the bus. A young gentleman, probably a college student, was sitting beside me. We had been conversing. As the bus left town we passed the area on the outskirts which is used as a bathroom. The odour was all but pleasant. This young man whipped a bottle of very strong perfume out of his shirt pocket so fast and sprayed himself. Then to be kind to me he sprayed me very liberally. Thanks!

It's time to tell you a bit more about the rainy season. In the hot season, the people plant melons and watermelons in the river beds. Some rivers dry up completely in the hot season but usually there are little patches of water here and there where they can plant something. They do very well because of the heat and water. Someone has to sleep by the melons or they would be stolen. The watermelons grow very large and are very sweet.

As the time comes for the rains to begin they start listening for a rumbling sound. They know that means the water is rushing down river from higher grounds. I have never seen it happen but was told it looks like a wall of water and floods the rivers. It also comes very swiftly. So as soon as it is first heard, they rush to remove their crops as fast as possible. They plant cucumbers and spinach in the river beds too. The Indian people are very clever and innovative. They make use of things we would never think of. I guess it's true, necessity is the mother of invention.

When the rains start in earnest, it takes only two or three days for the grass to come up and soon it is all nice and green. We had no lawns since it takes too much water. The grass grows so fast in the rains that people have to cut it or it gets too tall. Snakes hide in the grass. In fact, many people die from snake bites every rainy season. They lurk in the grass and the women grab a snake along with a handful of grass because they can't be seen that easily. As long as we had oxen (bullocks) we used our own grass to feed them. Later, we sold it to neighbours and others that had animals.

We had a nice gravel path from the bungalow to the road and planted flags on either side. I don't know if we have them in Canada but they look a lot like tulips. Glady and I watched one year to see how long it would take for them to grow and bloom. It took exactly four days after we got the first rain. They were about ten inches high by then and had buds. So we went out and knelt beside the plants and were amazed as we saw slight movement in the buds. It took about half an hour for them to be fully in blossom right before our eyes. That was so exciting, only God can do that.

Not everything became pretty during the rains. Feather pillows really began to stink. The mattresses smelled sour and felt so damp as we got into bed. Leather shoes would be covered with mildew by morning along with our leather covered Bibles. Cotton dresses in the closet smelled sour. So when there was a day without rain I'd open the closet doors to let a bit of air in. I found it very hard to fall asleep on a sour smelling pillow. So on one of my furloughs I discovered polyester filled pillows and took one back. I treasured it for it never soured on me!

During my first rainy season I got really depressed for it rained day after day. We did not see the sun for a month it seemed. I was sure we'd never see the sun again. My senior missionaries assured me it would come out again and it did. For three months I battled with depression. I don't remember any other rainy season when we got that much rain. Maybe it was just that I did not let it bother me as much, or perhaps it was because I knew what to expect. But really, the pattern did change, the rains came much later and often not enough. Many years the latter rains did not come at all or too late to save the crops. I then understood what the Bible means when it talks about the early and the latter rains.

Some years when they had planted their crops and the rains did not come on time the birds would eat the seeds. And you've never seen as many crows, mayna birds and squirrels as India has. Rats also forage for food in the fields. Then when the rain does come, they quickly plant a bit more. Often that's when they may even have had to plant the grain they had kept for food. It was heart breaking to watch.

When this happened in the Dhulia Dt. which was 100 miles or so west from where I lived, the people had no food because they planted all their grain. They would dig certain roots for food. But the roots were very bitter and made them very sick, sick enough to die. So they tied them to a piece of string or rope and put them in the river for about a week. They anchored the string with a stone on the bank. The flowing water took the bitterness out. Then they dried the roots in the Sun. After they were dry they pounded and pounded them on a stone to the consistency of course powder or flour. This they then mixed with water to make bread. The poor people. Some of the Christians had to do that too.

About 98% of our school girls came from that area. So we were very happy to take them into our school and hostel so there would be less people to feed at home. The main reason of course, was to give them the gospel and education so they could go back and teach their parents about Jesus. In several villages churches were started as a result of the witness of these little girls.

When some of the girls went home for vacation, usually the first one they witnessed to was Grandmother. She had missed the child so much so she would have her sleep with her. The girl would say, "Grandma, I always pray to Jesus before I sleep." So she prayed. In the morning she would sing to her. This was all new to Grandma and actually she was against it but she saw such a difference in the child. After a few weeks of this, Grandma's heart was softened and the child got her to pray to Jesus.

The girl would come back to school and tell us about it during the first testimony meeting in church. Meanwhile in the village Grandma would sing Christian songs and the family noticed such a difference in her. Slowly the family came to Jesus and a church might be started if there was not one already. I often refer to those girls as real church planters. The girlies may have been in first grade only at the time.

These girls as a rule did not come from Hindu homes but from the Aboriginal Tribes. Their religion is Animism. They believe that there is life or god in inanimate objects. For instance there's a god in a tree, or a chair, a mountain or in the earth. In some ways a lot like the New Agers nowadays here in America. In fact, I think they got it from India. What darkness!

Often when parents, or a father, brought a new girl for the first time I would ask if they were Christians. That is common to ask because each child's religion has to be entered in the school register. So, though ours was a Christian School we had to adhere to those same practices because we got government grants. If the father's answer was no, then I would ask if he knew that ours was a Christian school. He would say yes. I then proceeded to tell him that although we were not allowed to teach about Jesus in school, we did teach it in the daily Bible classes and in church. He said he knew that too. I told him that if his little daughter hears about Jesus and how He died for her and all of us, she may believe in Him. What would he say to that?

Then with a smile they usually said, "I know. I have watched the girls from our village that have been to your school. They come back transformed. I want that too but I am too old to come to school. So I am bringing my daughter. You teach her about Jesus and she will teach me and my family." Talk about an open heart and what an opportunity! Praise God.

I should say right here that we were required by law to teach Hinduism in school every day. Almost every subject had Hinduism woven into it. That was very hard for me at first. But in our Bible classes we would tell the girls that the things we had to teach in school were not what the Bible teaches.

The fact that we had to record each child's religion had its drawbacks too. The first information that was required to be written down when any child started school was ever after used almost like a birth certificate. It was called a School Certificate but it was more than that. It could never be changed that was a law of the Medes and Persians! Any change would bring heavy fines. That certificate follows a child through his Primary, High and College years, even into schools of higher learning.

Another drawback was that the Christian children were often failed in their exams and were not allowed a seat in the next class or school. The same often happens when looking for a job. They are required to give a HUGE donation (actually a bribe) before they are given entrance. It makes it very hard for them. It has become much worse in the last few years. Some would like to train as nurses, teachers or doctors. It has actually become almost impossible for Christians to get a seat in a medical school to train as a doctor, because of the high entrance fees. These are separate from the regular monthly fees during training.

Posing with my little family.

Some of the orphans I arranged marriages for.

CHAPTER 19

More Babies Arrive

Anand Lucas Hiwali was born July 15, 1951. His mother died. He was first taken to our Dispensary in Parola where the missionaries cared for him for eleven days. It was hard for them to be at work and care for an infant so one of them brought him to us on August 27. His name is Anand, which means Joy. However he was anything but that for a few weeks.

I kept him in my room for a few months because the two girls I had helping with the children were both very young. One was only 13. I often took him to the Baby Home so the children could see him and kiss him. They begged me to leave him there. They are just like our children here, they like babies.

Anand grew up to be a fine boy. When he was school age, he too had to go to Navapur to the Boy's Boarding. That was always very hard for them and for me. Anand is married and has two little boys. He works for the government at Ukai Dam as their Jeep Driver. To be a driver in India is a full time job. There are less cars and often people who own a car don't know how to drive. They just hire a driver. I had my Driver's License but never drove once. The steering wheel is on the right side and you drive on the left side of the road. I had no vehicle anyway but a few times it would have been a help to the missionaries if I had had the courage to take them to the railway station in their jeep at night.

ANOTHER BABY

Halsey and Ruth Warman (they were on the ship with me) lived in Raver. I had a letter from Ruth saying she had taken in a tiny infant and asked if I could take him. She had thought that they could keep him but it was not working out. So she brought the little boy on September 27, 1951, by train. She told me he had been born August 4 and was named Yohan Maltse. He now goes by John Malche.

Since he was not yet two months old, I kept him in my room too. He was a healthy baby for Ruth had given him a good start. When he was school age he too, left for Navapur. I'll say more about that a bit farther on.

Yohan was the only one of the orphan boys that wanted to attend Seminary to prepare to serve the Lord. The Lord leads each one in His own way. He had learned English in High School so that qualified him for Seminary, as all classes were taught in English. He then worked in Light of Life Correspondence School office in Chalisgaon for a few years.

One day I had a letter from Yohan saying he would like me to get a wife for him. That was altogether different for me. When our girls married the boy's parents always came looking for a girl.

So now my role was altogether different for I had to go looking. I started to pray about that right away and Yohan did too. I asked him if he had seen a girl he was interested in. He said, "No Mai, I want you to pick one. You know me so well." I prayed for several months but I had no guidance. I thought of this one and that one but there was no confirmation from the Holy Spirit that this was the one.

On a particular day, I had been quite concerned about not finding a girl. That night, I was awakened suddenly from sleep and the name Nira came to me as clearly as if someone had spoken it audibly. I knew Nira very well for she had been one of our orphans till she was 11 years old. Then her father came to take her back because now she was old enough to be able to help him at home. She finished her schooling and was now in nurse's training in a Christian Nazarene Hospital. She had one year left when her name came to me.

I was arranging the first orphan reunion to be held in Dharangaon and I invited any and all orphans (now grown up and married). There were several of the older ones I had never met.

Now I had to do a little scheming to get Nira to come too, so I could introduce these two. I wrote the Superintendent of Nursing and was told she could not get time off. Quickly I sent a letter back and told her that it was urgent that she come. If I did not make her arrangement now her Hindu father and brothers would marry her to an unsaved man as soon as she graduated. That letter brought results. She said she could come for two days. Well, that was enough! How I thanked God for answered prayer.

First, I took Yohan aside and pointed out the girl I had picked for him. He didn't really take a good look because he knew God had guided me. As far as he was concerned, she was the one for him. Then I called Nira into the bungalow and told her why I had invited her. She had no idea. When I broached the subject she at once said, "Oh Mai, you have no idea how concerned I have been because I know my father has someone picked out for me. I do not want to marry an unsaved man. I have cried and prayed to God that He would cause someone to have mercy on me and arrange a Christian marriage for me." She grabbed me and gave me a big hug. You can imagine how I felt. I knew it was God that had brought her name to mind.

Then I told her we would go to the verandah and I would point Yohan out to her. I asked her to think and pray about it and let me know her answer by letter. He was outside mingling with the others. He was too far away for her to really see what he looked like. But she turned to me and said, "I will give you my answer now. I do not want the superintendent to see my letter. My answer is, 'yes'." I was very thankful and arranged for them to see each other and talk. They did see each other but there was nothing to talk about!! I gave them each other's address and think they probably did write once or twice before they got married.

I say 'think' because I was going to Canada soon after for medical reasons and so do not know. Nira still had a year left, so the understanding was that I would arrange for the wedding as soon as I came back. However, I was detained longer than expected. They wanted to get married and why not? So Yohan asked Einer and Mary Berthelsen if they would be his parents and arrange the wedding details. They were only too glad to do so and they had a nice wedding in Dharangaon on September 20, 1978. I returned September 30.

Yohan, Head Cashier

They are both working in a large Christian Hospital, Yohan as head cashier and Nira as Nursing Superintendent. They have two lovely sons Timothy and Victor ages 19 and 17. All are active in church.

I said I would tell you more about when the boys left for Navapur. It so happened that three of the boys were going at the same time. Yohan, Anand and Santosh. I have not told you about the latter as yet. I had them sleep on the enclosed verandah of my home because I was taking them on the midnight train. Before they went to sleep I had prayer with them and committed them to the Lord and asked Him to keep them from sin.

Then each of them prayed but I will not tell you who prayed what. Their prayers were so much like their nature. The first one asked the Lord that the boys in Navapur not hit him. The second asked the Lord that there might be some sweets given out like there had been in Dhar. The third asked the Lord to help him be a good boy, to study hard and to live for Him. Bless their little hearts. I wept by the time they finished because they had burdens and they told the Lord about them.

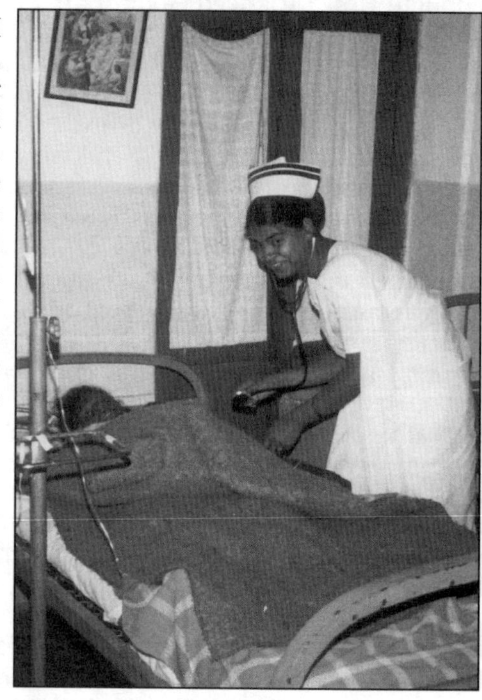
Nira, Nursing Superintendent

WELCOME BABY GIRL

On January 24, 1952 I went to the back verandah to get a drink of water when I saw a young girl sitting cross-legged on the ground outside with a wee baby on her lap. She was feeding the baby and I watched for a bit. She had a small medicine bottle with some milk in it. She poured some

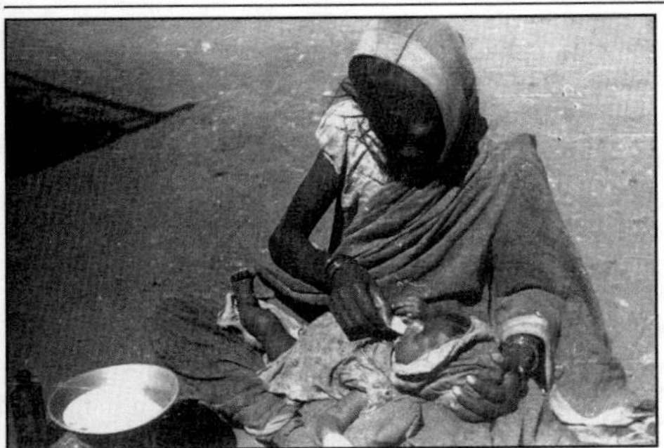
Baby Miriam being given her milk.

into a dish and scooped it up with a seashell to feed the baby. The girl's father was sitting not far from them.

I went to the door and said, "Ka Ho! What do you want uncle?" and gave him some water to drink. He then told me that the baby's mother had died eight days ago, and he had been feeding her and caring for her but he knew he could not do it much longer. He asked if I would take his daughter and raise her as my own. I thought for a minute and realized the Baby Home was full. So I said I was not sure I could for we had no room.

Then he got up and started to leave saying, "Her life is in God's hand (he meant one of his gods), I will do what I can. The rest is up to God." Then my heart melted and I said that we could probably put three babies in one cot instead of two. He held her out to me with the bottle of milk and the seashell.

She was born on November 23, 1951 so she was now two months old and very fat. I wasn't sure the mother had died because the baby was so fat and healthy. It could be because he said he had water buffalo so he had fed her milk. She was such a good baby and always happy.

The man and the older girl left but kept turning around to look at me holding the baby. My heart went out to him but I knew he must have a very good reason for bringing her. I got his name which was Edu Zaverlu. So I named her Miriam (after my youngest sister) Edu Zaverlu. I gave her a bath and put her on my bed to sleep. She slept a long time for she had been carried for miles in the Sun. I think she also knew that she had come home.

I saved the little homemade bonnet and top that she had worn that day. I gave it to her after she got married. In fact, I gave it to her just before I came home to retire. I still have the seashell. Again I say they are very innovative and can make do without the things we cannot do without. He had no baby bottle and nipple, no spoon and no soother but he had the most important, milk!

She went to Bible School. One time when I was on a long furlough, another missionary arranged her wedding with an evangelist. It was not very good for several years but the Lord turned his life around and he is serving the Lord. They have three lovely children ages 25, 22 and 21. Pray for good spouses for them.

TWINS ARRIVE

Doulat Gudade and his wife lived near Parola. He was a teacher if I am correct, no I think an evangelist. They had two boys and three girls when on April 18, 1952 twins were born. A boy name Santosh and the girl Asha. Asha means hope. Everything went well and then suddenly the mother died when the twins were nine months old. They were brought to Dharangaon four days later on January 27, 1953.

The three older girls were already in Dharangaon school so when their mother died, they just stayed on and were counted as orphans. The boys too were studying in Navapur. Kamal the oldest is married to a lay pastor and lives in Bombay. Vimal is married to a man that works in a war factory. How else to say it? He makes parts for ammunition. They have three girls. Shanta is married to Ashok Vankhede and has four children. Ratnakar and Samuel are married and work in another mission area.

I had lost complete contact with Asha for about twenty five years. When I went back to India for the last reunion in 1997 she came but I did not recognize her. She had grown up and changed so much. How happy I was to see her again at last. She is not married and does housekeeping for well-to-do business people in Bombay. By the way Bombay is now called Mumbai. When I write about Asha I think of another orphan Indhu Wagh who also lives in Bombay. She was married and has a son 25 years old. I don't know Indhu's address and have not heard from her or seen her since Atul was born.

So when I pray for our children, my heart is heavy and longs to hear from those that are silent. May God keep them in His care and may they stay close to Him.

ANOTHER BABY GIRL ARRIVES

About midnight on April 27, 1952 someone called my name. I awakened and recognized the voice of fellow missionary Miss Margot Kvaase from Navapur. She had a coolie with her and he carried a basket on his head with a 14 day old baby girl curled up in it. It looked more like a kitten curled up. I wanted to take the baby out and put her in a cradle, but Margot said to just leave her. She had cried for six hours on the train. We decided she probably had sunstroke. First, the father had carried her seven miles in that basket on his head in the heat of the day. April is very hot and just a thin cloth over her.

Then Margot told me the story. This baby's mother was Gangabai, one of our older orphans who was married to Bhanya Valvi in one of the villages. I had never seen her. Ganga Bai gave birth to this baby on April 13 and died right away. They had three older girls and one boy. Anyway, the baby slept through the night and seemed none the worse for all she had been through. The next morning I gave her a bottle of milk and a bath and she slept again. The father had named her Shevanti. Shevanti is the name of a flower.

Bhanya had kept three year old Leelavati at home. I guess he didn't want to be bereft of wife and two children in one day. How hard that must have been but they were Christians. The father worked in the fields so could not care for Leela like he wanted. On June 20 he brought her to us too. She did not want to stay. For one thing they spoke Mauchi so she could not understand us. She was so cute but kept running away. Dear little child.

Prabha holding baby sister Shevanti, Shanta holding Leela's hand.

Leela married Dayanand Chaudhari and lives in a village near where she was born. She does tailoring and sometimes teaches adult literacy. They have four girls, all of which have been through our Dharangaon School.

Shevanti went back to the village to her father when she was about thirteen. He was not able to keep his eye on her all the time and she fell in love with a Muslim, married him and had two children. He had TB so two babies died of it and Shevanti herself died in September 1978. The husband died also. That was a heartbreak for me.

Shevanti's two older sisters Prabhavati and Shanta were attending our school when Shevanti was brought and later Leela. It was a terrible shock and grief to them that their mother had died and later when Shevanti died so young. Prabha is married to a teacher, Aunsha Gavit who is now retired. They have two girls and a boy. Two were married when I saw them in 1997 and the younger is probably married by now too. Prabha was my hostel matron for quite a few years and I don't think I ever had a more faithful one. She loved all the girls so much and taught Bible Class and the daily things girls should know. Aunsha was very faithful too and he often preached on Sunday. He and the other teacher took turns during the last few years I was out there because we had no pastor.

MANJULA ARRIVES

Manjula Gaikwad was born on February 14, 1952 in a village near Parola to very young parents. The Mother was very sick and could not care for the baby so her husband took Manjula to the Dispensary in Parola at the age of two months. The missionary there cared for her for two months. During that time both the mother and father died, possibly of typhoid fever. So Manjula arrived in Dharangaon on June 13.

Manjula was a happy baby, and is still happy. She has a very winning smile. One of her arms is several inches shorter than the other but that does not hinder her in any way. She is married to Vijay Salve and they have two daughters Ruth and Mamta. They live in Dhule. She sews but also took a course in village nursing. Vijay had one leg amputated so cannot work much as there are no wheelchairs.

My cousin Iona Heppner was in Dharangaon for one year while I was on furlough and she took in two babies. One was Nira, the nurse I told you about. Then wee Nami Vasave was brought to her full of sores. Iona was suspicious that it might be syphilis but the local doctor did not think so. After several months she was diagnosed with that disease. She got it from her mother during delivery (or before). She received treatment but it was too late.

Her eyesight had been damaged, her muscle coordination was gone and she had some mental deficiency. Despite all that she was very cheerful and she too accepted Jesus. I was going on furlough and was concerned so made arrangements for her to live near Poona at Pandita Ramabai Mukti Mission homes. She was happy there but eventually started having severe seizures. She went to be with the Lord on August 13, 1988 at age 33. I visited her often and she always got so excited and told the other girls, "My Mai is coming to see me!"

Other babies were brought to us, as I said before. Prasad, Vijay, Vatsala are some of them. Others did not live long enough after they were brought to give them a name. They are in Heaven and God has given them a name. He knows each one.

Some girls came to us when they were older because their parents died. Kamal Ohol was one of about 14 years old. It was always harder for them to adjust and that was very understandable. I used to try to imagine myself in their place. She was born October 10, probably about 1935. She married Yonathan Naik, a teacher. They live in Shahada and have three boys. Yona is retired by now. If I remember correctly Kamal too had Bible School training as did most of our girls.

This "door of salvation" is painted on the church wall behind the pulpit.

A Hindu Temple beside the road.

CHAPTER 20

Vacations

I will tell you more about the rest of the orphans but for now I'll change the subject. While I was in language school I always went to Mahableshwar for the summer. When I finished, Doris and I went to Landour, Mussoorie for about six weeks so as to get away from the heat of the plains. It was exciting to go somewhere that I did not have to study Marathi. It was a long trip by train and by bus. The last mile or two we had to be carried in a Dandy by four men. It was uphill all the way.

Doris Frazer and I in our Sunday clothes.

Landour was 8,000 feet high and very cold up there. You can imagine how we shivered coming from 100 degree heat. The buildings are not heated up there either. Some guest houses had a fireplace which we enjoyed in the evening. When we came down for supper we brought our hot water bottles and placed them on a certain table. When we finished eating and socializing we picked up filled ones. We put them in our beds to warm them up.

I told you we were carried the last part because we could not stand the altitude and got very dizzy. Most get used to it after a few days. Leave it to me, I did not get used to it and had to enter the hospital. My blood pressure dropped dangerously low and I remained in hospital for about two weeks. The next year we went to Landour again but the same thing happened, only this time I was in hospital for three weeks. So I was advised by the doctor not to go there anymore and I didn't.

Annie, carried by 4 men in a Dandy in Landour.

The next summer I went to Kashmir with cousin Iona and several other Teamers. They went by bus which took about two days as I recall. For a reason I don't remember, I had to fly in. It was scary for the pilot was flying by sight not by instruments. It was so cloudy and foggy between the mountains. We could see him the whole time for there was no wall between him and the cabin. Sometimes, he stood up to peer through the fog. Several times I just closed my eyes and prayed. Maybe that's why we got there safely. I thanked the Lord when we landed safely.

I am bartering with a Kashmiri vendor.

There were no guest houses or hotels for us to stay in. We rented two tents and some men to be our cooks, guides and guards. We needed them because we were out in the forest. We slept two ladies to a tent. Iona and I in one. Viva Davis (Netland) and Marylin Monson in the other. There were a couple more tents with other ladies. Marylin and another lady decided to go horseback riding and would be gone overnight.

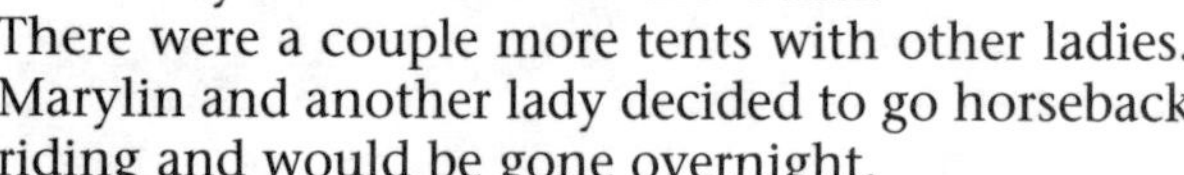

Eating cherries in Kashmir (note my paper hat).

Well, that night Iona and I were both awakened by what we thought was the growling of a bear. We had been warned they might come around. We moved our suitcases against the tent door (all the good that would have done!). We waited till morning but did not sleep. Then at the first appearance of dawn we opened the tent flap to see where the bear was because the growling continued. Then we realized that the noise came from our neighbouring tent. One of the ladies was snoring like I have never before or since heard.

We camped for about two weeks. Then we moved to a place called Srinagar where there was water and we rented House Boats. I don't remember how long they were but each had several bedrooms, a lovely sitting room and dining room. The House Boats were really quite quaint. All the wood had hand carved designs and was brown in colour. Each had a really funny name in English. Let me see if I can recall some names. They were Sunflower, Honey, and Christmas to name a few.

I'll digress a bit to tell you that all big trucks (they call them Lorries) have strange names, too. I've seen Merry Christmas, Halleluia, Earthquake, Sweetheart, and Happy.

When we rented a houseboat it came complete with servants, a cook and a 'cleaner.' They were pretty good cooks for they had been trained by foreigners. Some of it was British style but still good. At least we were able to get vegetables and fruit that we could not get on the plains. That meant a lot.

All around the outside of the Boat was a narrow board walkway. That was the only way to get around since we were on water. So whenever the servants walked around the outside it swayed and rocked the boat. I believe the ser-

I am opening some pork and beans tins for our picnic with cousin Iona beside me.

vants had some kind of quarters on shore where they slept.

All boat owners kept ducks for they were good fair for the foreigners. They really roasted them to perfection and served them with boiled potatoes sprinkled with mint and mint gravy. They got up early to serve us our chhota hazari but they had to do their chores first. One of which was to feed the ducks at 4:00 a.m. The ducks of course lived in the water all around us. The man would stand on the walkway and throw the feed out for them. Can you imagine all the quack quacks we heard every morning? That was one thing we did not appreciate, our sleep was disturbed every time.

Sometimes we noticed that not all parts of the duck were on the platter which meant they had kept a few morsels for themselves. A story was circulated up there that an Englishman noticed too that not all the parts came to the table. Usually it was a leg that was missing. He asked the cook about it since every duck has two legs! His answer was that when they go ashore they only stand on one leg. Pretty clever, eh? True said the Englishman but let me come with you the next time they are on the grass.

The two went over to the grass and the cook said, "Saheb, see they all stand on one leg. They are sleeping." Saheb replied watch them when I say, "Shoo!" Of course, they ran away on both legs. The cook said, "But Saheb, I did not say Shoo to the one I baked for you!"

Other boats would come around to all the houseboats. They were vendors selling vegetables, fruit, bread, flowers, woolen shawls, carved wood items and cloth. That was fun and exciting to look forward to.

Whenever we saw the flower vendor come, we started to giggle. He had a unique way of telling us that he had the best flowers. "Madam, Come see! beautiful, delicious, scrumptious, pretty, lovely, wonderful, flowers." I don't think we ever bought any. It was alright if he came during the day but once in a while he would come very early after the ducks had been fed. No, thank you.

There was a town across the lake but we had no way of getting there except by a boat taxi. These had a little canopy on top and benches for four people to sit. On one of our trips one of the ladies was pointing out something to the rest of us when her arm knocked another lady's glasses off into the deep lake. Well, she was as good as blind without them. The

On a boat taxi with houseboats behind us.

other lady felt terrible. When the driver heard what happened he said he knew a diver that would go in after them.

Well, he could not until the next day and found them quite quickly. They were caught on some weeds. When he saw how happy we all were he felt very rewarded. He only asked for the equivalent of one dollar. We had been praying that he would find them because this lady's vacation would have been ruined otherwise.

MORE VACATION

The next year Iona and I went to South India and en route we visited Amy Carmichael's Orphanage at Dohnavur. That was very special for us for we had heard Mr. Maxwell from Prairie quote her quite often. It was indeed a place of peace. Everybody was barefoot. It was a big establishment with a hospital and school. The missionaries rode from one place to the other on bikes.

They do a lot of singing and praying. They also teach all the children English as well as Tamil. Then they are equipped to work anywhere in India when they leave. That is one thing we did not do in Dharangaon and that I regret.

Next we arrived in the hill station of Kotigiri. It was nice and cool but not nearly as high as Landour. We had reserved a room at a lady's home. She had just the two of us and she needed the income. She was very kind but she let her dog roam around among the food too much. He looked like a Dachshund but his body was way too long and so were his legs. We asked her what breed he was and she told us he was a Dachsie gone wrong!

She was Scottish and loved to pray one of her Scottish blessings before meals. You know that one about, "some hae food and can't eat..." Then she'd ask us if we liked it. We did. I had never heard it before. She did not know the Lord and we tried to talk to her about salvation. But no way, she was a very good person and that was it.

On every hill station were churches and always one that was called the Community Church. So that was the one we missionaries usually attended. We got to know many missionaries and learned of the various ministries that were available. It was wonderful to be able to sing in English and hear messages in English. When I first went out there were around nine thousand missionaries total in India. That number began to dwindle sharply after about 8 years when a lot of visas were refused. I doubt that there are even one hundred there now.

One hot season Iona and I went to a different hill station called Kodaikanal. It was much bigger than Kotagiri but also in the South. There was a large school for missionary children. It was good to get to see them and get in on some of their programs.

It was that year one of our missionaries Rebecca Glanzer died suddenly. She was a nurse and had a ministry to Christian nurses in many parts of India. We Teamers had had a picnic on a Saturday and I remember how she came up to me and gave me a bear hug and said, "God is s-o-o good to me."

That evening she had a headache and the Doctor prescribed aspirin for her as she may have had too much Sun. It got worse and at midnight she called the missionary next door to her. She went in and prayed with her and told her to call if she got worse. She never called.

The next morning she went in with a breakfast tray and found she was gone. That was a terrible shock. We were called and I went in to see her. She had a lovely smile on her face. One hand under her head and other resting beside her. The doctors diagnosed it as encephalitis. They felt terrible that they had not realized she was that sick. There may not have been anything they could have done for her anyway. She went so very fast. It was God's time to call her Home and He was with her as Psalm 23 tells us.

I don't think I went far away to hill stations for my vacation anymore after those four or five times. For one thing, it was hard to get someone to stay with the orphans while I went away. Then too, I felt I could give them all my time for about six weeks. I could not spend the time with them that I needed to during school.

Iona went to Landour for that was where the Hindi Language School was. She studied and she took a few brush-up classes while she was on vacation. She did not mind the altitude.

After Iona returned, and our school and hostel were in full swing again I would go to her place for a few weeks vacation. It was not as hot there as in our area for they were farther north and a little higher. I always enjoyed that and I tried to pick up some Hindi on the side for that was what everyone spoke.

I'll never forget one of those trips. The trains were so crowded I had to stand for hours. I had my suitcase behind me but it was too high to sit on. After I could not stand anymore I managed to hoist myself up on it. Once I sat down the people moved in closer and there was no way I could get up again. I could not get to the bathroom nor to the food and water in my bag. Sitting so many hours with the pressure on my legs made them numb and I did not feel any pain.

When I arrived in the city I thought I'd never be able to walk because then the pain was so bad. I asked the Lord to help me and He did. When I arrived at Iona's place I felt very sick and had to go to bed. The next day she got a doctor who said I had thrombo-phlebitis. I was to stay in bed for a month or more otherwise the clots could break loose and go to my heart or brain.

Well, I did that and dear Iona took care of my every need. I was not even to lift my head to brush my teeth or eat. It was so hot that Iona spread the sheet loosely over me with the corners touching the floor.

I was reading and engrossed in the story when suddenly I felt something run over my legs. I looked and it was a mouse coming toward my head. I never had time to think and jumped up so fast and screamed. Iona came running and got me to sit down on the bed because the mouse was gone. Suddenly I started to cough and could not stop. Just when I felt as if I was fainting or dying, Iona called out, "Dear God, don't let her die. Please stop the cough."

My coughing stopped that instant. God answered her prayer. I lay down to rest while she tried to figure out what to do. We were both pretty sure that a clot had moved to my lung causing that cough. The next day she somehow got me to the doctor (since I had been up once anyway!) for an x-ray. The x-ray showed where the clot had been and passed through. Thank you Lord.

Dear Iona has been with me several times when I was in bad shape and she tells me she thinks I have more than the proverbial nine lives. One time she came to Dharangaon to spend part of her vacation with me. I had not been well so we both went to our Chinchpada Hospital to see Dr. Ormie Uptigrove. He prescribed Tetracycline but was not too sure I would tolerate it. He knew I had reactions to quite a few medications.

He suggested I take one right away and that his wife Freda (a nurse) accompany us to the station as we waited for the train to return to Dhar. The train was late and Freda saw signs on my face that I was having a reaction. She ran back to the house to tell Ormie and ask what to do. He said NOT to take anymore although it was an antibiotic with a wide range spectrum. Okay!

Iona and I left for home. It was very cold on the train. I guess we had not taken a sweater along and we were shivering when we arrived home about midnight. I made us each a cup of hot cocoa that someone had sent in a parcel. Then I did a very foolish thing. I thought since that medicine was so good, I'd take another pill and try my best to tolerate it. I am wiser now!

I might have been able to get away with it if I had not taken it with something hot. The hot drink dissolved it faster and into my blood stream, I guess. We both fell asleep. I awakened very soon not able to breathe properly. I managed to call Iona and she saw I was in serious trouble. I was tearing at my clothes and my neck trying to remove the tightness so I could breathe.

It had started to rain, actually it poured, but dear cousin got dressed and walked the mile to the Railway Station to try to phone Dr. Ormie on their line. There was no other phone that I knew of. He told her I had a throat stricture and that if it got worse she would have to do a tracheotomy. He gave her instructions on how to do it. She came back, sharpened and disinfected the butcher knife. She looked at me and went to her bedroom. I did not know what Ormie had said. I wondered why she did nothing as I felt I could not last much longer.

She had gone to kneel by her bed and tell the Lord that she could not do it. Then it came to her to try to call a local doctor. She awakened the two teachers who went in search of one that would come with them in the rain. She went back to pray.

Well, they got a kind doctor to accompany them on the back of one of their bikes. When he came, I guess I was almost delirious and asked him, "Who are you?" I did not know Iona had sent for a doctor. He was very gracious despite my ungracious greeting and gave me an injection. It must have been an antihistamine. He knew what to do and in a few hours I got relief. Iona and I were both very thankful. The throat stricture bothered me off and on for several weeks but not seriously though. I may have damaged my throat muscles by tearing at them so frantically that night. Believe me, after that I never again tried to be brave and tolerate medicine!

Iona is such a book lover and passed books on to others. She even ran a bookshop in India for several years. I spent more of my vacations with her and she gave me lots of good books to read each time. Especially when I had to be in bed for weeks, I sometimes read a book a day. I was so blessed and the time went faster.

Then I got convicted that I should read my Bible more even though I had my regular devotions each day. I told Iona and she did not bring any more books. I guess I read the Bible through twice then thought I could go back to reading more books since I never got time to read them at my station. Bless her heart, she teased me and said, "you'd better read more Bible!" Pretty soon she was back in my room with another armful of books. Iona "suffereth long" with this cousin. She is kindness personified. Thank you, Iona.

I want to tell of another vacation with Iona but first I need to give some background. In May of 1975 when I was on furlough I was in a car accident. I lived in the only high rise apartments in Abbotsford at that time. Across the street from me was Henderson Funeral Home on South Fraser Way. One morning I was on my way to speak at a Ladies' meeting at Central Heights Church. Just as I came to the road I saw work was being done and traffic was one way only. So I stopped behind the last vehicle which was a truck.

I looked in the rearview mirror and saw a woman in a big car coming behind me but she was looking at the buildings and not the road. I knew she would hit me and said, "Lord help me relax, so the bump will not be so severe as if I am uptight." Hit me she did, and pushed me partly under the truck. My head was bobbing back and forth because I got two hits, once when she hit and another when I got pushed under the truck. I had double concussion and landed in hospital for almost a day with partial paralysis of one side.

I did not realize I was in and out of consciousness so I wondered why no one helped me. Finally the ambulance came. I had my mail on the front seat which was alright except that the truck driver had come over and written down my name and address while I was out of it. The next day I got a phone call from him saying he felt God had allowed me to be pushed under his truck so that we would meet(?). Would I marry him? He married someone else.

Well, about a month later when I was out driving I'd suddenly forget where I was going. South Fraser Way was not as busy then so I turned off and asked God to give me back my memory. He did. This happened several times so I asked my doctor if it was alright to return to India just yet. He thought it would be okay as it was common to have brief memory losses after double concussion.

I left in September but I still had memory losses in India. Some were very scary. Iona and I were going to meet in South India to go to Dohnavur, Madras and Bangalore. She came from north India while I came from the west. I had made an appointment to see a specialist at a large mission hospital in the south in Vellore because of my memory problems . He had no good news for me. He told me the EEG test showed that the left lobe of my brain was affected and I could have seizures anytime. He gave me some pills and told me to always have a spoon nearby in case I had a seizure so someone could put it between my teeth!!

I started the medicine right away and took the bus (about a day's journey) to a town where the Salvation Army had a very well equipped hospital. Iona had a friend there so that is where we were to meet. Well, my head felt awful as soon as the bus started. I had no idea what was happening and by the time I got there I was almost out of it. I could not walk straight nor hold up my head. I tried to eat supper but could not even sit up anymore. The nurse noticed and called the doctor. It did not take him long to realize it was the medication that was to blame. He told the nurse I would not have lived till morning. He took me off the medicine and I was soon fine. I was ever so thankful.

To make a long story short, vacation was over and it was time for us to go home. Iona was not sure I'd get home by train and bus if I should have a memory lapse. So she advised me to fly from Bangalore to Bombay. I agreed. I had come prepared with bedding for the train and she teased me that my baggage did not exactly look like air luggage, especially the bag made of gunny sack cloth. The Lord guided her in saying that to me.

I arrived at the Bombay Airport and waved down a taxi. I told him that I had memory losses and asked him please take me to the Railway Station as I might not find it. Would he then turn me over to a coolie and tell him my condition and make sure he put me on the right train for Dharangaon. The taxi driver took me seriously and how I thanked God for it. Even in the gravity of the situation I had real peace in my heart.

This meant an all night ride on the train. I lay down and fell asleep. When I awakened I did not know where I was. Wherever I was, it was shaking and lurching! Eventually I realized I was on a train. But where was I going? Women and children slept everywhere. They covered their faces with the end of their sari. I thought I must know one of them, so I lifted a few saris but did not recognize anyone. It never dawned on me to look at my ticket. I sat down and prayed. "Lord, please tell me where I am going." It was amazing that I KNEW each time that I did not know. Does that make sense? I never felt lost. I felt each time that the Lord had me on a leash. He was in control of me and would not let me wander.

When I opened my eyes after praying, my eyes spied that gunny sack bag that Iona had made fun of. The coolie had stuffed it under the bench opposite me. Then it all came back to me and I made the trip safely. I had no more episodes for a few weeks. Again the Lord had helped me remember where I was. Then one day I noticed I could not do the bookkeeping. That concerned me and I quickly wrote a prayer letter and asked people to pray for me. Three people wrote back and said when they prayed the Lord gave them the assurance that I would recover completely. When I read them, I too got that assurance. I never had another episode after that.

However before that, I had notified our field chairman Einer Berthelsen about my problem also the Home Office. He and Mary came over and did my books for me. It was thought best I go home as soon as possible. Well, now I was well and felt I could stay. So I had an EEG done in Bombay which came out clear. But no, it was best I go home with the accompaniment of a nurse in a wheelchair. Margaret Vigeland was scheduled to go on furlough so she accompanied me.

All the tests done in Vancouver, Canada came out clear. There was no sign of any problem ever having been there. The Lord had healed me when those three people prayed and I knew it. How I thanked God for that. I also thanked Him for what I learned through those 14 months in India when He took care of me so graciously and wonderfully. He always had me in His hand and I was so aware of it. After ten months at home I was able to go back to the field with a clear bill of health.

CHAPTER 21

Registry of Orphans and History

I will start from the oldest but I will not have as much or any of their history, simply because I was not there and have never been able to obtain it. You must remember most were brought as babies and therefore they know nothing of their past. The only thing they or we know is what caste they came from and that we judge by their surname.

I will start with the oldest ones, some of which have died and some have died since I've been home.

- Grace Bai Valvi, *widowed, born 1913.*
- Margaret Ramji Valvi
- Premila Kothak *lives in Navapur.*
- Janki Bai Valvi *lives near Bhadbhunja*
- Timothy
- Ichha Bai
- Shevanti Reuben Vasave
- Padma McWan
- Saku Bai Jayvant Bhatt
- Anandi Bai Sane
- Sulochana Pawar *lives in Shahada, married with children.*
- Mrs. Manik Patole *lives near Navsari, Mother of Virmati J.Patil.*
- Lila bai Malge *lives in Navapur and is Stephen Pandit's mother-in-law.*
- Phulvanti Thorde, *a nurse, died May 15, 1991, 8 children. Palak Jagdhane, teacher, born 1923, died December 22, 1984, club feet, married, children.*
- Vasant Vairagard
- Santosh Bhalerao
- Lazarus Govande
- Madhukar Labale, *mechanic, married, 3 children.*
- Tolu Chintaman Padvi, *born November 1, 1932, 5 children, widowed.*
- Jaya Gulab Pawar, *born 1939, Auto mechanic, lives near Pune, Single.*
- Vasti Swarge, *wife of evangelist, 2 children, died January 3, 1978.*
- Daniel Walle, *born January 1, 1924, married, retired, 2 sons.*
- Baburao S. Katkar, *born about 1925, Air India employee, now retired, one son, lives in Bombay.*
- Marya Kika Valvi, *Pastor's wife, retired, widowed, children.*
- Baburao and Marya *are sister and brother. I know a bit of their history. Their parents were Hindus living in a staunch Hindu town and were quite well to do. They heard the gospel and became Christians. The townspeople became very angry and chased them out of town with what they could carry and their two small children. They walked from place to place and ended up in Amalner. There*

they heard that there was a church in town. They met the missionaries and decided to leave their two children in the orphanage till they could find work and acquire a home.

I am not quite sure how long they left them there, maybe about four or five years. By that time they were established and came for their children. The father went into the ministry and they were a Godly couple. Though Baburao and Marya were in the orphanage only a few years, they remain forever grateful. Baburao often visits village churches and preaches. Marya Bai has run a hostel for many years. Vijay, one of her sons, is a doctor in Navapur. Babu's son also works for Air India. When we have orphan reunions, of which we have had four, Babu is always present and is such a good influence on the younger ones. He is around 73 years old.

- Madhumalti Pawar, *born 1926, widowed twice, 6 children, lives near Chopda.*
- Philip Jaypal Patil, *born 1927, is a village Ayurvedic doctor, married to Viramati, 6 children.*
- Nami A. Chopde, *born 1928, husband a pastor, but recently widowed, had 3 children and adopted another.*
- Vijay V. Patil, *born July 29, 1929, teacher, married to a teacher, named Gangabai, 5 children, lives in Peint.*
- Rueben A. Patil, *born November 29, 1928, driver of a Hospital jeep, 3 children.*
- Shakuntala S. Borde, *born March 16, 1927, Nurse, 5 children, widowed.*
- Suniti J. Ardbole, *born August 6, 1930, widowed, 4 children.*
- Jidza R. Valvi, *born January 31, 1937, married, retired, 5 children.*
- Kamal Khare, *born July 20, 1931, teacher, widowed, 2 children. Her youngest daughter and husband died very young and within a few months of each other in 1999.*
- Shalini S. Chavhan, *born January 11, 1932, Nurse, married, 6 children.*
- Radha Gaikwad Robert, *born December 20, 1933, matron, widowed, 1 son.*
- Anandi V. Punekar, *born October 12, 1935, married, 2 children, lives in Pune.*
- Manohar D. Patil, *born August 26, 1936, medical doctor, practices in England, married to Elizabeth, 3 daughters.*
- Hira S. Pawar, *born March 1, 1937, widowed, 5 daughters, lives in Ahmedabad, Gujarat but seems to have disappeared completely. Makes me very sad.*
- Lalita Ahire, *born July 17, 1937, married, nurse.*
- Kalika J. Sane, *born November 12, 1939, 5 children, lives in Dharangaon.*
- Premi S. Moses, *born September 18, 1939, widowed, 3 children, lives in Surat.*
- Krupa S. Kshete, *born April 9, 1940, widowed, remarried, 2 step-children.*
- Suvarta D. Valvi, *born December 29, 1940, married to pastor, 2 children. I will tell a story about Suvarta when I finish this list.*
- Sugandhi Anil Christian, *born December 28, 1941, married, 2 sons, chief Public Health Nurse of a very large area, a Government job.*
- Vasuntika S. Ingle, *born November 25, 1942, married, 4 children, nurse in a mission hospital.*
- Nabha G. Gavit, *born October 13, 1944, married to a pastor, 3 children.*
- Hiraman J. Pagar, *born March 10, 1945, married to Mamta, 3 children, manager for Boys's Hostel in Navapur.*
- Manorama A. Gude, *born September 3, 1946, married to a doctor of a Leprosarium, she also works in same place, 2 children.*
- Mina A. Zadhav, *born March 20, 1956, married to Ashok, 4 children, lives in*

Dharangaon.

- Velza V. Chaudhari, *born June 26, 1952, 3 children, works for the government in the Police Department office, arranged marriage to a policeman (by someone else), it was very sad. Bless her heart she built a house for herself and the three children. That's unusual for a woman to do by herself, but she trusted the Lord to help.*
- Moshe Patil, *born August 17, 1942, married Jasmine, our cook, 5 children, died February 6, 1998.*
- Samuel A. Gudade, *married Sarita, 5 children.*
- Ratnakar A. Gudade, *born January 7, 1946, married Snehalata, 2 children.*
- Stephen Pandit, *married to Lydia, lives in Navapur, bus driver.*

Velza Chaudhari and her children.

I believe I have listed all the children now. There are a few older ones that I was not ever able to contact. There were no telephones and so it was impossible. I needed some contact and then follow up one lead after another. Once the older missionaries had retired or died there was no way to locate any of the older orphans. I should say too, that as far as I know there was no one who kept track of all of them after they were married.

Often people ask me if these children are Christians. Yes, they all profess to have accepted Jesus as Saviour. I have asked each one where they stand before the Lord and each has assured me that they are believers. But that does not mean that I have personally led them to the Lord. Many missionaries, hostel managers, speakers at special meetings and pastors have had a part in that.

I said I would tell you a bit more about Suvarta D. Valvi. She was found as a tiny infant in the brushes on the bank of the Tapti River. That river is between Dharangaon and Jalgaon. Someone went to the bathroom in the brushes and heard the cries of a baby. They looked and it was a baby girl with both arms and legs broken. She had been thrown from a moving train as it passed over the bridge. The Jalgaon police were called and the baby taken to the Civil Hospital there. The doctor set all four limbs and put casts on.

The baby must have been about a year old by the time she was healed. Then a female police officer brought the baby to Dharangaon to Gladys Henriksen. She was told of the circumstances under which they obtained the baby and how the nurses became so fond of her in the hospital. Then the officer produced a piece of paper which Glady was asked to sign. It was actually a receipt for the baby. It read in part: "I have this day....received a female child from the Civil Hospital, Jalgaon, by the hand of......." Then Glady signed. That was not on just ordinary paper. It had to have a Revenue Stamp affixed to the paper first and she signed across the stamp. Glady signed on behalf of our Mission. People who cannot write put their thumb print on the stamp.

As I said before, Glady and I helped each other out when one of us had to be away for a day or more. So when Glady was away I was in the storeroom in the hostel weighing out some grain that was to be sent for grinding. Little Suvarta was helping me. She must have been about eleven years old. There was another girl helping but when she left, Suvarta looked up at me with those brown sad eyes and asked, "Mai, why did my mother throw me out of the train?" I do not know if she ever had asked Glady that question. I gulped, turned around to move something, in order to send a quick prayer for wisdom to our Heavenly Father.

Then I turned back to Suvarta, drew her close and said, "Your mother did not throw you out of the train." I told her that her mother loved her very much and was holding her as they crossed the bridge. I continued that another woman or two must have been with her mother. It could be that her mother was not married and these women thought if they got rid of the baby everything would be forgotten.

I told her the woman did not have the courage to throw her into the river so they waited until there would be land below. They tore her out of her mother's arms and before she knew what was happening the baby was gone. There was nothing she could do. The train was moving very fast. Soon they were miles away. I told her that her mother cried herself to sleep every night. She probably prayed to her Hindu gods that they would watch over her. "Your mother often wonders if you are alive and where you are and what you look like".

That seemed to really comfort her. I could not be sure that that was exactly how it happened but I knew that such things had and were happening. I made sure I put the word "probably" into my explanation several times. The true and living God rescued her I told her and brought her to us so that she might be cared for, loved and learn to know Him. As I said she is now a pastor's wife.

The children often asked me as they grew up about who brought them, how were they dressed and why did they give them away. They felt unwanted and "thrown away". The next question then was, "What did you do first with me?" They wanted to know some history of their babyhood. I guess a sense of family. So I told them that I took you in my arms and held you very gently and kissed you and said, "Now you are mine. God brought you to me."

When whoever had brought you had gone I gave you a bath and put soft clothes on you, and some baby powder. Then I gave you a bottle of warm milk and put you on my bed to sleep. And you slept a long time. By now they would be smiling to think they slept on my bed.

Then after you awakened, I changed your diaper and took you over to the Baby Home to introduce you to your sisters and brothers who were brought here just like you were. The children felt your soft feet and hands and kissed you on your forehead. I recall now that when I took baby Anand over to be introduced I stood under a tree in the shade because it was so hot. Vivek, who was four at the time, pulled at my skirt and said, "Mai, come out from under the tree and show the baby to God." We did that for sure! Now Vivek is with God for he died August 17, 1997.

Suvarta and her husband Dadji Valvi.

Next I told them that I talked to the pastor about dedicating them to God. So that was done in church soon after. I told them how I dressed in a sari that Sunday and carried you forward and handed you to the pastor. He took you and held you up to God and prayed that Mai, (I) would have wisdom in bringing you up and that you would accept Jesus when you were still young and spend your entire life for God. Then the pastor asked me if I would promise to bring you up for the Lord. I promised and then he kissed you and gave you back to me. Then I would go back to my chair with tears in my eyes because of the awesome responsibility I had been given.

Each one of the children just loved to hear me tell that over and over again. Then they would tell the others just as if they remembered it all! As all children, they sometimes did not want to obey. If they insisted on disobeying I would remind them that I had promised before God, the pastor and the church to bring them up as best I knew how. And that included learning to obey me so that they could obey God. Then I would sometimes read Hebrews 13:17 to them. "Obey them that have the rule over you, and submit yourselves, for they watch for your souls, as they that must give account, that they may do it with joy, and not with grief: for that is unprofitable for you."

In an earlier chapter I told you that I asked God to help me to be very careful what I said to 'my' children. I did not want to say anything that I did NOT want them to remember the rest of their lives. I did not want them to have bad memories because words spoken cannot be "unspoken." Of course, I did not succeed. In haste I said words that hurt. Then I had to go right back and confess and ask for forgiveness. Bless their hearts, they were so ready to forgive. Isn't it wonderful to be forgiven? I know I was too strict, especially during my first few years in things that were not that important. Then I realized every child needs to be pampered and spoiled a little. For they were learning from me how to be future parents themselves.

There are some people who were not orphans in our Baby Home or School but when I write to all the orphans, which is twice a year, I include them too. I will tell you about them and give you their names.

Prashant A. and Sadhana Kambli, two children, Prashant was born October 1, 1956, son of our former pastor Ashok and Nalini Bai Kambli. They had another son and two daughters as well. They lost their parents quite a few years ago, and have very few relatives left. Prashant lives in Aurangabad.

Rev. Philip Wagh and wife Jasvanti Bai. If I am correct his parents disowned him when he became a Christian. His wife is an orphan from Pandita Ramabai Mukti Mission. Philip went to be with the Lord in 1997. She is left with four sons and one daughter who are all grown. Jasvanti lives in Satana.

Shravan Vankhede and wife Mankarna have five children. Shravan was our general helper when he was just a boy of 14 or 15. As far as I know neither have family left. They live in Nagpur.

My heart always goes out to folks who have no family. I think there should be no one that has to say, "I have nobody," when some of us know about their situation.

One thing the orphans have to guard against is not to call or think of their children as orphans too. It could become an orphan "caste." So I have always told them that the name orphan stops with them. Their children have them as parents.

The mission encouraged us to get supporters for each orphan child.I believe we succeeded in getting someone for each of them. Sometimes they were individuals, Sunday school classes or churches. In each case they were supported until they turned 18. We could not have done what we did without their faithful support. To those of you that were supporters and read this, I want to say again, a very big thank you to you. I hope that the account I am giving of them is a blessing to you, knowing that you had a very big part in them.

People often ask me how many orphans we have. That is hard to say for sure. I was able to track down names and addresses for eighty plus in about 1976. Since then several of the older ones have died and I have lost track of their surviving children if there are any, or a spouse. Now I write to seventy. I write a general letter twice a year, in Marathi, make copies and then add a note by hand on each one. Of course, in between these general letters there are those I write to when they need extra encouragement. Sometimes severe illness, a death, loss of a job or a wedding call for an extra letter. I always get invitations to the grandchildren's weddings but of course cannot attend. I try to send a card if I know in time.

CHAPTER 22

First Furlough

When my first furlough drew near, Miss Alice Zimmerman was stationed in Dharangaon to take over in the Baby Home. So I eased her into it, like Katie Iobst had for me.

S.S. Chusan

I left Bombay on the S.S. Chusan on March 6, 1953, via England. I arrived in New York on April 6 so that was one whole month enroute. I took a train to Detroit, Michigan and stopped off for a day or so to visit my one and only supporting church, Ross Bible Church. After that, it was so good to come back home to Mission, BC to see my parents and my sisters and brothers. There were now eighteen nieces and nephews that were born while I was away so there was a lot to catch up on.

The last two years in India I had infected tonsils. The Doctor said he would not take them out as I might need a transfusion. I had pennicillin injections instead. When I came home I went to the Doctor and he took my tonsils out on June 5. He ordered more pennicillin and I had a severe reaction. Fortunately it happened in the hospital. When I came to, there were several doctors and nurses around the bed. Dr. Dixon told me later that during the ordeal he had been quite sure there would be one less missionary.

I was discharged just in time to help my sister Rosa get ready for her wedding. She married Edwin Derksen on June 19, 1953 and I was honoured to be her bridesmaid.

I also had a lot of lower back pain for the last few years. So I went to Dr. Dixon about that. He tried various remedies but to no avail. So early in 1954, he decided to put me in a body cast for several weeks. I was in hospital to have it put on but because it rained so much it did not dry. So a fan or heater was placed near me to help it dry. I must have been in for at least a week. The cast began to rub on one of my ribs and cause pain.

The doctor said he would have to cut out a little piece but could not use the electric saw because the wall outlets were not polarized. I tried to find out from my friends what polarize meant but no one knew. Then my sister Tillie and her hubby Bill Crapo came to see me. The first question I asked Bill was what did polarize mean? He knew and told me I would get an electric shock if it wasn't polarized or grounded. Now I could relax. I finally knew what it meant.

My roommate was clever in writing little dittys and verses. So after they left, she had me step on a stool beside her bed. She could not get out of bed and I could not bend. I lifted my gown and she was busy writing on the back of my cast. She wrote :

"Dr. Dixon, I declare
I am so glad that you took care,
To polarize the plug you use.
For with one more shock,
I'd blow a fuse!"

Now we had a secret and we could not wait till my cast was dry enough so the doctor could cut out that piece. We were anxious to see his reaction. The day came and as anticipated, when the cast was exposed it had the desired affect. Lots of laughter erupted in that room. A call went out to others to come and see! That was good fun and did everybody good.

I was told I could do anything while in the cast so I decided to do some deputation work. I could not go very far for I had to be back to have it removed. I did however go to Castlegar to see the Woodrows and have several meetings. The cast had not done what the Doctor had expected. So exercises and a brace were tried but nothing helped. I did more deputation but I had to quit.

Then the mission advised me to go to Mayo Clinic in Rochester, Minnesota. So I went to Chicago while an appointment was made at the Mayo Clinic. I arrived at Mayo on April 29 and checked into a hotel for patients. The next day I registered at the Clinic and a lot of appointments were set up on an out patient basis for the week. I knew no one. Late Sunday afternoon I was out for a walk and feeling lonely. I saw a neon JESUS SAVES sign. I walked over and it was a Baptist Church with a meeting soon to begin.

I decided to stay. Before the pastor spoke he welcomed all the visitors as there were always a lot. You know patients like I who were there for tests and/or surgery. He had each stand and introduce himself. I said, "I am Annie Goertz, I am here from BC, Canada (they thought that was the North Pole!!) I am a missionary and will be having surgery," and sat down.

When the meeting was over, a lady came right for me from the farthest corner. She introduced herself as Elsiemae Buttles. She had been a missionary in China, got TB and had to come home after only a short time. She took nurses' training and now made a living specialing people after surgery who had no one with them. She offered to stay with me at no charge. She even had me move into her room so I would not have to pay at the hotel. All that was very welcome, of course.

My surgery was May 6, 1954. All Dr. E. D. Henderson said was that he would do a spinal fusion because I was born with a malformed lower spine. I did not understand it and other doctors did not know what that meant. I wrote to my doctor there several years later and asked for a written report. It read: "Findings were: Spina bifada occulta." Then he went on to explain how he rectified it as best he could and I quote, "At surgery, it was possible to get bilateral iliac bone grafts placed satisfactorily in the gutter on top of the laminae on both sides, extending from L-4 to the sacrum. These grafts were placed quite laterally on the sacrum because of the wide spina bifida occulta of the fifth sacral segment. In spite of this rather poor mechanical situation, she obtained a satisfactory fusion from L-4 to the sacrum." The surgery is 100% successful as far as I am concerned.

Elsiemae never left my bedside for the first three days and nights. She said she slept in the chair. She was simply wonderful and a real Godsend. We became the best of friends and kept in contact until the Lord took her Home. My roommate in the ward was Ruth Danielsen. She had cancer and they were fashioning a new nose for her. They used bone from her hip and skin from her chest. Not very nice looking.

She wondered how I could be so happy before surgery. I told her that I was a child of God and if I did not wake up after surgery I knew I would go to Heaven. She was in a denomination where they believe that you cannot be sure of that. So I had the joy of seeing her come to full assurance of salvation. Her nose job was successful but after many years the cancer came back and she died.

I was in the hospital for three weeks after surgery. You may wonder how I paid the bill. I did too! But I'll tell you what happened. God is so faithful to supply our needs as He has promised. When I was informed of the day and time I was to be admitted they asked me how I would pay. I said I did not know. They asked me what my salary was. I told them it was about $75.00 a month personal support. Could I put down a $400.00 cash deposit before I was admitted? I told them I would call the mission and ask if they could give me a loan. They did and wired it to the hospital. Praise The Lord! I paid it back.

None of the doctors charged me anything when they heard I was a missionary. Not even Dr. Henderson who did the surgery! I cannot tell you what gratitude I felt. I have asked the Lord to reward them, as only He can.

The pastor from the Baptist church and some members visited me regularly. I was so blessed. Elsiemae was sitting beside me when Dr. Henderson came in to tell me I would be discharged on May 27 and that the only way I could leave Rochester was by plane. If I could not do that, then I was to rent a room and hire a nurse to care for me there for three months. After that I could go by train or bus.

I had never been on a plane and was scared to fly. So I knew my options but where would the money come from for a room and nurse? Unknown to me Elsiemae had told the pastor. They held a collection and the pastor came and presented me with a plane ticket to Chicago!!! The ways of the Lord are always past imagination.

I must tell you I was still scared to fly, but since God had so miraculously provided a ticket, it must mean He would take me safely. He did. I spent three months in bed at the mission headquarters. Doris Frazer, who had been my roommate in India, cared for me even though she worked full-time at the office. On days when she could not, there was always a volunteer. I had my thirty-fifth birthday during that time. The office staff and board of directors all came up with cake and ice cream to celebrate with me. They really made my day! I could not walk stairs so they came up. There are so many kind people in this world. I meet them all the time.

After three months, I was able to fly home to BC. I had had a taste of flying and have loved it ever since. Good thing too because soon no one ever went by ship.

While I was still in Chicago I got word that my brother Otto and his wife Lynn had twin sons on June 25. They named them Robin and Brian. Brian is a doctor in Washington State. Robin is in construction.

On August 13, 1954, Mother had her first stroke. That hit me hard but she recovered well because it was a light one.

On September 15, Otto and Lynn took their not quite three month old twins to Scotland where Otto continued his medical training. A year later I stopped in Scotland to see them on my way to India. The twins were so healthy and happy.

On December 6 (Otto's birthday) Mother had a second light stroke. She again recovered well, for which we were all very thankful.

I was still wearing a heavy brace for my back but eventually I weaned myself off it because I could not wear it in India. Those were doctor's orders. I did some deputation meetings the rest of that year and 1955.

On September 9, 1955 I said good bye to my loved ones and left by train across Canada to the US. Isaac and Alma and their children met me at the train in Calgary to say good bye. The children gave me chocolate buds and one penny each. In Swift Current sister Miriam and her family came to the train to say goodbye also.

Later I crossed into the US to Detroit, Michigan and from there to Ross Church where they had a commissioning service for me. My sister Martha and hubby Art Douglas lived in Tottenham, ON at the time. So they came to Port Huron, Michigan to be present at the commissioning service and to say good bye. Little Ruthie was so sick.

From Port Huron I took the train to New York on the evening of September 19 and arrived early the next day. I took delivery of my luggage which my brother Sam had graciously taken to Vancouver for me before I left and shipped to New York

On September 21, 1955 I took the taxi to pier 90 and boarded the Queen Mary once again. We sailed at noon. It always depended on the tide as you know. My roommate was Mrs. St. Martin. This time I came prepared with seasick pills so did much better. On September 26 we docked at Cherbourg, France. Later that same day we docked at Southampton, England. I entered in my diary that I stayed on board till the next day.

I disembarked on September 27, turned my baggage over to a shipping company and took the taxi to The House Of Rest. I have entered, "oh how cold and lonely it is in my room." The hostess was very kind. I spent one night and a day there and took the train for Dundee, Scotland to see Otto and family as I have already mentioned.

On September 30 I boarded the S.S. Chusan for India. Miss Jean MacDonald was my roommate this time. We went past Port Said but docked at Port Suez and Aden. Then it was time to fill out Customs and Immigration papers.

CHAPTER 23

1955 Back to India

On October 15, 1955 we docked in Bombay. My cousin Iona and Katie Iobst met me. And bless my heart, I did not make another single entry in my diary all the rest of that year. I have no explanation for that. Almost as if I ceased to exist!

But I do know what took place for the most part because I had made notations elsewhere. I went straight up country to Dharangaon and stayed there one and a half months. It was very good to see all the babies, older children and the workers. I had been gone two and a half years so the babies were not babies anymore. But three new ones had been taken in.

Then I was stationed in Chalisgaon but there was no room for me until one of the missionaries went on furlough. So I went to Pachora to live with Miss Ethel Johnson for three months. There I went into town almost every day with a Bible woman. Often we went to the poorer section of town and gathered the women for a Bible Story. Of course, we sang first and that always drew a crowd. One time we sang a song about being thirsty for the water of Life. Then it repeats over and over I am so thirsty, give me water. The word thirsty sounds a lot like a plant called Tulshi that they deem holy. They often have one hanging outside by the door. While we were singing the woman of the house got up and gave the plant some water. So we had some explaining to do. Christian words and phrases are foreign to them.

Somehow a lot of beggars found their way to the bungalow. So Ethel gave them a few coins. Pretty soon she had a steady stream of them. Then she discovered that the first beggar had made a chalk mark on the tree as a sign to others that here was easy picking.

She used her head too. The next ones that came had to do some work first. Maybe pull weeds, or sweep the ground out front, wash the church floor, or sweep cobwebs off the walls. They had not expected that so soon they stopped coming.

From March 1, 1956 to July 1959 I was stationed in Chalisgaon. Louise Loewen and June McComb were both still there when I arrived. They left on furlough soon after so Jane McNally and I worked together for three years. The Light of Life Correspondence Course office was situated there. Our Team missionaries Don and Doris Hillis had started it. By the way it is still going. My job was to correct lessons and answer questions that the students had. Usually about the Bible but we got quite a few asking to go to America for college, or else asking for a wife. Some asked for money but most were very sincere in wanting to know what the Bible teaches. Many became Christians. It was in 1957 that Jane McNally launched a new magazine in the English language. It was called Light Of Life Magazine. I was there and worked alongside her in the same office. The title she gave me was Circulation Manager. That entailed getting a list of all subscribers, making address labels, putting stamps on, as well as mailing the magazine. The first edition of the magazine was actually mailed out on November 12, 1957.

Jane McNally, Louise Loewen and I.

A couple of times she asked me to attend conventions to try to sell subscriptions which I enjoyed. One was the Evangelical Fellowship of India convention in Vizagapatnam. When I returned she asked me if I was able to get any new subscribers. I said, "Yes, but just a few." She asked how many and I told her only forty-five. She was delighted and thought that was a lot. Whereas I had hoped I'd get one hundred! That magazine is still being printed and being used by the Lord. It's been in the hands of the Indians for quite a few years already.

Robert and Jean Couture lived in Chalisgaon for a few years too. They had a jeep and went to the villages with pastors and evangelists. Bob lives in Chicago and Jean has gone to be with the Lord. They have three children. On July 8, the entry in my diary says that there had been a theft at a house behind us. What a noise they made at 4:15 a.m.! The other entry was that a pregnant woman jumped into the well because her husband had beaten her so much. That was not the first time something like that happened. Some saw no other way out.

On August 18 I wrote that we were expecting company and I set up an army cot in Jane's room for the guest. I did this during my afternoon tea-break from the office. We had a severe thunder and lightening storm. I was wearing rubber thongs. I bent over to tuck in the sheets when lightening struck. A streak of lightening ran right across the floor where I was standing. As I leaned over, my toes touched the damp stone floor and the lightening ran up through my body and out of my hands. It threw my hands up in the air. It hurt! I was in shock for a few seconds and not able to move. I thanked God for saving my life.

On April 23, 1958 I entered that the temperature was 111 degrees. The next day the same. On April 25 it was 112 degrees. I wrote, "It's burning hot. Used a wet sheet over me at night and hung a wet sheet in the window." By April 28 it was only 102 degrees. It was such a relief. Then a heavy thunder storm came and in a few days it was only 96 degrees.

On May 5, I entered in my diary that a parcel came from Canada from my sister Tillie and hubby Bill Crapo. It contained an orlon sweater, a dress, belt, footlets and green sockettes. When a parcel came it smelled so good when opening it. So fresh and clean these parcels meant a lot.

During my first ten years or so, people were able to send parcels and we actually got them in good shape. But in later years, we had to tell family and friends not to send any because they did not reach us. That was almost heart breaking when they had sent something we needed very much and it did not reach us.

On another day in May, I noted that I took all the children on a picnic to a garden in town at 7:00 a.m. I do not remember that at all. The time of day is what strikes me now! It must have been because it was so hot during the day, 107 degrees. I wonder what I fed them. They liked a "peeknik".

That same day Sonubai came to see me. She lived in a village about four or five miles away. She knew I had some medicines. I gave her some aspirin for her problem just to take her through the night. The next day I was going to take her to a doctor. She had an engorged breast, worse than any I have ever seen. Her baby had died and evidently did not know what to do to avert her problem. She had a very high fever, as I remember it was 105 degrees.

Come morning I went to call her to go to the doctor. She replied, "No, I am not going to a doctor. You go and ask God what you should do. He will tell you." With slow steps I went back to my room, knelt by my bed and told the Lord what Sonubai had told me to do. That instant I got my answer. Go and look in your home remedy scribbler that mother gave you, that one about an onion plaster.

I went and looked and there it was, lightly steam finely chopped onion, melt some bar laundry soap into it and mix with a spoonful of thick cream. Spread the mixture between two very thin pieces of cloth and apply. I prepared it, applied it and asked her to lie down for a rest so it could work. She fell asleep and slept for many hours. In fact, she slept so long I got worried that she might have died from whatever she had. I went to check and she was just awakening. She told me that the pain left as soon as she lay down. We took the poultice off and the breast was absolutely down to normal. Even her temperature was down to normal. We thanked God together. He had healed her. She could not read or write but she had implicit faith in God.

Then I went to the cloth shop and bought some cloth to have some dresses and panties made for Sonubai's two little girls who were completely naked. Oh, they may have had some rag string tied around their loins and perhaps a string of beads around their necks.

The rest of the day was spent in finishing preparations on messages I was to give that weekend in Manmad. Doris Bailey, whom I knew from Prairie, was heading up a school and hostel there. I have noted that a Mrs. Pingale received assurance of salvation during my first message. I remember well how happy she was. The next day I spoke on "washing feet" and one of the teachers cried out loud and said she must go and ask for forgiveness from someone. What a joy it was.

On June 14, 1958, I took the train "Pathankot" to Bombay to meet my cousin Iona Heppner. I have told you about her already. There was a dock strike so her ship the SS Carthage was not able to dock the next day. They had to stay out in stream and come ashore by small boats.

The next day we did some shopping for her as new missionaries need to get some 'must' things before going up country. I went to a dentist to get some teeth filled. The dentist's son David, thirteen and a half years old had died, so he just put some temporary ones in and I had to go back in ten days. I did not blame him for having me come back though it was a long trip.

Iona came to Chalisgaon with me for a few days so I could get caught up on news from home. She also brought lovely things from home. Then she went to Dharangaon for a few days to meet the missionaries there. After a few more days with me, she went to Chikalda to be housemother at our TEAM children's hostel. We had a school there too for those children.

Two holy men bathing in ghats in Mathura.

In July, Evelyn Bates (now Garrison) and I left for our vacation in Naini Tal. We went via Mathura and Khatgodam. We stayed at the YWCA. We had no doctor at our own hospital at that time so I had to go to another Mission Hospital in Bareilly to have my physical exam. One of our missionaries, Sara Mae Harro, a nurse was helping out there at the time.

Turtles in bathing ghats.

We had a short vacation and on the way back we stopped in Mathura to see some of the sights. One was a temple near the Jammu River. We watched as many people, including "holy men" came to bathe in the river in order to have their sins washed away. The river was considered holy. Some people drank the water. We saw huge turtles and I mean huge! I would say they were about three or four feet across their backs. We heard that some got bitten by them if they came too close. It gave us the shivers.

After I got back to my station, I had word that on August 29, my brother Isaac who lived in Three Hills (with his family) had been badly scalded. He was working in the boiler room when suddenly one boiler exploded. His life was in danger. About six weeks later I had a letter saying that the tide had turned and Isaac was making a remarkable recovery. It was hard to be so far away when things like that happened. The church in India prayed much for him and that was a great comfort.

CON ARTISTS

I could tell you many stories about con artists that came quite often. Some sounded so real, we got taken quite a few times. It is difficult to turn people away just in case they really are in need.

I'll tell you of one Mr. John from Ceylon supposedly. He had his sick wife and child with him. He had an engineering degree from Sholapur and was on his way to Assam to take charge of a big project there. He had all his documents to prove it. He did not have quite enough money to take his wife and child. So he wanted to leave them with us for a few weeks till he could come and collect them. She had fallen on a banana peel on the Railway bridge at the station and broken her two front teeth.

He never asked for money and that's how he got me. Then Louise Loewen, (she was back from furlough), came for coffee break from the office.It sounded fishy to her. She listened to his story and believed it too. Then Jane came and she too was skeptical until she talked to him. So we decided to give him money so he could take his family. Also we were going to give them a blanket and food.

All of this took time. Then Clayton Kent came over from Pachora. He said, "what have you here?" We told him the story and he said we women were too easily dooped. Then he listened to his story. Soon he felt in his pocket to see if he had some money to add to ours.

Then it happened. Clayton suddenly thought of a way to test his documents and honesty. On some excuse, he got him to sign his name. CAUGHT! It was HIS signature that was on the documents telling him to come to Assam.

So, of course we did not give him the money. He got upset and said he would get the police because we had not kept our word. We told him that was a good idea. So he took his family and left suddenly.

I kept that document with his signature under the glass on my desk. I figured sooner or later he would be back with the same story. And so it was. He came to Dharangaon several years later when I was stationed there again. He had the same family, same story. I quickly called the police and they put him in jail. They left the woman for us to care for. That was not a good idea and I took her to the police station too.

They had no cell for women so they put the whole family on the train without tickets. They knew they would be caught by the ticket collector and most likely be locked up overnight. That's not the end of the story. I was on my way to Bombay a couple of years later and this man carried his wife into the ladies' compartment and asked me to see to her. I recognized them both. I went over and asked her to show me her teeth. Sure enough those two teeth were still missing. I then told her that I recognized them from the two times they had been to see us. She said nothing but when the train stopped at the next station she jumped up, took her bed pan and got off the train as fast as possible. She probably got her hubby to carry her into another compartment. I never saw them again after that.

Another man came to see us and gave his name as Dr. Joshi. It was late and so we gave him a blanket to sleep out on the verandah. I was dubious about his story to begin with. During the night he got up and left, taking Jane's army blanket with him. I went to the station early in the morning and retrieved it. The train had not left yet.

Early in 1959 I went to Dharangaon to celebrate Gladys' birthday. There was no train to come back to Chalisgaon so I came by bus via Amalner and Dhulia. I had to take a horse tonga in Dhulia to go from bus depot to train station. We always agreed on the fare before we got in. I had done that and all was fine until I paid him. Then he demanded more. So I gave him a bit more but he wanted more and more. I got very scared and later realized he had had too much to drink.

He grabbed my little suitcase that I had borrowed from Louise and tore it a little because he thought I had money it in. I finally grabbed the bag and ran inside the station master's office begging for protection. The man followed me. The Station Master called the police and took him out. By then I was scared to go the rest of the way by train as it was night time. So they gave me police escort. I was very happy about that until the passengers asked the police what I had done. They did not know I understood Marathi. They thought the police were taking me to jail, I guess. The police explained the situation to them and I felt better.

That incident had scared me so much that I lost my voice completely. When I walked into the bungalow I could not speak to the girls. I had to write down on paper what had happened. My voice came back by morning. I had some nightmares during the night. After it was all over, I wondered who might have been praying for me just then.

The women in the church had women's meetings too. I guess the missionaries brought that in. It was a real help to them. In March I started to teach them the Lord's prayer. Usually it was repeated at the end of every meeting in every church. So I decided to teach one sentence in each meeting. It proved to be a real blessing especially to me. I told them that the Lord's prayer is not like a lock to close every meeting.

One of the ladies that was helping in the office had a fever. I checked it a few times each day. After about the third day I figured the pattern of fever (rise and fall) indicated it was typhoid fever. So I gave her an antibiotic. It had the desired affect but I wrote to our mission doctor and he said to bring her for a blood test. Then he ordered complete rest for her for a few weeks. I don't remember if he agreed with my diagnosis or not!!??

About that time Viva Davis one of our mishes was going on furlough so I started out for Bombay to see her off. I went to the station in the evening. Every train that came through was full with no way to get people to open the door from the inside. The doors are always locked by passengers at night. I sat at the station all night until 6:15 a.m. when the Calcutta Mail via Allahabad came. Then I got a place to sit and reached Bombay safely and saw Viva off.

For my next vacation I went to Landour with Glady and Margot Kvaase. There was an Evangelical Literature convention at that time. I went one day but got severe tummy troubles (which are better not described) and so had to miss the next day. I wanted to go so badly so went to the doctor for medicine. He gave me a dose of Opium. It worked right away. I was so glad I started out for the meeting place but the last part was very steep so I ran.

I arrived and sat in the meeting. It was not very long before I got dizzy and began to shake. I could not hold my head up. I got up and went out into the foyer. By then I could not stand anymore and there was no chair, so I lay down on the cold stone floor. One of the missionaries had seen me stagger out so followed after a few minutes. She said I had turned green(?) in my face. She was concerned and called someone to send word for the coolies to bring up a Dandy. They carried me to the hospital. There I was met by the Doctor that had given me the opium.

He could not help but smile when he saw how I looked but he also felt bad because I had reacted to it. Running down the hill had caused it to enter my blood stream too fast. So he and someone else lifted me onto a stretcher and let me sleep it off. I was there the rest of the day. So don't mention Opium to me.

When I got back from vacation Zoe Anne Alford came to visit me. She is a dear friend of mine and we still correspond. She was a professor at Yeotmal Seminary and I often wrote to her to ask for advice. She is a dear prayer warrior too. She lives in an assisted living complex in Texas.

Margie Rodin came to visit about that time too. She was a nurse at our hospital. She had the gift of hospitality and was always so gracious. She made you feel as if you were the only guest she had had in a long time.

Just before the rains set in it was time for Cholera shots and Tetanus/Typhoid shots. In the hills I had received smallpox vaccination and a polio shot.

In the middle of the monsoons I awakened one morning and saw a big red spot in front of my eye the size of a quarter. I went to the eye Doctor in town. He said it looked like a detached retina and told me to go to our mission hospital. He gave me some drops in the meantime. I took the train at midnight and arrived at the hospital the next morning. Dr. Al Holt was the doctor and his wife Carol a nurse.

Dr. Holt examined my eye and said it was all clear now but that I could have gone blind. I was glad that all was well. When I arrived back home the folks wanted to know what the doctor had said. I told them. They said that after I left they, the Christians, had gone to church to pray. They prayed until the time they knew the train had arrived in Chinchpada. Bless their hearts. I believe the Lord answered their prayers and healed me before I got there.

A story just came to mind about a time the Bible woman and I went into town to meet and teach women about the Lord as we often did. That day we went to a well-to-do widow's home to visit with her and another woman that was staying there.

The widow was very interested and it seemed she was seriously considering becoming a Christian. But in the end she said, "When I die, my children will break up the floor in this room and bury me with a sack of salt right here. Then I'll always stay with my children in their home. When our feast days come, they will spread shortening on the very spot I am resting, bring flowers and break cocoanuts. But this woman (pointing with her finger towards her) says she will become a crow when she dies." With that she flapped her arms and made a noise like a crow and laughed. How our hearts ached for both of the women.

Then I said, "God says, dust you are and to dust you shall return. But not for ever, your bodies will be raised when Jesus returns. The saved will go to Heaven and the others to Hell." Her facial expression changed, the Lord was convicting her. But she hardened her heart and said, "Now I've listened to you both sing and I've listened to your story, now I want to eat. I am hungry." So we got up and left. Our hearts were heavy and we prayed for her. Then I was transferred and I never heard if she was visited again or not.

CHAPTER 24

Move to Parola

On July 27, 1959 a wire came from our field chairman, Roy Martens. He asked if I would move to Parola to work in the dispensary with Zaida England. I had trained a young Indian man to do the work I had been doing in Chalisgaon so that freed me up.

Two days later I moved with bag and baggage to Parola. Elcho and Millie Redding had been working with Zaida but they were leaving. The young people had a lovely welcome party for me and I was given a beautiful fresh flower garland. I appreciated it very much. I did some Bible Womens' work now and then until I got worked into the dispensary routine. I made a note that on a certain day I gave ten injections.

Zaida eased me in gradually and soon I was giving up to one hundred injections some days. My lesson on how to give an injection was to practice on a sweet lime. I could not believe that I would actually give injections. I, who was so scared of injections! I remember at Prairie I almost fainted just at the thought of getting a dic test for TB.

A lot of injections were vitamins for skin disorders like eczemas and rashes. I was loathe to give an injection when I could not find a spot where there were no sores. However, the next morning the patient would come back and show us how much his skin had cleared up. I could not believe my eyes. After that it was a joy to do it for I knew they would get relief.

At first, I was so careful to be sure to use a sharp needle and to give it quickly so it would not hurt. Of course, some had to be given slower. If it did not hurt, the patient would ask if I was sure it would help since he had not felt it. I assured them that it would help just as much and that I purposely tried not to hurt them.

When we gave medicine and it was not bitter, they doubted it would work. For instance cough syrup is usually sweet. Many pills have a sugar coating too, though they are plenty bitter inside. Malaria medicine was very bitter so we put it into gelatine capsules. If they could not taste it or was not unpleasant to swallow they were doubtful about its potency.

The medicines were made up into doses for each day and wrapped in small pieces of newspaper. Most could not read, so this helped ensure that the medication would be taken properly. Even so, some thought if I have to take it all anyway, why not take all of one day's doses at one time. Easier to remember, no? As happens in our country too, if you feel better after a few days, why take it all? Better save some for another time, or else share with a loved one!

All of you know that I am not a nurse, but I have always been very interested in nursing and medicine. I sometimes kid about having had the training and experience but no degree! Whenever I was stuck and did not know what to administer, I went on my knees and He guided me. At least I never killed anyone. One day in Parola it came pretty close to that though. Zaida asked me to give this one more injection and then go for my afternoon tea break. Then she would take her turn after I came back.

By the way, because of the heat we regularly scheduled our morning coffee break and afternoon tea times. We needed to stop and get some fluids into us. So I returned from my tea and Zaida met me at the door to say it was a good thing I had gone first. The man I gave a penicillin shot to had keeled over as soon as I left. She had been in the other room but heard the thud and went running. She recognized him as the last patient and at once administered another injection which brought him around. I would not have known what to do and he might have died. Praise The Lord he lived!

I always prayerfully did my best in treating patients. But I know that sometimes my best would not have been what my two doctor brothers Otto and Edwin would have done. And the dear Lord probably overruled my mistakes more than once. I am thankful for that. Shortly after I came to Parola, Zaida decided to have TB inpatients. There was so much TB in that area. That way we could administer the medicine ourselves as well as the injections. So often they stopped the medicine as soon as the cough stopped. That made them immune to the medicine quite quickly. There was a much higher rate for patients to be cured if they stayed.

We got some rooms ready (I believe six) for them and put a metal folding bed in each room with a mattress. In a small back room was a place where they could bathe. Three stones served as a stove to do the cooking. Some family member always stayed with each patient. They did their cooking, bathed them and did their washing. That holds true in all hospitals or dispensaries. It is probably done because of the caste system.

I enjoyed the medical work very much. Often it took just some simple medicine to make a very big difference in their recovery. I felt so very rewarded. The patients were so grateful too. One of our evangelists would take time every day to give them the gospel. Tracts were used too. Those that could not read would find someone to read it to them. It was so good to see most of the patients (if they were well enough) and their family all sitting in a huddle listening to someone reading the tract or Bible to them.

After supper I often went to the TB Line, as we called it, and talked with each patient about the Lord Jesus. During the day I was too busy in the dispensary. The patients that required the longest stay were sometimes the ones to become Christians. That was always a great joy. They knew nothing of Christianity before they came but their hearts were touched because of the love they experienced. After the patients were discharged, they got regular visits by an evangelist and/or Bible Woman.

One patient who became a believer was Popat. Popat means a parrot. To help us in the evangelization of the patients we often loaned them a phonograph. It came from Gospel Recordings. It was a small metal box with no motor. You had to turn the handle to make it play. So nothing could go wrong with it. It was a bit tricky to get them to turn the handle at the right speed.

Popat loved that phonograph. He begged to take it home when he was discharged. We thought that was a good idea for he could return it in a month when he was to return for a check-up. He came for the check-up but no phonograph. We reminded him of it. Yes, yes, he would bring it back for we told him we wanted to loan it to other villagers. Another month went by and Popat showed up but again without it. But he would return it, he said.

That was the time I talked to him about bringing it back. He said you want to take it to other villages, don't you? I want you to know that I have played it for everyone in my village. And after work, I take it to a nearby village that he named. Then I take it to another one and so on. So what is the difference if I take it to the villages or if your preacher takes it? So let me keep it, please, he asked. We had another phonograph so I let him keep it. I can't remember if it was ever brought back or not. I did not worry for I knew either way the gospel was being given to those that had never heard. God, bless dear Popat if he is still living, keep him strong in his faith and witness.

We were very thankful for the films called, "King of Kings" and the "Jesus" film. Someone brought the King of Kings film over to Parola and we had a lot of people from town come out to view it, as well as all the TB patients. At any given time we had quite a few families camped somewhere on our compound. Some had to stay over for another injection or treatment of some kind for a second day or more. These people attended too. We did not have any outward evidence of the Lord's working in their hearts that night. We know the Holy Spirit is faithful and we trust they have not forgotten the message of God's love.

While I'm on the subject of films, later on I had a group come to show the Jesus film in Dharangaon. We had advertised a lot and we had our own school girls too. All was in place and there was a lot of excitement. The children called it "cinema".

We had set the time for 8:00 p.m. but you know what happened? At 7:50 p.m. the power went off. I sent someone to the Power House to ask if it would come on soon. They could not give us any promise. The group sat and waited and waited. Finally at 10:00 p.m. the lights came on. A shout of joy went up. I must say though that the Indian people do not get as agitated about some delay like that like we do in our country. They have time and are very gracious.

Everybody sat very quietly through the two-part films. I dare say that most of the people had never heard the gospel story like that. The town was a very staunch Hindu town. If we had a preacher give the same message they would not have come.

I was sitting on a chair to one side. Beside me sat one of our orphans Miriam, on a rug with their three little children. When the scene came on where they nailed Jesus to the cross her 5 year old daughter jumped up, came and curled up on my lap. When I held her close she said, "Grandma, right now I would scream if I did not know the rest of the story. But I know that Jesus rose from the dead and He is alive. And He lives in my heart." What a wonderful testimony from my little granddaughter Sujata. She is 26 years old now.

While I was in Parola, Gladys Henriksen sent word to us that Cholera had broken out in Dharangaon. She asked us to come as soon as possible to give injections to all the girls, staff and compound people. So we went by taxi because we had a lot of stuff to take with us. I believe we gave injections to about one hundred seventy-five people that day. It was a back breaking job but we were so glad we got it done before anyone got cholera.

Two village women grinding grain.

We had a real heartache concerning one of our orphans girls while I was still in Parola. She and her husband had three lovely children. Another woman seduced him and he allowed it. So he left his family and moved in with her. Of course, the church could not stand idly by and they talked with him time after time. But he felt the Lord had given him love for this other woman and saw nothing wrong with it. The orphan and her children were sent back to Dharangaon where they were cared for and protected.

After a few years the other woman kicked him out and then he had no place to go. So he wanted to come back to his family. She did not want him back. There was a lot of prayer going up for the situation. He was taken where he could work at a secular job and receive some counselling from a missionary.

Eventually, the missionary was convinced that this man had truly repented and would not commit a second offence. The missionary then suggested to him that he get a gift for his wife, a sari. A meeting was arranged for husband and wife. The missionary was there as go between. The result was that they went back together. They had another child. The man has since died. His wife, the orphan is still living and this year will have her 70th birthday.

CHAPTER 25

Move Back to Dharangaon

When I finished my first furlough, my doctor stipulated that I not go back to Dharangaon for a few years. He wanted my back to heal completely before I did that much lifting of children. That is why I was stationed in Pachora, Chalisgaon and Parola.

But now a need arose in Dharangaon and I was asked to go. Ethel Johnson who had been our field treasurer went on furlough, so Gladys Henriksen was stationed in Pachora to take her place. I moved from Parola to Dharangaon on November 10, 1959. I was very glad that Glady stayed for Christmas and she moved on December 31. The move was very hard on her, the girls and everybody because she had been there a long time. In fact, ever since she arrived in India.

I have noted in my diary that the church gave Augusta Swanson and me the right hand of fellowship early in January. I guess that meant we were now members of the local church. Soon after that I had entered in my diary Augusta took the Sunday morning service and also several prayer meetings in the absence of the pastor. Further, on January 13, 1960, I wrote that, "today is Augusta's 69th birthday and I completely forgot about it and did not celebrate." The Baby Home had been closed a year or so earlier which meant we did not take any new babies anymore. The ones that were left were being cared for until only one was left. That one then went into the girl's boarding because it did not pay to keep two staff on for one child. The reason we stopped taking babies was that the government so often threatened to send all missionaries out of the country. We did not want any babies handed over to the Hindus for them to bring up as Hindus.

So this time my designation was School Principal of the Christian Girl's School as well as Hostel Manager. We had seven standards (grades) and four female teachers. Three of them taught two standards each. The fourth was the headmistress who taught only one standard because of the extra work.

Four teachers and I.

At that time I was THE school board of one. It was up to me to pay the teachers. I also hired new teachers and when necessary I had to let them go. The latter was the harder job. Several years later a school board was formed and that made it much better.

Once a month all the teachers in town had a teacher's rally. The schools got a holiday that day. They rotated the rally from school to school. I had only been in as Principal for a little over a month when it was our turn to have it. I made note that we served sixty-three cups of tea and supari. Supari is a mixture of roasted seeds, one of which is anise seed. It also had some finely chopped beetle nut in it. I never ate it. If they insisted, I picked out some of the anise seeds. They liked to come to our school because they said it was cleaner than theirs. A few days later was Republic Day. That meant a lot of celebrations in town and in the schools. Usually a program in which our girls took part too because they sang very well.

The Indian people have a unique ability for drama or skits. One of the subjects in our school was just that. Sometimes, the headmistress sent for me to come and observe during that period. She would divide the class in groups of six or seven girls and tell them to come back in five minutes with a skit. They did. I was always amazed at their creativity in such a short time. They were always very good.

That was not the only time I sat in on classes. I used to slip into classes anytime to see how the teachers were doing. Also to see if there were any students that needed encouragement and whether the students were being treated with respect. Sometimes I suggested to the teacher that she smile a bit more and not shout quite so much. Likewise I would encourage the shy girls to take part and speak up. Maybe I was too hard on the teachers but I felt every girl was capable of learning something and certainly most, or better all, should pass with a good grade. If one teacher had a lot of students failing, I would sit in her classes all day every day for a while. Often I could see where the problem lay and be able to remedy it. Encouragement for any of them went a long way. I need to do more of it now too.

One day when I sat in on Miss Marya Padale's (headmistress) class she taught that there was a rabbit in the moon. I said nothing there but later that day I said, "There's no rabbit in the moon. There's a man in the moon." She insisted there was a rabbit. So we went outside and she explained to me where the ears were and the rest of the body. I looked and looked. All of a sudden I saw the rabbit! Now when I look at the moon, I have a hard time finding the man in the moon. All I see is a cheeky rabbit!

Very often I would make a note of the temperature outside. Some mornings in January it was 50 to 56 degrees Fahrenheit in the mornings. That may not seem cold and here in BC it's often lower than that. But when there is no heating in the homes and the people wear such thin clothes they feel the cold. I did. I was in a second hand store just this morning (February 8, 2000) and saw so many lovely sweaters and jackets. My thoughts immediately were, oh that I could buy a bunch and take them to India. Fortunately, there are organizations in the West that send used clothing to foreign countries. I wrote to the Lutheran Relief Service and asked for clothes. How wonderful it was when they sent me a few bales of clothes. I never knew what might be in them. One time I got two bales of heavy winter overcoats.

At first I wondered if I should get someone to rip them apart and make blankets of them. That would have been a tedious tough job. However, the lining could have been used too to make blouses or shirts. Nothing would be wasted. Then one of the men suggested they wear them in the evening and then sleep in them at night. Wonderful! That was the best suggestion. They did that only during the cold season which lasted a month or so. The rest of the year they would put them underneath their sleeping mat.

Another time I asked for clothes from another organization. We were able to make use of all kinds of strange apparel by ripping the seams and having the tailor make them over into proper clothes. By the way, hardly anyone makes their own clothes. The cloth is taken to a tailor. The price depended on how fancy or how simple a pattern you chose and the cost of the cloth.

Well, there were quite a few bikini sets in one of those bales. Now I was stumped and embarrassed to tell anyone that those things were being worn by women in my country. I felt I could not waste them either. Well, ask the Lord I did. Then it came to me to sew two of those little squares of cloth together so it was thicker and then use them as pot holders. In that way, I had several sets of pot holders to give to the women to use when cooking. My motto always was, waste not, want not.

The women had never seen pot holders except those that saw them in our kitchens. They get along with a lot less than we. So when they want to remove a hot pot from the fire they may use a piece of crumpled up paper. More likely they will use their sari or even their petticoat. Since they cook on an open fire on the floor it is very dangerous. Often the clothes catch fire and the woman dies from the burns unless someone is around to rescue her and put the fire out.

We had only two outside toilets for the girls in Dharangaon and that was not enough. Gladys' uncle died in Chicago and had left her some money in his will. She gave it all to build toilets inside the girl's boarding. Actually, it was built on the outside of the high stone wall that enclosed the boarding. Then they made a hole in the wall for a door into that part.

Walter Engblom and Les Buhler came over to get it started. Then they came back at regular intervals to see how it was going. In between their visits I was in charge. First the soak pit had to be dug and lined with cement. It was quite an ordeal and I learned a lot. They installed seven lovely white ceramic toilets in little cubicles. They were set into the floor so the top was flush with the floor then they squat on them.

We really rejoiced when it was finally finished and working nicely. Then something happened. We had forgotten that most village people use leaves or stones instead of toilet paper. Where there's enough water they take a little jug of water along to wash with instead of using leaves and stones. The water "treatment" is actually very sanitary.

We had forgotten to educate the girls when they returned from their villages that they must not use stones. So in a few days the toilets were filled with stones, sticks and leaves. They flushed them but the stones would not go down. There were too many!

I sent word to the sweeper caste to please send a sweeper to remove the stones. Their work was to clean all latrines and toilets in our town every morning. So one came and I told him what needed to be done. He came back in a short time to collect his pay. Then I went to inspect his work and my heart sank. He had not picked out the stones and other rubbish. He had taken a thick iron rod and rammed it in there until he broke all the toilets so that the rubbish fell out down below. He had done that with all seven!

You can imagine how I felt. What unnecessary loss! There was nothing I could do but ask the Lord to provide more money so we could replace them. It took almost a year but we were able to replace them. Believe me, every time after that when the girls went on vacation we locked the doors to the toilet until we could remind the returning ones and teach the new ones how to use them. We always kept a big barrel of water right there for them to use. I also provided the tin cans needed.

We had a deep open round well. The water used to be hauled up by a pail on a rope. It was dangerous for the girls to draw water and too heavy as well. We were able to raise money for an electric pump to be installed. We got two long pieces of train rails and put them across the mouth of the well. The pump was screwed onto them and a tiny wooden platform built so we could walk to the pump. It used to make me dizzy to walk on that because the well was 85 feet deep.

The same two missionaries had arranged for us to build a big water tank beside the well way up in the air. Then we pumped water into the tank and had pipes running underground into the boarding house and my house, as well as a few extra taps outside.

The water had to be pumped up so far, especially when the well was almost dry. That put a strain on the pump and it broke down often. Sometimes several times a week, other times not so often. I just dreaded these words, "Mai, the pump is not working." Then we would have to have the girls help us pull out 85 feet of pipes and there were two sets of them! One took the air down and the other carried up the water. They were so heavy.

I am not sure I can explain it now but what broke was usually at the bottom where the two pipes joined. After the full length was lying on the ground we repaired what was broken or had come undone from the vibration. Then we reversed the whole ordeal. I shed tears over that more than once. I remember praying a few times, asking the Lord to please "heal" those pipes down there. It was so hard to pull them up and let them down again, pipe after pipe and putting the couplings on each one.

Have you heard of God's servants getting weary IN the work but not weary OF the work? When that pump broke down I groaned and became very weary in the work. It might take us all day to fix it, or more if a new part was needed. Sometimes it necessitated a trip to Bombay. We all got so weary. At such times especially I would ask the Lord to please tell folks at home to pray. I am sure they/you prayed. Thank you.

If only the motor was involved and not the pipes it was much easier to fix. My general helper and I both learned a lot about mechanics. In fact, after a while I fixed clocks, watches and electrical appliances. I'm not so sure I knew how to but it had to be done so I'd say, "Lord, help me." And He did.

One day near the end of 1960 I wrote an entry that Royal and Mabel Paddock came for a few days to help with the pump and pipes. Several of the missionary men came to help us fix the pump and pipes. What a relief that was. While he worked on that, Mabel and I took their jeep and went to a village to see Augusta Swanson who was camping with her evangelistic team. We took her mail to her too.

While I am on the subject of camping, Augusta demonstrated how to prepare meat so it would keep in camp without a fridge. She made a lot of little Swedish meat balls and fried them in deep fat. Then she filled a quart jar, or jars, with the meat balls and poured the hot fat over them till they were covered and closed the jar. Then in camp she would take out a few meat balls for her meal and she used the fat for whatever she had to fry. The meat never spoiled for the fat preserved the meat.

Augusta taught me many things but one I want to tell you about now was how to cook food using very little fuel. While she was growing up in Sweden her Mom did the same as mine, not cook too much on Sunday. Do on Saturday what you can. Her Mom would just bring the potatoes to a boil on Sunday morning in a metal pot and then bury the pot in bedding. She did the same with the vegetables and meat. The meat however, took a bit longer. When they returned from church the meal was all ready to eat.

That gave me an idea. Our school girls would get up in the morning early to cook the porridge. The dear young girls were sleepy and sometimes they did not awaken in time so they would put too much fire under it and burn it. Or, they could not get the damp wood to burn and so the porridge was not done.

So I had a square wooden box made and lined the sides and bottom with sacks filled with hay or grass. Then the girls would bring the big brass pot of porridge barely to a boil. It took about five girls to carry it to the hay box. They set it in, put the lid on and piled a few more sacks of hay on top. You should have seen it in the morning. The pot was so hot they could not touch it. They used the pot holders I had made (remember?) and carried it outside to the waiting girls to serve it. It was always done just perfectly- never burned and never half done. Most of all I was glad the girls did not have to get up at 4:00 in the morning.

As I told you before, I do not have a middle name, nor do my sisters. But when I did something as a young mish which I should not have done, maybe something not culturally correct, Augusta would ask me to sit down. Then she addressed me as, "Anna Maria, what you did was not culturally correct or whatever." Whenever she called me by that name I knew I would receive a very gentle and kind rebuke. I was very thankful she did that.

The strange thing is that when I was graduated from Prairie Bible Institute, they wrote my name on my diploma as, Annie Marie. I guess those two names just went together easily for some people.

In August of 1960 we had special meetings in Dharangaon and Miss Jean Ramsey was the speaker. She was a precious lady. At one of the meetings orphan girl Leela Valvi broke down while listening to a testimony. She realized she was not a believer and could not go on. I talked with her later and she was born again. How wonderful those occasions were.

On November 29 of that same year, Leela's sister Shanti, who was two years older came to me and said she just could not keep from telling lies. When I

Margot Kvaase teaching village women.

asked how come, she told me she was not saved. So it was good to be able to pray with her while she asked God to make her His child. She is married to a male nurse and they have three children.

My teeth began to bother me so I went to Bombay to have them filled. I don't know if I was short of money or what but I stayed at the Victoria Train Station the next night. I just snatched what sleep I could on the bench or floor. It did not make any difference both were hard.

I took the train back to Dharangaon and a jeep full of ladies came for afternoon tea on their way somewhere else. Ethel brought her friends from the United States. That was always a happy and welcome occasion to see other white people. Nell Gibson came over the next day and was going to take the train back. However the train had derailed so she stayed another night.

It was quite common not to be able to leave when you had planned. Trains derailed and buses broke down. So we usually brought along a toothbrush at least. One of our missionaries, I will refrain from giving her name, always was very reassuring when we were stranded at her place. "Don't worry I have a guest tooth brush. I always sterilize it after the last one." The dear lady sterilized a sterile brush over and over again, for none of us ever used it!! None of us had the courage to tell her so. It became quite a joke amongst us. She was a very good missionary.

CHAPTER 26

Second Furlough

On March 26, 1961 I sailed on the SS Chusan from Bombay. I had to change ships in England. I arrived in Vancouver, BC five weeks after I left Bombay. Those trips by sea took a long time but I appreciated that time. It served as a time of rest and also as a time of debriefing myself.

Debriefing is a word that is used a lot these days by missions and corporations. It was most recently used by my mission when one of our missionaries who had been kidnapped and held hostage for nearly eight months was released. The mission arranged for a debriefing for him, his wife and two teams of people who worked around the clock to gain his release. They demanded millions for his release but in the end nothing was paid. We thank God for that but they did cut off one of his fingers.

All that, to say that a long sea journey to and from the field is very beneficial to the missionary. I like flying but the change from one country, climate and customs to another is too sudden. I know we will never go back to the old way but it had many benefits. There was time to be alone to think and pray.

Before leaving on furlough there was always so much to do. There was one or more, to turn the work over to and they had to be trained. My stuff had to be packed to a certain extent so someone else could move in, in case I could not get back. In those days many visas were refused. The good byes were very hard on me too, especially when I worked in the Baby Home.

I particularly remember this furlough because two of the orphan girls were very upset that I was leaving. They cried a lot the last few days (I did too, in private) and more so when I actually got on the train. I stood in the doorway as the train pulled away and suddenly those two grabbed a hold of the train and ran along side the train as it moved faster and faster. I called to them to let go or they would get killed but they held on. Fortunately, one of the men saw them and outran the train and pulled both away. He told me when I came back (1 1/2 years later) that he thought they would all go under the train for they would not let go. Their Mai was leaving, I was leaving my children. I almost jumped off the moving train. It was very, very hard.

Arriving home was wonderful, especially to see my parents and family after so many years. You soon find so much has changed. I think the first thing I noticed was that I did not know how to use the phone. I was afraid I would ring a long distance number by mistake, so my sisters or Mother would do the dialing for me.

The electric stoves and washing machines scared me too. How would I remember the different settings? I was afraid I would blow up something if I hit the wrong button. A few of my friends had electric garbage disposals in the sink. Unthinkable that was possible! I was watching one lady put the garbage into the sink. Then she said, "Now you push the switch." I said, "it might break." She said, "no, go ahead." I pushed it, there was a terrible noise and it did break! She assured me it would have broken if she had operated it too.

My first furlough I was so hungry for salad dressing. First chance I had, I bought a small jar. As soon as we got home I opened it, sat down and ate the whole jar in one sitting. My mother kept saying, "Child, you will get sick. Eat some now and eat the rest later." I felt I'd get sick if did not eat it all! Then I was satisfied, and I did not get sick. But I NEVER did that again.

The next thing I wanted was a soft ice cream cone. My parents took me to town to Dairy Queen and ordered three cones. There were three sizes and three different prices. They ordered theirs and went to sit on a bench on the main street in Mission City. I asked for the biggest they had. I had no idea how big it would be. When they gave it to me, I'd swear (?) it was a foot tall! I was embarrassed of course, but also looking forward to having s-o-o much.

I took it and went outside to join my parents. Remember it was soft ice cream. It started to lean to one side. By the time I got to the bench I was laughing so hard. I had to hold on to the top of it with my other hand to keep it from falling on the sidewalk. My parents really enjoyed that and wished they had a camera. Mother asked, "Do you think you have a big enough one?" I did and they never stopped teasing me about it or the salad dressing.

When I arrived on furlough, I thought I had nothing to tell about the last term. I was so tired but after a few weeks I could look back objectively at what had been done. And not just think of all I didn't get done. I was able to line up some stories and messages to give to the churches, Sunday School classes and women's meetings. I was amazed at what God had done.

Here's an example of when I tried to help in Pioneer Girls Class. I was assigned a table, some girls, lace, colored paper, some bits of cloth and, "here's the glue gun you will need." What's a glue gun? I had never heard of nor seen one. I felt like crying but I didn't. I pulled myself together and I helped the girls make some cute Valentine hearts.

On the field I used a lot of object lessons but never anything that cost anything. The main reason being there was nothing available. I used things that they would in turn be able to use in their villages to teach their parents or villagers. I used sticks, if there were none, I'd break twigs or branches off the trees. I used stones, leaves or straw. I could use newspaper but I knew they could not use that in the village. We'd gather little scraps of rags and use the rags and sticks to make some dolls. The children enjoyed them just as much or more than children do Tickle-me-Elmos here at home. I even brought one home. We used the dolls in telling a Bible story. They represented different characters. The children always enjoyed that.

When I needed to draw I did it in the sand or on the dirt under our feet. To sew something together we used thorns. If it had to be tied, we'd pick some tall grass and use that. Grass is stronger than you might think.

People had invented some new words while I was gone. You know, words like cool, gross, goofed, neat and others. I had a hard time trying to use the word goofed at first. But I "mastered" it (do I get a reward for that great achievement?). It is rather a handy word! There were many more words or phrases but I got so used to them that now I can't even remember which ones they were.

Another thing to get used to was new foods or dishes. Goulash for one. Lasagna, zucchini, yogurt, quiche, stroganoff, dip, mocha and pizza to name a few.

I was staying at my sister Hulda's place for a while. I was still a bit hesitant to go to church and meet so many people. So I stayed home that Sunday. Before they left,I asked my sister something about lunch. I don't remember exactly what I asked but she said, "Well, we are having ozzie for lunch." You may be sure I did not try to make it for I had no idea what kind of dish it was.

When Church was over they came home. They brought the speaker home for lunch and he was introduced to me as Mr.———. We put lunch on and started to eat. I kept looking for a new dish to appear. When there was a lull in the conversation I said to my sister, "I thought you said we were having ozzie for lunch." She smiled and hardly knew what to say. She said, "Excuse me, Annie. The speaker's first name is Ozzie." She and I were terribly embarrassed and I guess everyone else was too. But we all had a good laugh and Ozzie took it good naturedly. What else could he do? So I have always remembered that new dish called Ozzie.

Let me tell you one about pizza. When our new pastor's family arrived at our church I told them I would babysit their two children Richard and Rebekah, ages 14 and 12 as I often did for any of my pastors. This happened after I retired though.

Their mother had fixed several dishes and put them in the freezer. By the way, a deep freezer was new to me too. After a few days I said to the children that I liked pizza very much and I thought I would go and pick some up for supper. I asked Richard which one would be nice to get. He did not come up with a favorite right away so I said, "Shall we get it from Pana go pole us?" I saw his mouth twitch as if he wanted to smile but dare not. He did not want to hurt me. I said, "I did not say that right, did I? Go ahead and laugh." He very politely gave me the correct pronunciation and then we all had a good laugh. For those of you that don't have that pizza chain in your area, the spelling is, Panagopoulos. Now you say it!! Did you do any better?

Television was new to me too. One furlough I invited myself to Isaac and Alma's home for Christmas in Alberta before going to BC. En route, I had spent about five days in Norway on my way home to visit two of our retired missionaries, Margot Kvaase and Marie Christensen. It was all in my ticket. Did not cost any extra!

Well, I watched TV at my brother's. It made my eyes and head ache at first. One night we all watched hockey. It was a first ever in my life! I got quite taken up with the goalie, only I did not know that's who he was. I thought it was rather cute the way he squatted or did the splits every time the puck or any one came for him. With all that gear on, he looked different than the other players. I'll exhibit my ignorance and tell you that I thought he was a clown. I was fascinated by him. But I did not say anything until I heard my family start talking about their salaries. It sounded to me as if he got too much for his antics. Finally, I piped up and so sweetly said, "Do you mean they actually pay a guy to play the part of a clown during the game?" My nephews were lying on the floor watching the game. When I asked that question they just roared and rolled with laughter. When they could talk they very graciously explained the game a bit to me. I was thankful!

I am missing the diary for the years 1961-62. So I don't have any more memories of that furlough except that I know I had more surgery and recovered well. I also travelled a lot for deputation meetings and was always glad to gain new prayer supporters. I rejoiced when people were saved when they heard me tell of my conversion. I've discovered that a lot of people look for and depend on feelings when it comes to salvation.

One more thing about my first furlough. I had not seen my youngest brother Joe since he was sixteen years old. He grew up, got married and was living and working in Toronto. I sent him word as to when and where I was arriving. I actually got off the bus not far from their home. Not seeing anyone I started to walk toward their street. All of a sudden this big man came toward me but I dodged. He knew me but I did not recognize him for he was over six feet tall and a big man.

Then half crying he said, "Annie, Annie I am your little brother Jonah. Don't you know me?" I felt bad I had walked past him. He understood, we embraced and cried together. I had a few days with him and his wife and had a lovely visit. He had come back to the Lord and we had lovely fellowship.

Manjula and I in 1978.

CHAPTER 27

1963 Back to India

Each furlough I visited every one of my brothers and sisters, no matter where they lived. I could usually work it in somehow with my speaking itinerary and that was a great joy.

This time I decided it was time to see Sam and his wife Florence in Ghana on my way to India. Our furloughs had not coincided so it had been quite a few years since we last saw each other. I was able to do it on my ticket at no extra cost. Praise The Lord!

In my diary on January 5, 1963 I noted, while at my parents I received my visa for Ghana and it was good for 28 days. However I only intended to stay about 9 days.

On January 9, my sister Tillie took me to Bellingham to buy an air pistol. I discovered it was not a very good idea. It was for one of our missionaries who had trouble with goats and pigs in her garden. I had a permit from the RCMP but the customs people did not look favourably on the permit nor on me. I guess it looked too real. I paid duty on it and vowed never again to try to bring a 'weapon' across the border.

Before I left, the Cedar Valley Mennonite Church had a recommissioning service for me. Rev. P. Froese, Rev. Pankratz, John Pankratz and Mr. Peter Klassen laid hands on me while I knelt and prayed for me. It was a precious service. Tillie and Bill had a farewell for me at their home and gave me a stainless steel coffee perk. The day before I left, Isaac and their twin sons came to see me from Alberta. Isaac was always "Johnny on the spot."

Mother packed a small suitcase of frozen farmer sausages and frozen strawberries for me to take to Sam and Florence in Ghana.

January 26, 1963 I left from Vancouver by C.P. Air via the Polar Route. First came my goodbyes to family and I found it much harder this time. I'm not sure if it was this trip or another one, when my cousin Daisy and Joe Gardner and family came to see me off. I was crying so hard. Their son Dale was only four or five years old. He came to me and said, "Auntie Annie, you don't have to go away. You can come and stay with us." He thought my parents were sending me away or I did not want to go. Bless his heart. It blessed my heart too. I remind him of it now.

I was still crying when we took off. Then I dried my tears and asked the Lord to watch over all my loved ones till I returned. I looked ahead to my term of service and I was very concerned that I be the missionary God wanted me to be. "Lord, it is my sincere desire that you use me in India. If you can't, I'd rather You let the plane go down than that I not be usable."

The plane stopped in Edmonton before heading north but there was a bad snowstorm and very icey so we were not allowed off. One of the pilots came to the cabin and sat down near where I was sitting. I turned to him and asked, "Sir, if it's so icey that we can not get off and cars can't go, how will you be able to take off on that mirror of ice?" His answer turned out to be a powerful sermon which has often helped me in difficult situations. It was "Madam, our take-off is not dependent on where we are parked. We have the power and the thrust within." Thank you, Pilot. Thank you, 'Heavenly Pilot' for that lesson. Jesus, Saviour, Pilot Me, is one of my favorite songs.

It was so cold going over the North Pole that all water froze on the plane. The crew had to put out bottles of lotion and perfumes to wash with. I got so sick (allergic) of that smell, it was so strong on everybody.

When we landed in Amsterdam, I decided to buy two boxes of chocolates at the Airport for Sams. I knew how he would appreciate them. I didn't read what was on the labels, just went by the pictures. They looked so delicious.

I arrived in Accra on January 28 and Sam and Flossie were there to meet me. The frozen foods mother had sent were still frozen. Then the chocolates came out, Sam took one and bit into it thinking it was solid. Out ran some runny stuff and it smelled like what we do not drink. It ran all over his shirt, pants and tablecloth. He was so shocked that Flossie and I began to laugh. We also read the label and it said, "Liqueur centres." I was shocked at what I brought the missionaries!

Well, Sam would have no more of those. So I said, "Let's open the cherry chocolate they will be okay." We did. Sam was our sampler. Very innocently he bit into the cherry. Out ran the same liquid as before, more on his clothes. By then we laughed till we were almost hysterical. John and Vi Bergen lived downstairs and called up to ask if we were crying or laughing. Sam thought he should report me to TEAM!

My time went fast. Howard O. Jones was there holding meetings. We all attended and were asked to help with counselling. I had the joy of being with two African ladies when they asked Jesus to forgive their sins. Sam and Floss were with African Challenge Magazine at the time. When it came time to leave they gave me a bunch to hand out to the passengers on the plane.

February 6 was my departure day. We arrived in plenty of time and I checked in with Ghana Airways. It so happened this was their maiden flight. Is that how you say it? When 5:30 drew near a lady came to say they were almost ready. The just had to put food on the plane. I was surprised that she told me personally instead of announcing it over the PA system. Then, in a short time she came and said, "Let's go, Miss Goertz." I followed her, and Sam and Flossie did too. I looked around for the other passengers and walked slower. The lady said that this was this airlines' first flight and I was the only passenger. I think it was Sam who had told me earlier that it was a Russian airline but called Ghana Airways. I said goodbye one more time and kind of hung on saying that I was scared. Flossie in her inimitable way said, "not to fear, God was with me."

I knew that but it was no comfort to me at this time. Flossie did not know about my prayer on CP Airlines at the beginning of my trip. Mother used to say to us, "if you say 'A' you have to say 'B'", meaning finish what you start. So I had to go. I hugged them both one more time and left to what I thought, might be my death. I was scared to say the least.

Remember I asked the Lord to let the plane go down....? The setting now was perfect! How did I dare to think that the Lord would down a whole plane full of passengers because of me. Yet here was His chance, He had me all alone on the plane, except for the crew.

The plane sat way out on the tarmac so they took me there by bus. I was glad it was that far for I had business to do with the Lord. I said, "Lord, you know since I'm the only passenger, the Russians can open up the hatch and drop me out and no one will know what happened to me. I know what I prayed Lord and I meant it, but please make me usable instead. I don't want to go down."

Don't you wonder what went through the Lord's mind about that time? Want to know what happened? I'd like to keep you in suspense but you know I did not go down, right? Before the bus got to the plane the Lord had answered me so graciously. He said to my heart, "Annie, I know the Russians do not stand for what you do. But I have chartered one of their planes to take you, my ambassador to India, to proclaim the Gospel they do not believe in." That was all I needed. After I got settled on the plane, I told the Lord that I was dedicating myself to Him anew and trusting Him to use me.

Can you imagine how I felt with so much attention from one steward and two stewardesses, all Ghanian? The three pilots were Russian. When they came on board, they came up to me, tipped their caps and had big smiles. They brought me a drink of juice right away and sat down with nothing to do. I handed out my magazines and they all sat and read and read. For a bit I thought I might not get any food. (^_^) Do you recognize that as a smiley face? My friend Joye tells me that is how the Japanese print one. Thanks Joye.

Not to worry, I got lots of food. We stopped in Kano, Khartoum, Asmara and Aden. During the night one of the pilots came out and asked me to join them in their lounge where the extra pilot slept. It was lovely. They had reclining chairs that were very comfortable but I thought I'd be more comfortable in the cabin with the crew, so I did not stay long.

Every stop we made I had to get off and it was night! No other passengers ever got on at the other airports either. But it did not matter to me anymore though. I learned that night the Russian planes always park way out from the Terminal. I had to be bused to the Terminal when they escorted me off the plane. As I left I turned around and said, "You won't go without me, will you?" By the time I did that three times one said to me, "If we had one hundred passengers, it would be possible to leave one behind but since we have only you, we will know if you are on board or not."

I had a scarey experience at one of the airports that night. I went to the washroom and as I proceeded to walk out the seemingly very friendly female attendant turned rooster on me! She ran toward me and tried to grab me. I ran as fast as I could but she followed me, shouting something in a language that sounded like Arabic. She followed me all the way into the waiting room. I kept on running. She was dressed in black from head to toe with only two holes for her eyes. She was a Moslem. She finally retreated. Some of the passengers told me she wanted a tip. Well, I had no money that she could use so I avoided using any washrooms on that trip the rest of the night except when on the plane.

We reached Aden at 6:30 a.m. the next morning and said our fond farewells. The mission had booked me in a hotel from 7:00 a.m. to 11:00 p.m. in Aden. I had a good rest then I boarded an Air India plane around midnight and flew the rest of the 1,910 miles to Bombay. I arrived in Bombay,(now Mumbai) at 5:45 a.m. I was very dizzy when I set foot on terra firma and remained dizzy for several days. My cousin Iona met me and we left for Dharangaon that evening where Gladys and Ethel were awaiting us. The girls were all lined up by the gate and put a garland on me as was their lovely custom.

I settled in quickly. My eye had bothered me since I left home so I went to Chinchpada Hospital as soon as possible. There Dr. Maynard Seaman did a small operation on my lower lid where I had a cyst. That took care of it but it was hard to see because I had to keep it bandaged for a week. I wrote in my diary that when I was on the train a gypsy woman came to me and gave me a good whallop. I don't remember why. In Dharangaon I noticed there were a lot of bedbugs in the hostel so I sprayed all the rooms with DDT. That was before it was outlawed.

It seemed Satan was really busy in Dharangaon. The first church board meeting I attended had a blow-up. The senior pastor had retired and he was to hand over to the younger man at this meeting. But it was so hard for him to let go. I thanked God that the pastor fixed it up later.

Next the teachers came and handed in their resignation one after another. In a way I brought it on by making a new rule but it was needed very much. The teachers (all single women) had been told that they could have a student help them in their home with some housework for an hour a day. Then those girls did not do work in the hostel like the others did. If the girls did some of the hostel work, it cut their fees just like at Prairie, I guess.

This rule had been made long before I ever came on the scene. I noticed though that when I returned, the girls were kept working for hours, even at night. They fell asleep in school as a result. I requested the teachers to please stick with one hour a day or else hire a local woman. Even if they resigned they would still teach till the end of the school year May 2. That was a government rule.

When school closed I left for vacation to Coonoor in South India. Margot Kvaase, Marie Christensen and I travelled together. Once I got rested a bit I wrote a prayer letter asking people at home to please pray for a resolution to the teacher problem. It was always refreshing to be able to attend an English speaking church in the hills and meet many missionaries. We had picnics for it was easier to buy food suitable for a picnic. We had a convention with Major Ian Thomas as speaker. His messages were on the corn of wheat that has to die in order to bring forth fruit.

I stayed home one day in order to pray all day about the teacher situation. The next day I got typhoid and cholera shots too, so was sick for a few days. One day in May many of us missionaries went for a picnic to Nonsuch Tea Estate. The owner gave us an interesting tour of the plant. At one place we saw the men walking all over the piles of tea. I remember I was not very thirsty for tea for a while.

While in the hills, I had a telegram from one of our workers in Dharangaon telling me that my house had been broken into and a lot was taken. I did not go home right away because the damage was done. When I did arrive in Dharangaon on June 2 at 2:30 a.m. I was not anxious to enter the house at that time of the night so the station master put up a camp cot outside the station where I slept till morning.

When I did come to the compound the workers and girls were so serious and close to tears. We all went in. I looked around and said, "my things are gone but you are all here. I am glad that none of you tried to protect my stuff and put your lives on the line." I told them it is just stuff. Other mishes gave me a sheet and towels so I was very able to get along. They did take my new camera and a diamond tipped fountain pen that was given to me as a very special gift. I did not notice that it wrote any better than a regular pen, it had sentimental value though.

I started to look for teachers and wrote letters and sent wires. I was able to persuade one of the teachers to stay and be headmistress. She did stay and was a very good one. That relieved my mind a lot to atleast have one former teacher remain. I had three others I was waiting to hear from but no word came. I got discouraged and decided to do some ironing.

Do you know why I got discouraged? I told you a few times in the earlier chapters that I believed that if God could forgive my sins and let me know they were forgiven, then nothing was too hard for Him. I could trust Him for anything and with everything. That was still true. But I now had my eyes on the teacher situation, the broken pump, thief trouble almost every night, my leg in a cast, a broken big toe, and two more problems besides. All this loomed big in my eyes. My eyes were now off the Lord and on my problems. No wonder I was discouraged!

Now back to my ironing. My cousin Iona was on furlough and had attended our TEAM conference in California. Rev. Wilbur Nelson was the speaker. He talked about problems and entitled one of his messages, "Nevertheless". His text was taken from 4 verses which I'll write down for you, in which that word appears. Hebrews 12:11, 2 Timothy 2:19, Luke 5:5 and Matthew 26:39. Iona knew I had problems so she sent me the tape.

I had not had time to listen to the tape before, (do you blame me?) but now I had time while ironing. Mr. Nelson told of some of his problems. He said we may be serving the Lord with a true heart and all of a sudden the roof caves in. We live in a cruel, heartless world, sometimes a downright savage, jungle world. Nevertheless! In Christian service there is an ebb and flow. We must examine ourselves to ensure the fault is not with us, if it isn't then just keep on. Don't try to escape the trials. SUBMIT to them. But more than that ACCEPT them. Yea, EMBRACE them as something precious allowed by God. Nevertheless Thy will be done, not mine, as Jesus said in the last verse I gave you.

By then I was crying and began to realize that perhaps the Lord was answering my prayer and making me usable. I turned the iron off and knelt by the couch right there in the living room where I was ironing. I named each of my problems before the Lord and told Him that I was submitting, accepting and embracing each one as a precious gift from Him. I asked for forgiveness for having taken my eyes off Him. I knew again that nothing was too hard for Him. The school was His and I knew He knew exactly what He would do.

"Well, what happened?" you ask. School started on June 7 as planned. As far as I knew I had only one teacher but that was not my worry now. Wonder of wonders, the former headmistress felt she could not leave me in a lurch so she returned to help me for two weeks. Isn't that just like the Lord? Praise The Lord! At the beginning of a new school year all schools have only half day school for the first few days. On June 8 one teacher came. Praise The Lord! On June 10 the remaining two teachers came. One was accompanied by her father. Red letter day! God had answered.

But wait, the next day one of them got scared and said she could not handle two classes, so her father took her back home. It did not throw me in a dither for I did not want any teacher that God had not sent. I knew He would send just the right one for us.

On June 15, He did send a very sweet teacher. She was a dear child of God and was such a blessing. She had so much patience with the girls in her classes. They loved her.

A few days later Olga Noreen, one of our missionaries and a nurse came to visit me. Only the Lord could have known how much I would need her the next day. Sushila Eirao, one of the orphan girls climbed up on to the metal drum we had in the girl's toilet area for them to use. She straddled the drum with one foot on each edge and reached up to fix something on the roof or whatever. There were electric wires up on the roof and she touched one by mistake. Some of the plastic covering was gone from the wire and made it live. She got a terrible shock because she was standing on metal with bare feet. The shock threw her into the drum which was full of water. Some girls were nearby and used all their strength to throw the drum over on its side or she would have drowned.

They screamed and everyone within hearing came running. When I heard what had happened I called for Olga. Sushila was lying on the ground with her tongue out,eyes rolled back and convulsing. A terrible sight. Dear Olga knew what to do. We called on the Lord to revive her and He did. Her hands and feet were badly burned and took a long time to heal. When I was in India three years ago she mentioned it again. She said, "I was dead but God resurrected me." She certainly did look almost dead. She is now married to a teacher and teaches adult literacy to women in their village.

A few days after that, the police came to get a statement of the stolen items from me. I appreciated that but nothing was ever recovered. I really did not expect it would be.

By the end of June an Inspector came to inspect our school. She was very friendly. On her previous visit she had asked me to teach the girls a prayer to repeat after they saluted the flag each morning. I taught them a general prayer. All I can recall now is this, "........thank you for the birds that sing. Thank you Lord, for everything." She asked the headmistress to have the girls recite it for her which they did. Then she looked at me and said, "I meant the one from the Bible." I had been afraid to teach the girls the Lord's Prayer because of government rules. Then she told me that her parents had sent her to a Catholic school where she had learned it. She now thought every school should repeat it each morning. That was a real surprise to us.

The next entry of interest was that we had a church business meeting, AND it was very good. It lasted two and a half hours. The Lord worked since the last one I told you about. In all fairness I must tell you the senior pastor came to appreciate and support the younger pastor, Rev. Ashok G. Kambli.

Quite a few years later Pastor Kambli sent word to me one Sunday morning about 7:00 a.m. that he was seriously ill. He asked if I would preach at the 9:00 a.m. service so I went over to see if I could help. It seemed to me like a kidney stone attack. I assured him I would take the service and I'd be back afterwards to see how he was.

The unusual thing was that as soon as the messenger said I was to speak I decided to speak on, "Nevertheless." I led the singing, took the offering, and prayed. When I opened my eyes I saw the pastor and his wife had slipped into the service which surprised me. I took the main points of my message from the tape and applied it to my experience as I related to you a couple pages back.

When the service was over I shook hands with folks like you do after you have, "preached"! When I got to the pastor he told me the pain left just as suddenly as it came. He said the sickness was for the glory of God. He went on to tell me that the message was for him. He had had so many difficulties lately, and never enough money. Tears came to his eyes, (his wife's eyes too) as he confided that he had been ready to hand in his resignation. He had thought he must be out God's will or why else would he have so many problems.

He went on to say, in Marathi, "Tari pern" (which means nevertheless) I will serve the Lord." And he did serve the Lord faithfully until he had a stroke and the Lord took him Home. The Lord allowed me to go through those trials and be comforted, in order that I might comfort others the same way.

I mentioned this pastor had felt there was never enough money. Well, one year he and some evangelists were camping in a village near Dharangaon for a couple of weeks. A very rich man had invited them to set up camp near his house. Our men must have slept outside because the pastor said he was not able to sleep much at all. The rich man was so afraid robbers might come during the night and rob him, or worse still, kill him that he came out every hour to check on his goods. He made a lot of noise to scare robbers away.

Our pastor told me the man had everything he wanted except sleep. He decided it was better to not have anything because one could lie down in peace and sleep. If you have nothing nobody wants it. Our pastor was not greedy, I don't want to give that impression. Their salaries were very low because the people had no more than he.

One day his wife Nalini Bai came and asked me if I would teach her English. I told her I knew she could already read and write it, all she needed was to learn to speak it. So I told her if she was really serious I would speak only English with her from that day forward. She took me up on it and became very fluent. So much so, that about five years later she had worked her way up to a headmistress position for an all English medium school in Malegaon. The enrollment was close to a 1,000 I believe, or even more. She had twenty teachers under her. I was very proud of her. Practice makes perfect as the saying goes. She and her husband were Godly people.

I had ordered typhoid serum to be given before the rains started. We usually gave typhoid and tetanus together. The serum came and on July 6 I gave one hundred twenty injections to everyone on the compound. I made a note that I was "all in" afterwards.

The rains started that night. On July 14 I wrote that I gave forty-two more people their injections. In August the government sent some men to vaccinate all of the girls, workers and staff against smallpox. The next day they came back and vaccinated any and all people off the compound that wanted to come. The leader of the group asked to buy a New Testament. He had one but someone had stolen it. As far as I know India eradicated all smallpox. Job well done.

In the rainy season so many of the girls got scabies, well not just our girls but most children. It is very contagious and also very painful. At one time I had forty girls that came for dressings twice a day. The only way it would start to heal was to wash the scabs off before putting sulphur ointment on. You can imagine how that would hurt. I felt so sorry for them, some cried and I joined them. It took so long to heal because they got reinfected. I don't know what book I was reading at the time but there was a sentence in it that comforted me. It was, "For this I have Jesus". I would repeat that to myself as I spread the ointment and bandaged their hands. If they touched their feet the scabies would spread. The poor dears.

We never knew what a day would bring. One morning I got word that the septic tank for the boarding had overflowed. Can you imagine what that was like? The sweepers could not come till the next day to fix it. I was so thankful for the sweeper caste that did any job. After we got that cleaned up, eighteen of the girls got streptococolus (Sp.?). Not from the septic problem though. The sores were so contagious too. The doctor gave me medicine for it and they all recovered. I spent many an hour bandaging their legs. It was hard without bandaids but we managed. A few days later some of the girls got staph infections. That called for injections so I was busy with that. You can see that I got lots of medical practice.

About the same time, two of the men were cutting grass that grows very tall in the rains. They came across a small cobra and killed it. They always had to be on the lookout for them. In fact we all did. About one month later Shamuel killed a big cobra in the girl's boarding. One night one of the girls was awakened by something falling on her. She sat up and saw it was a three foot snake. It was a bit stunned by the fall from the tile roof above. That gave her time to quickly push it off and scream "sap" (snake). The other girls heard her and grabbed a stick and killed it. The girls were used to that from the villages they lived in. Quite a few times we killed snakes in the boarding room but as far as I know, no one was ever bitten. I am very thankful for that.

One day, while everyone was in school, I went into the kitchen to check on the food. I had to go through one of three rooms to get there. The Lord guided me in which one I chose. Just as I was going to go through the door onto the verandah and into the courtyard which lead to the kitchen I saw a rope hanging in the doorway.

I thought to myself that the girls had put it up there to swing on. I was going to pull on it and see if it was strong enough for that. As I reached for the rope, a snake fell at my feet with a bit of a thud. I screamed, "sap" and the men came running with sticks and killed it. God's timing was perfect for just about a second later I would have grabbed it's tail and it would have swung around and bitten me.

Scouring dishes, pots and pans.

Another time I had hired some men to do some whitewashing in the Baby Home. Only now it was being readied for the hostel superintendent to move in. It was getting sort of dark and the electricity was not on. I took my flashlight to go and inspect their job. I was standing in the small room which was used for bathing, (not a toilet) and I thought I heard, "sss sss". I turned ever so slowly because if there was a snake it would strike if I moved quickly. About twelve inches from my right foot was a huge cobra coiled ready to strike. It's head was near the hem of my dress.

I tell you, you can do what you could not do otherwise, if your life depends on it. I grabbed my skirt (it was a full one) and held it without moving it too much, took one big step away and then ran. I ran out of the door screaming, "motha nag, motha nag". That means big cobra. Joseph came and killed it. He was very good at it because he was quick, strong and unafraid.

When some of my friends heard I was writing my story, they said, "don't just write about all the good things. We want to know the other side too." So in this chapter I have told you some of the problems and trials. As I was going through my 1963 diary and some of the others, I was reminded of some problems that I will not include. I did not write very much about them in my diary. Someone reading them would not know what happened. I feel when problems have been taken care of they are best left under the Blood. If I write them down in detail I feel it's documenting them. Then they are like feathers which after they are scattered in the wind cannot all be found and put back in the bag. Then Satan can have a hay-day.

CHAPTER 28

Thieves

For several years thieves bothered us almost every night. I think I had a pretty good idea who was behind it but that did not help. There was nothing I could do, except maybe make it worse if I said something to that affect. Sometimes it's better not to let on you know. The thieves would bang on the teacher's doors several times some nights. The teachers were all single girls and roomed in twos. I put electric buzzers on the inside of their houses so they could push the button to buzz in my room. Then I could shine a bright flashlight over there but they were scared to do even that.

Sometimes, they took hinges off a door at night. One night they removed the locks. The doors were bolted on the inside though. The teachers never knew when they might break in. It was very scarey for them and all of us.

One night they removed the bricks from the corner of a house. I guess they tried to get in that way. So every day I was busy getting things repaired and putting extra bolts inside everyone's doors. I had given every household, each boarding room and classroom a big bamboo stick to keep behind the door for three reasons. One, to kill rats; two, to kill snakes; and three, to chase a thief. Little chance the third one would be used. The thieves often carried knives or long sticks with a scythe tied to the end.

I kept two big dogs. I kept them chained during the day and let them loose at night. Being chained made them fierce and often the thieves would strike at the dogs as they tried to keep them at bay. They cut them with the scythe on the head or leg or wherever they could. Then I had to become a vet and treat the dog's wounds with antibiotic. I felt sorry for them because they were innocent.

Some nights the thieves would rattle the doors to the boarding. That scared them very much. Finally, I went to the Police Station to report it. They said they would send the police to make several rounds during the night. They came for two or three nights and then no more. I went back to report the matter again. This time they suggested I get a scribbler to hang on a nail just outside my back verandah, with a pencil tied to a string. They would instruct the police to sign their names and time when they made the rounds.

That only lasted a few days too. There was no mistaking whether they came or not. They were scared too, for all they had was a stick and a whistle. They banged that stick against anything hard and made a lot of noise. They blew their shrill whistle and yelled, "A ho, A ho". It almost scared us away too! Some nights when they thought they saw someone, they'd come to my back door and call, "Bai, come with us. We saw someone." A few times I stepped outside but decided that was not very wise.

One night I was sound asleep, which was unusual those nights, when I was awakened by what sounded like Mother's voice calling my name. I sat up to answer her but all was dark and I knew it must have been a dream. Then I thought maybe she was sick and needed me to pray. Just as quickly it came to me that she was praying for me. I must be in danger. I listened and heard loud noises coming from the boarding. I jumped up and grabbed my police whistle which I always kept under my pillow on a string. I threw the string over my head, grabbed my flashlight and ran to the back screened in verandah.

I saw about five men dressed only in shorts and they looked shiny(I learned since that thieves put oil on their upper body so no one can grab them and catch them!). They all had long sticks and were trying to break down the doors of the boarding. At that instant I blew my whistle in several loud bursts. I am surprised I was able to do that because I was shaking so much. I shocked them and they just shot across the verandah and behind the boarding. I kept blowing my whistle till I almost fainted. I finally went back to bed when I heard no more.

In the morning, my cook Moses, was all excited and told me they had been robbed while they were sleeping. Evidently they had not locked their door. These men took most of their clothes and things. Then I knew that after I had scared them they had gone to his place. I felt so bad. But at least they did not get into the boarding or harm anyone physically. The Lord had awakened me and I thanked Him.

Another night, I heard noises but I could not see where they were. I walked the screened in verandahs on the front and side of my house almost all night. My whistle and flashlight always with me. I was overcome with fear but later realized it was Satan. Over and over it came to me, "Annie, you are alone. There is no phone. You cannot call for help. If people at home knew you were in danger, they would pray. But no one knows and so how can they pray? You are alone, all alone." Morning came so slowly. Repairs had to be made the next day. The thieves had done more damage. There were so many buildings and I could not see them all from my house which may be a good thing.

About two weeks later I had a letter from a missionary in Singapore. Her name was Minna Allworden. She and I were both from Prairie and were on the same ship at one time. We used to correspond for a while but we had lost contact.

Minna explained that one day while she was working the Lord burdened her to pray for me. She gave me the date and I checked in my diary. It was the exact time that I had been in such danger. I felt like saying,"Ha ha, Satan, someone did pray even though she did not know what was going on with me. God told her to pray and I was not alone, God was with me the whole time."

That was not the end of Minna's letter. She had never had an experience in her life before where she was so burdened to pray that someone's life be saved. She wanted to know what had happened but did not know if I was at home or in India. She asked the Lord to help her get my address.

That night she got a very severe toothache and knew she had to get to a dentist. There was none in her town so she took a trip to a city where she knew there was one. She also knew missionaries there that she could stay with. As soon as she entered their home, she saw my prayer card on their shelf. She said, "oh, there's Annie Goertz. God has answered my prayer for I need her address very badly." The mishes told her they did not know me. They had no idea where the card came from. It was just suddenly there after another couple had left. It must have fallen out of their baggage somehow.

These folks took the card and said she could have it since she knew me. They had kept it with their other missionary prayer cards instead of throwing it away. Doesn't that give you goose bumps? God had them preserve it till Minna came! That's how much He cares. Dear reader, He cares for you and has complete control of your circumstances. You may be disquieted. God never panics. Trust Him and tell Him so. He knows exactly what He is going to do for you.

That seems to be why Minna had to have a toothache so she would go to where she could get my address. Hadn't she asked God for it? It was such a blessing to those missionaries because she told them how she had been burdened for me. It was a great blessing to Minna and certainly to me. I cried for joy when I got her letter. I wasted no time to tell her how God had protected me. Minna is with the Lord now.

I know there must have been many times when people were burdened to pray for me but did not write to tell me about it. When they did I always checked in my diary. One time I was telling a story about how a lady in Moose Jaw prayed for me and my life was saved (I shall relate it later). My dear friend Frances Hall raised her hand and asked me what had happened on July 8 in a certain year. I could not remember right off of course, but told her I would look it up when I got back. I also told her that I probably would not find anything outstanding on that day's entry and I did not.

It came to me then, that many times I must have been unaware of imminent danger but God knows and He burdens people to pray. When we are aware of danger we are careful. So on that July 8 I may have been in greater danger than any of these other times. The Lord alone knows and that is all we need to know.

One day the thieves bothered us so much the teachers came and said they did not think I should be alone at night. I agreed that I would ask the matron for two girls to come and sleep in the living room close to my bedroom. I was very tired so I asked the girls not to awaken me if they heard the thieves. They promised but a few hours later they were by my bed calling in a loud whisper, "Mai, Mai, they are by the back verandah. They are trying to come in." Before I was wide enough awake to hear what they were saying I started to say, "I did not want to be awakened...." but stopped short. Maybe it was really serious. I jumped up, grabbed my whistle and flashlight and ran to see if they were really there. They were and I scared them away with my whistle. God again protected us.

A couple of nights later I was suddenly awakened by the noise of the screen door on my side verandah breaking. Again I jumped up, opened the door drapes just enough to push my flashlight through to shine on them. The screen was rusty so I could not see anything but they thought I could. They pulled the iron bar out from where they had wedged it in the door and ran. I heard their footsteps and a loud thud. I wondered what they had dropped.

I have never been able to figure out why I did what I did. I waited a few minutes and went out to see what they had dropped. I found a triangle shaped slab of stone about 5 inches long and one inch thick. One point was as sharp as a knife. They had filed it. I brought it in and put it on my trunk by the door and went back to bed. I was not really afraid but I closed the door to the verandah and went to sleep.

A few days later I heard how thieves broke into Ethel Johnson's place when she lived in Raver. It was at night and they removed the bricks from one corner of the house to get in. They had a flashlight with a very bright beam. They went straight to her bedroom to awaken her. First they took her glasses and house keys then asked for money. She told them to get out and that's when they used a stone (just like the one I picked up) on her throat to cut a big artery. She had a jeep but she was bleeding so much, so how could she get into town to the doctor? She awakened the evangelist who lived down the hill. She gave him a few towels to press on the cut to try to stop the bleeding while she drove several miles. The doctor was able to suture the wound and save her life even though she bled profusely.

When I heard that story I could not stand to look at that stone anymore and got rid of it. That's when I was gripped by real fear. I could not sleep even though I shut all doors and windows for safety. It was so hot and there was no air.

We had so much trouble that I decided to put iron rods across all my windows. I also had heavy expanded metal put on top of the screen already on the screen doors. The general helper and I did it by ourselves and it was very hard work.

I was still afraid when night came. One late afternoon I sat on my bed and looked out west through the open door. I felt I could not stand to see the sun go down one more time. I started to pray and ask God to not let the sun go down. Would He please stop it so I could get a few hours sleep? I opened my eyes, looked up and saw the sun was indeed on its way down.

I closed my eyes again and pleaded earnestly that the sun would stop its course. I even told the Lord, "Lord, you did it for your servant Joshua in the Old Testament (Joshua 10:12,13,14). I am your servant too, I am so very tired and so afraid, I cannot take another night, please Lord."

When I opened my eyes the sun had disappeared. India does not have a long dusk or dawn. If you see the sun starting to go down, you'd better run for your flashlight or light the lamp. So I said to myself the Lord did not stop the sun for me. But just as quickly a verse from the Psalms came to mind, something about being afraid. The Holy Spirit brought it to my mind.

So I lit a lamp and looked up the verse. It was Psalm 56:11. "In God have I put my trust: I will not be afraid what man can do unto me." I read it several times and then I said yes, I have put my trust in God but I am still afraid. Then I read the Psalm from verse 1 and came to verse 3. "What time I am afraid, I will trust in Thee." So I put "But" in front of "What" and it read, "But what time I am afraid, I will trust in Thee." Then I realized God answered my prayer but not my words. He helped me to trust in Him rather than solving my fear problem by making the sun stand still. He could have but then I would have wanted Him to do it every night!! I am so human.

I cannot tell you that I was never afraid after that. I was, for the problem of thieves continued unabated but it was different. It was not a question of whether I'd be afraid ever again. But when I was afraid I would trust God. At the very beginning of our problem I had hired a watchman but he made one round and fell asleep till morning. I found great comfort in the knowledge that God never sleeps nor slumbers, Psalm 121:4. Actually the whole Psalm is so reassuring. It was our dear Mother's favourite Psalm. She quoted it so often to us in German. It has come to mind many times since then.

The watchman slept all night as I told you, so I told him I would not need him anymore. He took his roll of bedding and went home but that was not the end of him. The next few nights he hired people to come to our compound to throw stones at our buildings. That was to prove to me that we needed him. We did not let on about the stones and eventually they stopped.

One night the thieves cut a hole in the window screen of our teacher's house and took some bricks out of the wall. In the morning when I got up, there lay the bricks on my back step. After about two years of this one of our workers left and I put another man in his place. That stopped the thief problem!? Coincidence? No.

Prayer card picture for third term.

Annie turned nurse just for fun.

CHAPTER 29

Various Topics

Once again I was ironing my clothes in the living room for that was the only place I had a power plug. A power line had much heavier wiring for ironing and heating water with a plunger. Suddenly, a man stood before me. He was barefoot so I did not hear him come in. I ushered him out to the verandah because I had no idea who he was.

I gave him a chair to sit down and he started to weep. He was a railway worker from Chawalkheda. He told me his 20 year old son had just died from some serious illness. He had heard there was a Christian church here so he wanted a minister to take the service at the grave side. He told me he was a Christian. Our pastor was not home but I said I would tell him and he could come early in the morning. It was late afternoon now so I suggested he go home and have the grave dug. Before he left I gave him tea and prayed with him.

Everything went off as planned. This man was most appreciative and became a friend of our pastor who would go out to have a gospel service in his village. From then on he came to town almost every bazaar day to see us. If the pastor was home he would go to his house and pray with him. If not, then he'd come to my house. We always gave him,(or anyone that came) a cup of tea then we prayed with him and he went home encouraged.

He did this for several months. One particular bazaar day he came as usual. I talked with him, gave him tea and then I waited for him to leave. I was so very busy, a group of girls were waiting for medicine. The headmistress needed to talk, my cook wanted a list and money to do my bazaaring, and a few other things I cannot recall now. I guess he sensed I was busy. I actually felt so pressured that I really forgot about praying with him. I no doubt did not give him my full attention. So he got up to go but stopped. He then turned around and looked at me. I asked him if he wanted to say something. He said, "No, but I thought you would pray with me!" That hit me like a brick. I invited him back in and I prayed. Then he warmly saluted me with folded hands as if in prayer, the Christians do that when they leave and say, "salaam".

I felt so smitten. I had not realized, for one thing, how much it meant to him to have contacted some Christians to pray with him. He and his wife were far from their native home and the only Christians in their village. I felt so ashamed that I had been too busy to pray. I was also ashamed that I had unknowingly let him feel I was busy. When I think of it, I can tell too when people are too busy to stop and talk. I asked him and the Lord for forgiveness.

His wife invited Pauline Holbrook (who was living with me for a short time while learning the language) and me to come to visit her so we went by train. They had raised a part of the earthen floor at one end of the room to make a little platform to sit on. So that is where we sat. Our hostess had just set out our cups of tea and some sweets between us. Along came their goat and squeezed in behind us. It must be where she liked to rest. Suddenly, her droppings were all over the platform just barely missing our cups of tea. It almost turned my stomach but Pauline saw humour in it. She said in English to me, "Oh, baked beans too!" Well, that started us laughing. We were so embarrassed because the lady wanted to know why we were laughing. I guess I said something funny about the goat and then it was okay. We were almost hysterical. We just could not stop laughing even though we knew it was so impolite.

Eventually, we were back to our neighbourly chatting. The hostess came over and pushed the droppings aside with her hands and sat down. Then I read a portion from the Word and had prayer with her. Pauline did not know any Marathi. The lady was still very much grieving the loss of their son and was hungry for fellowship. A month or two after that the Railway transferred them to another place and we lost contact with them. That man taught me that I must deal with the person at hand and not sit and think about what I still have to do after they leave. Jesus was not frustrated by interruptions. Rather, they were appointments.

ANTS

Little red ants were everywhere. One day I was bitten on my eyelid by such a tiny ant that my eye swelled shut. Another night I got no sleep because my bed was full of them. At first I thought I had the itch or something. When I shined my flashlight between the sheets I saw lots of ants. I had to take off all the linens and shake them in another room. Not just once but several times that night. That happened quite a few times.

Usually I had the legs of my dining room table sitting in little tins of water or DDT powder. Also in the pantry the pinzra (screened in cupboard) had to sit in water or even kerosene. Any place where there was food the ants found. I had some peppermints in my purse when I returned. I did not use my purse in India so put it away. When I did look at it the ants had eaten the peppermints so only a few crumbs were left.

I had noticed for several mornings while I stood in front of the mirror by my dresser to do my hair that there was a tiny brown streak down the front of it. I wiped it off and there it was again the next morning. After about a week, I decided to investigate where it originated. It came from the small top drawer.

I checked and checked and finally moved the Ex-Lax container to see what was underneath. As I lifted it, it felt light. It was empty and I knew I had not used any. When I opened the small carton, the little squares of silver paper looked intact. I put my finger on one and it collapsed. I touched each one and they were all empty. I could not figure it out. Then, it dawned on me that the little red ants must have carried it all away leaving that brown streak down the front of my dresser.

Then I began to wonder if they ate it or if they just carried it away to store for food. I could only imagine what must have happened to all those innocent, little, industrious ants had they actually eaten it. Then I began to laugh,

I laughed so hard that Glady and Augusta came to ask what was so funny at six o'clock in the morning. When I told them, they laughed too. To be sure you probably are too! Have you no heart? Being a tenderhearted woman, I wondered if I should set out some anti-cholera tablets in that drawer for my little thieves (possibly patients by now!).

Then there were big red ants, or black ones, called mungarla. The small ones were called mungi. The big ones seemed to have a pair of scissors in their mouth. They preferred to get you between your toes. They made a neat incision that would bleed a lot. After that they sucked the blood and it was sometimes hard to pull them off. It was painful too. You can imagine how children screamed when they were bitten.

LICE

Augusta, Gladys and I were having breakfast when Augusta turned to me and said, "Annie, I think you have lice. You are scratching your head so much. Let me have a look after breakfast." I told her I thought I had heatrash because it WAS very itchy.

School girls checking for lice.

She met me on the side verandah. I had long hair in those days. She spread some newspaper on a trunk out there. I bent over and she began to comb. I thought I heard little clicks on the paper as if something was dropped on it. I was afraid to look until she said, "Annie, your head is crawling with lice." I looked and sure enough there were lots on the paper.

That scared me to think I had so many bugs. I raised my head and started to run through our house. I wanted to get away from them. Augusta stopped me and told me that running would not get rid of them. She assured me that since they had not killed me so far, they would not now. She waited till bed time then put DDT powder on my head and tied it all up in a bandana. Now the lice tried to get away from me! They ran around on my head all night. In the morning I washed out the DDT and many had died. But there were nits that were not killed by the powder. They hatched that day and another DDT powder treatment went on again that night. Pretty soon I was rid of them and very thankful. I did get them one more time although I tried to be very careful.

You know, I am sure that lice multiply very rapidly like bedbugs. Mother used to say if just one is missed, it can become an adult, a mother, and a grandmother all in one day. I believe that.

Another way of treating lice was by rubbing kerosene into the hair. That was a sure kill. The women and girls in India prefer to sit down and pick each other's lice and nits out by hand. The school girls would sometimes sit in a row of six or seven, each one cleaning the head in front of her. It reminded me of another species that does that but now I am naughty. Sorry!

CHAPTER 30

Watering Banana Plants

The girl's bathing place.

Indian bananas are so sweet and juicy and we all liked them very much. One of those was often our dessert at the end of our meal. They were cheap too in those early days, usually one dozen for 3 annas. Now they sell them by the kilo and they are more expensive. I decided it would be nice to have bananas of our own. So I asked our neighbor across the road for three plants which he willingly gave me. I planted them near our well where we had a small section I called our oasis.

Someone before me had planted a hedge in a circle beside the well. In that circle were plants with big leaves which were used as a vegetable and very nutritious. Where the hedge came together were two weeping willow trees making an opening as it were. Goats liked those leaves but they did not like the hedge. There was a bit of a gap in the hedge so that is where I planted the banana plants. The oasis needed water and we got that from the waste water from the boarding. There were three taps in the compound near which we built small stone platforms for the girls to sit and take their baths. A high stone wall enclosure gave them privacy. We built gutters around the bathing area and guided them toward the well in an underground sewer system.

The soap was not that good for the plants so we dug a deep pit and lined it with cement. On one end was a hole for the dirty water to enter. Then the soap settled in the tank and cleaner water ran out a hole at the opposite end, higher than the intake one. That water then ran into the oasis. Again, underground for about 25 feet and above the ground the last 5 or 6 feet as it entered the oasis between the two trees.

When school was in session there was always enough water to keep our little spot green and lush. When the girls went home only the orphan girls were left in the boarding, anywhere from ten to fifteen. That was not enough water for our plants. So every hot season the banana plants dried up. They revived when the girls returned and also with the rains. This had gone on for several years and it was not the way to grow bananas.

I decided I would go out each morning and evening when the town water supply was turned on for one hour. I opened the three taps full blast to water the plants so they did not dry up. There was one hitch to my plan. The chickens used to go and scratch for worms in that last 5 to 6 feet which was above ground. I had a nice little canal opened but the chickens disturbed it so the water ran all over the ground instead of into the oasis. So I was compelled each time to go with a stick to try to shore up the canal so all the water would not be wasted. That was quite a ritual I went through for a couple of weeks. Then something happened so keep the above details in mind.

Early every morning I had my devotions in my room before breakfast. Then I just asked the blessing on the food and ate. I had a Daily Light from Zondervan Press which someone gave me. It had morning and evening daily readings, all Scripture nothing else. I never used it unless I had guests. Then I read from it before we ate.

However, on May 24, 1969 I broke custom and took the Daily Light and read it before I ate. I don't know why I did but I soon understood. When I got to the second line I read, "In all their affliction He was afflicted, and the angel of His presence saved them:.." Isa. 63:9. When I read the part about the angel, it just seemed to almost lift off the page. I might say it stared at me. It seemed it was for me but I did not understand.

I asked the Lord why was He giving me that promise because I was not in any danger. I was not going to travel anywhere. In fact, I was going to get the orphan girls to help me sweep the three classrooms so they'd be ready for the opening of school in a few days. I also thanked God for the privilege I had of working with the school girls and orphans and seeing them come to Jesus. I asked the Lord to prepare their hearts as they returned. The phrase, "and the angel of His presence saved them" stayed with me so I did not read any farther.

I thanked the Lord for the food and had my breakfast. It was going on eight o'clock and that's when the town water was released. So I went out, grabbed my stick that was leaning against the wall and off to the boarding to open the three taps full force. I hurried to the oasis because the water would be flowing all over, as it did every morning.

That morning there was no water, not even a trickle. I had opened the little canal and kept looking between the two trees to see if it was coming. Nothing came. Had the orphans turned the taps off by mistake? No, I could hear the water splashing in the boarding. Then I remembered that two huge bullfrogs lived in the tank and they loved to sit in the big hole that let the water run out.

I went to the tank, moved one slab of stone (six slabs covered the tank so no one could fall in) to the side a bit. Sure enough, there they sat, big and flabby and closed the hole completely. I talked to them, "I thought you were the culprits. Now get down off of there and stay out till I water the oasis." Then I rattled my stick against the inside of the tank and they jumped into the water. I hurried back to the two trees to scratch some more but still no water.

Back to the tank to scold Mr. and Mrs. Bullfrog again. They were up in their perch. I rattled the stick really loud and again hurried back to my little spot. Now a trickle of water came through. I scratched some more just for something to do. This time I went inside the hedge. I looked up again for the water. I saw something but not water. Here came a huge snake right for me between those two trees. Its head about 3 feet in the air, the rest of its body galloping.

Snakes run down on the ground zig zag as I had seen dozens of times. Just at that split second I said out loud to the Lord, "Oh, that's why you gave me that verse!"

That's all I remember for I passed out in front of the snake. Not from fright because there was no time to be afraid. It was that snake that kept the water from flowing out. It was a hot day and it was cooling itself in that moist sewer. My stick had frightened it out of its repose.

I came to about five or six minutes later on my back. I should have been on my stomach because I was bent over forward when the snake came for me. With all my heart I believe that is where the Angel came in. He must have laid me down on my back. If I had been bent over the snake could have wrapped itself around me.

There I lay on my back looking at the clear blue sky. I was surprised that I was still alive. I thought I should have been in Heaven because I thought it was a cobra. I knew that if one gets bitten you'd be gone in five minutes in most cases. Unless of course there was someone right there with anti-venom serum.

Then I said out loud, "Get up quick, why do you lie here? That snake must still be around." I got up but I staggered. I was very weak. I looked for the snake but could not see it. I did not look very hard, you may be sure! But I was not going to walk out between those two trees where the snake had come. So I climbed over the hedge. It was almost impossible because it was waist high. I managed and fell down on the other side. I could not walk so crawled on my stomach to try to get away from the snake in case it was still looking for me.

I crawled a distance and stopped. I could not call for anyone because I was too weak. BUT GOD! At that very moment the deaf-mute daughter of one of our workers, Sudina by name,(that family had six children, three could talk and hear and three could not) was at the water tap by the side of the boarding filling a pail of water. While it was filling she looked around and saw me. I heard her yell, "AAAAAAAAAA." That brought the pastor and his wife out of their house. We all knew what that yell meant and responded.

They asked her with motions, "What?" She formed two circles over her eyes with her hands. That was her way of saying me, it signified I wore glasses. Then they asked, "Where?" She made a crawling sign and pointed to me. Bless her heart. She was an angel too! They came running and asked what happened. I told them a snake had come for me. When I said snake, they inspected all my exposed skin to see if they could see two holes where the fangs would have gone in. They saw nothing.

Then the pastor asked what kind of snake it was. I told him it had a yellow stomach and markings all along his back but the head was not spread out like a cobra's hood. It was about 15 feet long. He said it was an azgar, that means a python. Cobras are not that long. Pythons are related to the boas they do not bite but constrict its victim.

The pastor and his wife helped me up and steadied me so I could walk back to my house. My legs and knees were all scratched and bleeding from crawling over the hedge. Nalini bai brought me a pan of water with soap to wash my legs. Then I put on bandages. I was weak and could not do any work that day. In fact I lay down quite a bit even though I had planned so much for that day. Nalini Bai asked if she could take the girls and clean the classrooms. I gratefully accepted her offer.

When I was alone in my house again, I was thinking about the verse the Lord had given me that morning. He had fulfilled it by sending the Angel to save my life. Yet I felt part of it was not fulfilled. You remember it said, "saved them" and I was alone. I said to the Lord that His Word is so specific. He could have given me the verse from Psalm 46:5b which came to my mind then, "God shall help her, and that right early (8:00a.m.!). Of course, the Lord did not give me my answer then but He did later.

In the summer I took the orphan girls for a walk each evening about 5 o'clock. I could not that day but dear Nalini Bai came and asked if she could. They went across the road to walk in the neighbour's orchard. They were not gone very long when they came back all excited. They were talking at once and I could not understand what had happened. I asked them to sit down and one tell me the story. I got the story that there was a 6 foot trunk of a tree that had fallen into the shallow irrigation ditch by the row of papaya plants. Sushila bent over to lift it out so the water could flow better. Her hand was about two inches away when the COBRA moved! She came so close to being killed.

Then I asked the girls to listen while I told about the verse the Lord had given me before I had the encounter with the Python. I told them of my talking to the Lord about why He gave me a verse with the pronoun "them" when I was the only one saved. I said that I now had my answer, for both Sushila and I had been saved that day. We had prayer together as we thanked the Lord for His protection. I was satisfied but there was more to come!

The next morning my cook Moses came in to make my breakfast but before he started he called to me. I went to see what he needed. He told me how the night before he and his family were seated on the floor having their devotions. Their eyes were all closed for prayer except for 5 year old Daya. She held her hands over her face but her eyes were open as she peeked between her fingers. We've all done that! Suddenly she screamed, "sap"(snake). There they saw a three foot snake crawling in through the open door toward where they were sitting.

Where could they go? The only door was behind the snake. There was one window but it had bars across it. One of them managed to sneak behind the snake to grab the bamboo stick from behind the door that I had given them for just such occasions. However at the cry 'SAP' the pastor had come with his stick and killed it.

I told Moses (in Marathi we call him Moshe) about the verse the Lord had given me and how He had fulfilled everything in that verse by saving not just Sushila and me that day, but also his whole family.

I've told this story in many Sunday School classes across the country. When I come to the place where the snake was in the doorway and no place to run, I'd ask the class what they would have done. Most often the answer was, "I'd pray". One boy stood up so straight to give his answer. I reiterated the dire situation of no window or door to escape through. He calmly said, "I'd make another door." I guess he thought he'd just push his head through the wall. I appreciated his answer. He won't let anything stop him in life! May it be with the Lord's enabling.

There's more to this story. That day my neighbour to the South of us sent word for me to come for tea and sweets. Their field is between our compound and their house. They used to have a cotton gin too. They were of the Jain religion. They are even stricter than the Hindus about not killing an insect or ant because it might be one of their reincarnated ancestors.

She had heard about my python encounter and wanted to ask me if we had killed it. She then related to me how there was a huge mother Python and her two young who lived down by their well in the middle of the field between us. The mother was close to 30 feet long, she told me. The mother often came around their house but she would shoo it away and steer it toward the well. She was sure the one I saw was one of the baby pythons. She wanted me to promise not to kill it if it ever came back. She had called me to introduce them to me, I think.

Talk about shivers up and down my back! To think a python family had lived there all those years and we never knew about them. We knew a lot of our chickens were never seen again if they spent too much time near or in that oasis. But we thought dogs killed and ate them. Think of all those years when any one of those snakes could have crawled into one of our staff houses or the boarding while everyone was asleep. I know that Angel of the Lord must have watched out for snakes more often than we knew. He protected us from dangers seen and unseen. Praise the Lord! Isn't it wonderful that we have a God who never slumbers or sleeps? He even knows when we are awake, worrying and planning when we are supposed to be sleeping. Someone remarked, "Why should we both be awake?"

There's more! But a bit of background first. You remember when I got the $50.00 to attend Summer Institute of Linguistics at Caronport-Briercrest Bible School? Good. Mr John Cunningham had a radio program in Moose Jaw. Somehow we got acquainted and he asked me to come in to read a one minute testimony over the air.

I did and started out by reading what I called my favourite verse from Psalm 34:1. "I will bless the Lord at all times. His praise shall continually be in my mouth." Then I told briefly that I was headed for India. A Mrs. Elizabeth Graefer from Moose Jaw had heard that program. It so happened that the same verse was her special one. She hired someone to bring her out to Caronport to meet me. I was working in the kitchen when she came and we were introduced through the window above the counter.

She gave me her name and address. Then she asked me if she could pray for me. Why of course, she could. I'd be ever so grateful to her. Then she asked, "May I pray for you three times a day, Annie?" That brought tears of joy to my eyes, as I assured her how much I would need her prayer. Well, she prayed faithfully and also corresponded with me very faithfully. On furloughs I always visited her.

About one week after my Python incident, I had a short letter from Elizabeth. All it said was, "Annie, what happened to you at such a time and date? Are you very sick? Are you short of money? Were you in an accident? Is Satan attacking the work in a real way? Please let me know as soon as you get this. I have to know because God told me so clearly to pray for you." Later on she told me that she had felt I would die if she stopped praying. I might have too. Well, that letter made me cry so much I could hardly read it. Just tears of joy that God loved me so much and would talk to people so many thousands of miles away to get them to pray. That experience, as well as others like it have strengthened my faith so much.

I came home on furlough the end of 1969 and visited Elizabeth again. This time it was in her hospital room. She was dying of tongue cancer. It was hard to see her suffer so much but harder still for her. I talked for a while and then prayed with her. I asked God to ease the pain and discomfort. I also reminded Him (as if He needed it) about how often that now very sick tongue had spoken my name in prayer. Then she asked me to kiss her goodbye for we would not meet again here. I did but it was hard, for the odour was very unpleasant. I knew she had to put up with it all the time which was harder.

I sometimes wonder what happens when a faithful prayer warrior goes Home. Does the Lord raise up someone else to take their place? My parents prayed for me so much too and now they are gone. I would like to thank those of you that read this, for praying for me. I know more prayer went up for me than I will ever know. And God answered.

At this point I want to tell of a very young prayer warrior I had, and still have though she is grown up and has a family. On one of my early furloughs I visited in the home of my second cousin Elsie (Bergen) Doell and her husband John. Their children were all small at the time. Little 4 year old Carol took a liking to me and I to her. I had a plastic lizard with a magnetic head and a magnetic pencil. I could make that lizard do all kinds of things in order to attract shy children. It worked every time. Many of you reading this might remember it.

I took Carol on my lap and told her stories and let her play with the lizard. Then I asked her if she would pray for me. She promised and her mother told me she did that before every meal for quite a while. One day while they were having supper Carol suddenly put down her fork, put her hands over her mouth and cried hard. They pulled her hands away, thinking she had bit her tongue. She insisted she did not. Finally, she was calmed down enough to tell them that she had not prayed for Annie Goertz. They bowed their heads and she prayed for me.

Thank you Carol, you are a sweetheart. Thank you for praying then and now. Now it is my turn to uphold you as you battle cancer and MS. You are putting up a brave fight. I love you and do pray for you and your family.

Back to some miscellaneous items. I have noted in my diary that Pauline and I had taken our radios to the Post Office to register them. If I remember correctly we each paid Rs.2/00 for a one year licence.

That was the same day, November 23, 1963, that President Kennedy was shot. The papers were full of that very sad news. India mourned his passing very much. The next day I was in school sitting in on six-month exams for first and second standards. Word came that all schools were to be closed for half a day in honour of President Kennedy. So we closed the school and continued with exams the next day.

I felt our girls needed milk but we could not afford to give it to them. So I wrote to a relief organization in the USA and they sent me quite a few cases of powdered milk. Some of the girls liked it but others would not taste it. When I asked why not they told me they had heard this was milk from wild cows who lived in the mountains. Whenever a cow walked over a certain kind of stone, the milk automatically ran onto the stone. Then someone(?) came along and scraped it up and put it into tins. No wonder they didn't want it.

I used to mix it with water but one day I did not have time so I just gave them each a big spoonful in their hand or dish to eat it dry. Well, they loved that. It tasted sweeter and seemed like candy.

The corpse sitting in the foreground is the grandfather of the lady in white standing next to me.

CHAPTER 31

Queen Elizabeth Visits India, and "Hodge-Podge"

Pussycat, pussycat, where have you been? I've been to Delhi to see the Queen! I got quite a surprise when a gilt-edged invitation came from the Canadian High Commissioner in Delhi to come and meet the Queen on January 25, 1961. Soon I discovered that I was not the only one thus honoured. All subjects of Commonwealth countries, who were in India were invited. That was exciting! Some accompanying instructions told us of the dress code to be observed. Ladies were to wear hats and gloves. I had a hat but no gloves so I borrowed some from Augusta. When I came back and returned the gloves to her I said, "Augusta, look into the eyes that beheld the Queen!"

My cousin Iona Heppner, Helen Penner and I travelled the long journey together. The trains were so crowded (when were they not?) we climbed up on a top shelf called a berth. The women crowded in down below. There was no way to get down without treading on people. When we arrived in Delhi, we allowed the women to get off first then we let ourselves down gently. One woman did not get off because she was sick. As I touched the floor my hands were still holding on to the berth, she vomited right down the front of me.

When I got off and the girls saw me I was at a loss as to what to do. A kind and resourceful water vendor called me over and said he would pour water on me so I could try to wash the vomit off. Bless his heart, he saved the day. Most of the vomit was gone but not the smell. We got some coolies to carry our bags to the Railway Station ladies' waiting room. There I changed clothes, washed the dress and hung it up to dry. The station was going to be our "hotel." The Queen's and the Republic Day Parade the following day filled all the guest houses. We slept on the floor like many others.

Then the next day we had our baths and got dressed in one of the bath places. It was kind of hard. Then with all our finery on, we got a taxi to take us to Government Place. The red carpets were laid out in circles. We all stood around those circles but off the rugs. The Queen and her retinue came along. They had given special coloured ribbons to every seventh person, I believe. She evidently had a list too and shook hands with only those persons. The one closest to where we were was Margaret Willems from Saskatchewan. The Queen knew all about the wheat province. She was about a foot from us and I felt I wanted to reach out and shake her hand but that was forbidden. She looked lovely.

When that official function was over, we were all invited to a different place for a reception outside. Table after table was laden with food we had not seen for years like turkey, ham, various kinds of salads, cakes and ice cream. Too many to mention. But we had stiff competition for the food from the crows. So they had stationed well starched and turbaned chefs at intervals around the tables to wave flags on long sticks.

The following Day was January 26, India's Republic Day. A parade was scheduled every year in Delhi,(and elsewhere). This year it was special because Her Royal Highness was visiting and she would be riding in her chariot as well with her husband.

We went to the office of Tourism for free tickets so we could have a seat near the front. Iona, Helen and I went over but when we asked for three, the man said there were none left. We were very disappointed but asked again. His answer was the same so we just sat there and wondered what to do next.

Suddenly, I thought of a little story Mother had told us about her Father. When things did not go the way he had expected or when the price of a commodity had gone up before he could buy it, he would say, "When it rains gold, the poor man's saucer is always turned upside down." So I told the man behind the counter that story. At once he reached under the counter and gave us three tickets. We thanked him profusely and left. He had wanted a bribe which was often the case, but we never gave any.

From there we went directly to the "maidan" (a huge open area) and found our seats. It was hot to sit in the sun for so many hours but it was worth it. Pandit Jawaharlal Nehru was the Prime Minister at the time. He and other dignitaries walked in the parade. It was exciting for us and I have no idea how many thousands of people were there. Pandit Nehru's daughter Indira Gandhi later became the Prime Minister. She was very good as was her father.

We had slept (or not slept) at the railway station for two nights and were ready to sleep in a bed with a bit more privacy. We searched and searched but every place was full so back to Tourism we went. They gave us the name of The Ceylon Buddhist Pilgrim Refugee Home that was right close by and I guess we qualified as pilgrims!

We went right over and discovered it was run by Buddhist priests! You know the shaven heads and saffron robes! Now what were we to do? We were a bit leery to say the least but they were most gracious. They spoke English and within minutes they brought us three steaming cups of tea. That greatly refreshed us then we were ushered into our quarters which were really quite nice. Lovely clean sheets and our own bathroom so we decided to settle in.

They brought us a delicious fish dinner right to our room. Everything was lovely. They even brought us boiled water to drink. When night came, we decided it might be good to drag one of the cots in front of the door. We had two very refreshing nights. At check-out time, we wanted to pay them but they would not take anything. Oh yes, I remember we did leave them Rupees ten total for our whole stay! Then we all went back to our homes. Iona lived close to Delhi, Helen and I in Maharashtra. All in all it had been a very interesting time away from our work for a few days.

I told you Mrs. Indira Gandhi became Prime Minister after her father died. She was coming to our area to inspect some dam or an irrigation project. On her way she was going to stop in Dharangaon because it was an old British Fort town.

I heard about it when the local police came to call on me and ask if Indira Gandhi could stay in my house for a couple of days. I thought that was alright. I would welcome the Prime Minister but they said I would have to move out so they would move their stuff in. That meant her maids, cooks and Gurkha for her security. It would not be safe if I stayed. I guess for her, anyway!! I was quite willing to say yes then thought I'd better ask for permission from our field chairman. I sent one of our men with a note to Nasik.

It was a good thing I did because he said no. He pointed out to me that as missionaries we cannot enter into anything political. She was heading the Congress Party so if we put her up, it would look as if we were endorsing her party. I could see that. I had thought I might have a chance to have a visit with her but it would have interrupted our work so much and we probably would have had to close our school for her security. So, I've seen the Queen of England but not the beloved Indian Prime Minister.

From Queen to Prime Minister to a Sadhu (Holy Man)! One day the girls came to tell me that a man had come onto our compound and he was leading a very big elephant. Elephants were scarce in our area so I went out to speak to the Sadhu to see what was up. He said he was travelling through our area and he and his animal wanted to spend the night here. I knew that meant we would have to supply fodder for the elephant and that was a big order! Sadhus do not have a good reputation so we were afraid to keep him on our yard.

I made tea and had it taken to him while I prayed about what to do. Then I remembered that we had to have permission from head office in Nasik to have someone out of the ordinary stay with us. An elephant was slightly out of the ordinary! I went back to him and told him he would have to spend a few days in town somewhere while I sent a note to Nasik for permission. That settled it. He said he did not have that much time to wait for a reply. I was very relieved.

I told you before about the bales of clothes and the milk powder I received. Well, an organization called CORAGS was able to send me lots of Bulgar Wheat for our hostel. It was cracked wheat which we used as porridge for the girls every morning except Sunday when they had chappatis and tea. That was such a help as the price of grain went up and was rationed.

Another item they sent us was cheese in one gallon tins. At first the girls did not like it but later they really liked it. When the tins were empty I gave each family a few. They called the tinsmith who made lids for them. Now they had a rat proof place to store their flour, sugar or lentils.

Whenever I opened a small tin of jam or fruit, I saved the lids very carefully. The rats often chewed through thin boards that held the verandah screen in place. Sometimes the boards would rot from the rain so I would nail those lids over the hole, one on the outside and one on the inside. We wasted nothing!

Sometimes we had Evangelistic teams come from a Bible School to help our pastor in the villages. Our own students in training were usually sent to our mission stations for their practicum. The leader of the team was a widower. While he was at Dharangaon he asked if I had a girl he could marry. I had several so I asked one but she said no. I asked the next one who also said no. I asked a third one and she said yes. Then he said one of the stipulations was that she must be able to speak English. This one could not but don't worry all three got married later. I did change the method quite a bit but I'll tell you more about that a little later.

I had a very sore throat for a while so went to Chinchpada to see our doctor. He said it was strep throat and I would have to wear a mask. He gave me two of their gauze masks that were used for surgery. I wore one everywhere I went, and that was into town too. A few days later a gilt edged invitation was delivered to me by the Jain people. They were having a special meeting and invited me. They had seen me with my mask and thought I had joined the Jain religion. You see, they often wear a mask because they do not want to swallow a gnat or fly while talking. They sometimes drink through a mask too. I sent back a thank you note and declined the invitation.

We needed some masonry done in the Baby Home so I hired a mason by the name of Joseph. He was a Muslim and had a lovely wife and large family. He used to watch me care for the children in the Baby Home. One day before he went home he said to me, "Mai, when you go to Heaven and take all these children with you, will you take me too?" I told him I could not and I could not even take the children. Each one has to go by him or herself. That surprised him very much. He wondered why not. I told him that Christianity is not like any other religion in the world. I told him he was born a Muslim and Hindus are born Hindus but Christianity is about Jesus Christ. We accept Him as our Saviour and that makes us a Christian.

The next day he told me that he had gone home very sad. He thought about it all night and asked me more the next day. I asked our pastor to talk with him and he sold him a Bible. The third day he came back and told me he had hardly slept at all because I had said he could not go to Heaven like he was. In his fitful sleep he had a dream. An angel came down and said, "Give me your finger, I will hold on to it and take you to Heaven." Joseph argued with the angel and said, "You give me your finger and I will hold on to it. I am sinful, so you may drop me."

The angel insisted he would not drop him. So up they went until they reached Heaven. God stood up and looked over the edge and asked the angel who he had brought this time. He said, "I brought Joseph." God waved his hand and said, "No, no, he cannot come up here. He is sinful. Take him back down again." So the angel did as he was told.

Joseph felt so bad that he was denied entrance into Heaven. He realized that what I had said was true but he wanted to go to Heaven. He took a ceremonial bath that night and decided he would ask Jesus to be his Saviour. Then he looked at his wife and children sleeping peacefully and knew if he became a Christian they would all leave him which was hard. He might even be poisoned but oh, he wanted peace so badly.

He battled that for a while. Then

Joseph and his young son.

the decision was made, he would kneel down and denounce his religion and accept Jesus Christ. After that he lay down and had peace. But how could he be sure? He told God that he would lie down to sleep. If God had really accepted him, would He give him another dream or vision.

He lay down and fell asleep. The angel came back and gave him the same instructions as before. Up, up they went to the edge of Heaven. God asked who he brought. He told him it was Joseph again. God said, "Now his sin is gone but it is not time for him to come yet. He must come here later." so back to his home they went.

The next day he came and told me all about this. He was so happy. Now, I do not believe that everyone who has a dream or a vision like that is saved. I have noticed that sometimes God reveals Himself that way to some people who have no other way of finding out about Him, especially those who cannot read or write. In Joseph's case I believe He did get saved that night. He was a changed man. He read his Bible and other Christian books I gave him.

At one time he was staying with his son in the city when he was not well. He was lying in bed and reading the book I gave him, "I Dared To Call Him Father." He was crying, so put the book over his face so his son should not see his tears. However the son did see them and took the book away saying, "It's too hard for you Papa to cry when you are sick."

To go back a bit, he asked me if he should tell his family and relatives that he had become a Christian. I just read him Rom. 10:9 -13. He said, "there are no two ways about it, are there?" and I agreed. He went to the city on business and stopped in another town en route, to witness to relatives. He sent me a postcard from the city and told me that they had ridiculed him. What should he do now? I prayed much for him. He remained true as far as I know.

Not long after this, their little baby girl was very sick. She was about a year old. She could not keep any food down. He asked me to come and pray for her. I told him to wait till Augusta came home so she could come to pray. The baby got worse so I wrote a note to our Doctor and asked Joseph to take her and the note there. Joseph would not go. He wanted me to come and pray but I was hesitant. What if I prayed and the baby was not healed? Would his faith waver?

A few more days went by when he arrived at my place with a bullock cart. He asked me to get in and come to his house. He told me he thought it was too hot to walk so he brought the conveyance. There was nothing I could do but go.

He asked the driver to wait to take me back home again. When we arrived at his house, his wife sat on the floor just inside the door. He told me to wait until he called his children. They came and he told them all to bow their heads then he took his cap off and said, "Everybody be real quiet, Mai is going to pray for the baby so she will get well." As soon as I said Amen, the tea vendor was there with a cup of tea. I drank it, he thanked me and escorted me back to the cart.

Many things went through my mind. "What if, what if..? then what will happen?" My mind was not on my work. The next morning I saw Joseph come but he was looking down. "For sure she has died," I thought. He told me with a big smile that she had not vomited once, nor had diarrhea since I prayed. She was sitting up eating porridge when he left! He said that he knew she would live if I prayed for her. After that they called her my child. Years later when she got married I was an honoured guest and he told everybody the story.

His wife died after the children grew up and he took it very hard. I sometimes thought she had been saved too. He sold his home and moved to Bombay to live with one of his children. When it came time for me to retire in 1984, he heard about it. He came back to Dharangaon to say good bye but by this time was an old man.

Over a cup of tea he asked me if I was going back to America to take charge of my fields and houses again. I asked what fields and houses? He said, "Your father was a farmer and surely he left you some of it!" I said that my father had sold everything and he was in Heaven. He could not believe I had nothing to go back to. Finally, I drew the size of a postage stamp in my hand with my finger and said, "I do not own even the size of this on this earth." He looked sad. He was quiet for a bit and then he smiled and said, "Mai, the God whom you have served for over 36 years will provide something for you. I know that." That certainly seemed like a prophecy, for today I own a lovely condominium which I paid for in ten years. God is no man's debtor.

My condo is not an expensive one but well built and I feel safe. When I retired, I had no money. Well, I should not say that, for I had a little more than $100.00 cash on hand. I was going to rent the smallest apartment I could find but God had other plans. A couple I had known for about ten years, offered to let me live free in their spare condo. They gave the keys to my sister to give to me when I came home. Praise The Lord ! But I did not know that till I arrived here.

After two years they wanted to sell it to me but I did not have what was needed so I moved out and rented an apartment. It bothered me to pay rent and have the money go down the drain as it were so I began to look for a condo, without any money.

To make a long and precious story short I will tell you that when I found one I liked, the owner asked how I would pay for it. I told him I had a pension. Well, that did not impress him very much. I needed a down payment, he told me. Where was I going to get it? I said, "from the Lord." He said I must borrow it from someone. I told him I had asked the bank and they refused because I did not have enough pension to repay it.

He thought for a bit and then said, "you must ask from your friends." I replied that I could not do that. I had never asked anyone for money and I would not start now. He wondered how I got my support so I told him I had asked God who provided without me ever mentioning support to anyone. Well, he thought times had changed a bit and no one would know I needed money if I did not ask. He meant very well and I did not blame him at all.

He mentioned three people he knew had money and asked if I knew them. I did know them so I let him convince me to do my part while he and God did theirs. With a heavy heart I made appointments to see them. God so graciously overruled. Would you know that each one said they would like to give me a loan but could not right then? One had it all invested and he would lose a lot if it was taken out early. Another was going to help his son build a house. I will leave out the third man's reason.

You know something? You have no idea how relieved I was when they all refused. I was not hurt or disturbed at all. I had known I should not ask but I did. I felt that my Heavenly Father wanted me to only ask Him. Well, the owner went and asked another couple if they could help me. They at once offered to loan me $18,000 for ten years, interest free. A few days later a widow asked me if I was ever going to buy a place. When I said I was looking she asked if she could loan me some money at 5% interest. I could repay it within ten years so that took care of the two loans. (^_^) However, I still needed a down payment.

The money came from three different sources so I had $17,000 for a down payment! Who has that much to pay down even if he has a good job? The owner said he would reduce the price by $10,000! When I went to the lawyer to draw up the papers he would not take my word for it that the loan was interest free. He called the man to confirm. I was able to tell the lawyer that God had done it all, none was my doing. Well, what could he say but wish me more luck!

Now back to Dharangaon again. Girls came to our school from various places but mostly from the Aboriginal Tribes. A Hindu father brought three of his daughters to us from a different area. A few days later I had a letter from him saying that his wife died while he was away. I guess we will never know why because she had been perfectly well when her husband left with the girls. I thought perhaps it had been too hard on her that they went so far away.

Whatever the cause, he told me not to tell the girls until holiday time in about four and a half months. He would then tell them when he came to take them home for three weeks. I was afraid their hearts would break and thought it would be better if he came in between to tell them the very sad news. But he let it go because he wanted them to be able to study unhindered.

Well, these little sisters were so receptive to the gospel message. They had never known of a God that loved them. Pretty soon the middle one received Jesus as Saviour. Then the oldest one and finally the youngest. It was a joy to see them grow so strong in their new found faith. They prayed for their parents to become Christians too. I was very glad that they became Christians because I knew that the Lord would help them face the sad news ahead.

When their Father came for them and told them the news, they cried of course. They arrived home and he set a lovely meal before them. One of the girls said, "Papa, we want to thank God for the food. We have learned about Him and we love Him." The father said, "NO, you cannot pray to a strange God. Our gods are in that corner of the room. You all bow before them and then eat."

His daughters refused to bow before the gods (idols) and would not even face that way. He begged them again but they refused. Then he said, "Alright, then you go without food." They answered kindly, that they would rather not eat than to acknowledge those gods. They did not mind going without food because Jesus meant more to them than food. He was stymied by the strange yet strong witness that they gave. Eventually, he put the food before them again and let them eat but they prayed first.

They came back after vacation, finished the school year and did very well. The next year when it came time to come back he did not allow it. We felt very bad and prayed a lot for them. I discovered that he had put them in a Hindu boarding. I was in their city for a conference and went for a walk. Suddenly these three girls broke away from the rest that they were playing with and clung to me. They told me they had always continued to pray to God and to trust Him. They wanted to come back to our school. I have no idea where they are now. I am sure they are all married. Whenever I think of them I pray that God will watch over those three little lambs. They endured persecution for the sake of Jesus and they were not the only ones.

Palak's (born with club feet) wedding picture. His orphan brother Daniel was best man. On left is Pastor A. D. Chaudhari.

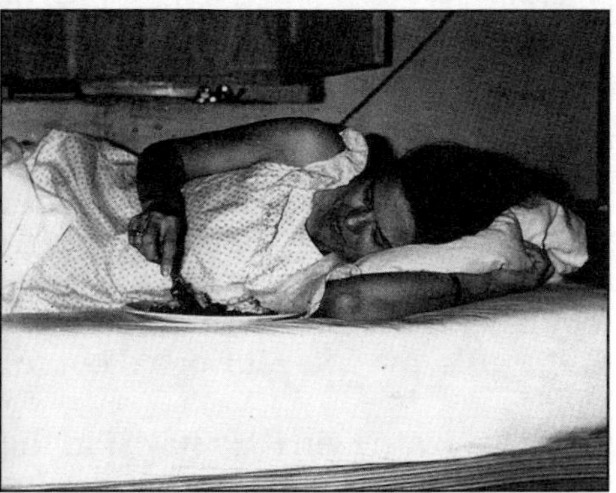

Eating while lying flat as per doctor's orders. Remember the mouse?

CHAPTER 32

Move to Sakri

The Dharangaon School was closed for about two and a half years. When I returned from furlough I was asked to go to Sakri which is more in the area where some of our girls came from. Sakri had a boarding for High School girls on the mission compound. We had some High School girls in Dharangaon but this was just for High School girls. It was going to be very different for me. There were around forty-five girls that attended the High School across the road from us. Later the number was increased to sixty girls. These girls would otherwise have been in Hindu boardings so we tried to avoid that. Their parents wanted them to be where they would receive Christian teaching.

We had daily Bible Classes for them but here we had to have them in the evening because High School started very early in the morning. An Evangelist was stationed there and he took the Sunday morning services.

We did not have a table or chair for the front of the little chapel so we used to carry them over from my house for the service. We received some later on though. I really wanted a little stool that could be left there for when I needed it. I often sat beside the girls when they ate and yes, I tasted the food. Usually just one bite. Makes me hungry now for their food. I did that just to keep the cooks on their toes.

My nearest neighbours were Leslie and Verna Buhler who lived in Pimpalner about seven or eight miles away. Their son Dan was home from school and one day heard I wanted a stool for the boarding. He set to work to make one. His father helped him as Dan was not very old. I really appreciated that. Another time Dan brought us a puppy for the girls in the boarding. I was not as enthused about it at first, but the girls loved it. All worked out for the good, as I will tell you.

That dog grew up and was well fed and loved by the girls. He stayed in the boarding all the time except for his "outdoor" privileges. I had gone away for the day on business. When I walked on to our compound all was quiet, all windows and doors were closed tight which was unusual for daytime. Not one girl in sight anywhere and not a sound.

I went and knocked on the main door. Someone opened it a crack and I asked what was going on. The girl did not want to tell me but the matron came and told me that the dog had ran out on the road and was killed by a truck. They were all so sad and that's why they were all inside. I did not realize how devastated they were until it came time for our Bible Class that evening.

I went into the boarding with my Bible and lesson in hand. I had to walk through their sleeping quarters to get to the chapel(which actually doubled as a sleeping room as well). Usually the girls were seated in neat rows and had started their singing. Tonight there was no singing and I noticed quite a few girls lying on their mats with their heads covered. I could see they had no intention of coming to class. I uncovered the faces of a few of them and asked if they were sick. No answer but I saw they were crying.

It dawned on me just how sad they were. I stood for a minute not knowing exactly what to do. Silently I prayed for guidance. I believe the Lord guided me to put aside the prepared lesson and instead talk about losses that come our way. I said out loud, "Girls, too bad you are not coming to class because I am going to talk about the puppy." Suddenly there was a flurry of blankets being thrown back as they all came to class.

We had a blessed time as I tried to explain to them that all through life we will have problems, disappointments and even death. I used the scriptures to point that out to them. Some will be small, some will be big but I told them how I had enjoyed seeing them take good care of the dog as they played with him. Now he was gone through no fault of theirs. It happens often I said, to dogs and cats, even goats that go out on the road. It's one thing to lose an animal we love but someday all of us will lose members of our family, some sooner, some later. We had a time of prayer and their little hearts were comforted. I used to do that whenever something unusual came up that I had to deal with. I needed to prepare them for what life might hold.

Little did I know that in a few months, on November 9, 1976 I would receive a telegram from my sister Rosa informing me that our dear Mother had died November 6, 1976. I grieved because I would not meet her when I returned to Canada. She would not be there to welcome me with a smile and a big hug. I would not hear her words, "Welcome home, welcome."

I'll tell you what happened immediately after and then how I used the occasion to teach the girls about the death of a child of God, the death of a Mother.

When the telegram came, I went out on the verandah and called to the evangelist who lived with his family just on the other side of the wall. He acknowledged me and I went back to my room to think and cry. About half an hour later he called at my door, "May we come in?" There he was with his wife, the general helper and the matron. He carried his Bible and they all came in to sit down. He told me they had wanted to respect my privacy for half an hour but now they had come to cry with, and comfort me. He read some of the familiar portions of Scripture that relate to the death of a child of God. Then he told me how sorry they were that I was too far away to be able to go home and be with my family and he prayed.

The evangelist prayed such a comforting prayer. It went something like this. "Dear Heavenly Father, Mai has just received such hard news from home that her mother has died. Mai is our sister in the Lord. We are sisters and brothers in You. Since we are sisters and brothers, it is also our Mother that has died. So Lord, while you are comforting our Mai, please comfort us too because we need it. We are all very sad." Then he talked of Heaven and the assurance of meeting again with Jesus. They were probably there about 45 minutes. They all shook hands with me and left. They had truly comforted me. How I thanked God for the bond we have in Christ.

The next day was November 10 and the telegram had stated the funeral would be that day. I sat down in my favourite chair to have my own service. I sang some of Mother's favourite hymns, especially, "There's No Disappointment in Heaven". I read 1 Thess. 4:13-18 and sang another song. I prayed and of course there were many tears but I was not without hope. The Lord was so present and He comforted me though I was 10,000 miles away from the rest of the family. I felt the prayers and love of my family and my home church, Grace Evangelical Bible Church in Abbotsford, BC where Rev. Ken (and Sandra) Quiring was the pastor at that time.

Mother had missed our Father so very much after he died. So though I grieved, I also rejoiced with both of them. They had been married on that very date in 1904. In my mind, I could picture Dad standing beside Jesus waiting to welcome his bride, just like the groom stands besides the best men. That's probably not the way it happened in Heaven, but it comforted me that they were together again on their original wedding date!

The boarding girls had lots of questions about where my Mother was now. What was it like to die? Was my Mother afraid? After a week or so when I could talk about it a bit easier, I told them we would devote one Bible Class to the subject of death. It gave me time to study and ask the Lord for wisdom. I remember using the blackboard and drawing something that was supposed to look like a wall.

We, the living, were on this side of the wall. On the other side of the wall was Eternity. The wall represents death but the wall is not a dead end. As we come to it, the door opens and we pass from this life to the life beyond. We are not alone though because Jesus sends His angels to carry us through the door called death. Then immediately we see the Light of Heaven and Jesus. That is where my Mother was and she was not afraid. How could she be afraid when the angels carried her and told her they were taking her to Jesus? That is how it is going to be for all of us when we die if we have accepted Jesus as our Saviour.

There was more to the lesson that day but this much will suffice. You may not picture death the way I did, but that is how the Lord comforted me and how I related it to them. You should have seen them smile! I always felt my responsibility to take the need of the moment and help the girls understand it in a way that would help them as they grew up to be women of God. In many ways, I was the Mother figure for them for about ten and a half months out of each year. I must be able to give an account to their mothers and especially to God.

Remember, I was still in Sakri where these things happened. There's another "hands on" lesson to learn at the end of this next story. One day the evangelist asked me to take prayer meeting as he did now and then, as well as the Sunday morning services. I was all prepared for prayer meeting when one of the girls named Payli came and asked if she could give her testimony first. She had it all written out neatly so I agreed. I did not know her story so was very glad to have a chance to hear it. Payli had braces on both legs and walked with crutches. She was a very sweet girl with a BIG smile.

Payli gave me a copy of her testimony so I will try to translate it as closely as I can, as well as add what I learned later on. She writes, I was born in an

Animist home in Patsamba (means five mangoes). My condition was very sad and difficult because I was born with deformed lower limbs. My mother thought the evil spirits were punishing her by giving her a child like me. I was born in the shape of a ball. My left leg was twisted around the right side of my neck. My right leg was twisted around the opposite side of my neck. My arms were sort of entwined among my legs.

When the midwife saw me she showed me to my Mother. My mother shrieked with horror and fright. She told the woman to quickly choke me but she put me aside while she took care of my Mother. Then she took me outside to....But as tiny as I was, I opened my eyes really wide and stared at the woman as if to say, "what are you doing?" The woman released her fingers from my throat. She took me back to my Mother and told her that I just would not stop breathing.

My Mother tried to starve me to death. She also tried to poison me in order to get rid of the curse on my family. I don't remember ever sitting on my Mother or Father's knees. None of my family or relatives loved me. There were kind neighbours who were won by my smile. They would take turns asking my mother to sit down while they held me for her to nurse. They also got my arms straightened out by massaging them. They did the same for my legs but my legs would not bend at my knees. When I got a little older I learned to walk on four legs like a dog, meaning she walked on her hands and feet. I got around the village that way and the neighbours gave me food and clothes when I came around.

As I grew I began to wish I had never been born. Sometimes I would go away from the village and I'd look up and cry to God and ask Him why He made me this way. You gave me life, you can take it away, I would tell God.

Even in my condition my parents enrolled me in the village school where I suffered at the hands of the children. I finished standard four, for that's as far as the school went. I never knew anything about the true and living God and my parents didn't either. I did not know any Christians. Then one day a couple of TEAM missionaries named Wayne and Evelyn Saunders came to our village. They brought some pastors along who could speak our local Mauchi language. They all lived in tents.

Mrs. Saunders stayed by the tents while the men went out to preach the gospel (only I did not know that that's what they were doing). I was walking on all fours like a dog and went to see Mrs. Saunders for something to do. When I came around the side of her chair she was startled. I smiled and talked to her. She asked if I would like to go to Dharangaon to attend a girl's school. I asked my parents for permission and they readily agreed for they were glad to not have me around. Mrs. Saunders got me some clothes, a small tin suitcase and took me to Dharangaon.

There I gradually learned about a loving God. I wanted to love Him too but could not. I was bitter. If He really loved me, He would not have formed me this way. So I listened to the Bible Stories, the prayers and sang the happy songs. When it rained and all the girls were running to school from the boarding I would get wet because I had to go slower. Often one of the girls would just scoop me up and carry me.

Katie Iobst was in Dharangaon at that time. She had visitors from the USA.

One man was an orthopaedic surgeon. When he saw me walking across the yard he asked Miss Iobst who or what I was. After she told him a bit about me, he asked her to call me so he could examine my legs. He smiled and said, "If only I could do surgery on her, she'd be able to walk upright." He promised to go back home and send money for my surgery if there was a hospital that could do it. She told the couple about the Christian hospital in Miraj.

He did send money very soon and I got permission from my parents to go far away to Miraj. Before I go on with that I want to tell you once I left home for Dharangaon, my parents told me not to come back. All the other girls went home for holidays but I stayed.

My parents gave permission gladly. I had to have someone with me to cook for me and wash my clothes as was standard procedure in India. My brother Mohan and a pastor accompanied me. I stayed in that hospital for two years because I had multiple surgeries on my hips, knees and feet. I took my books along and studied in between surgeries. I am very grateful to my brother for staying with me. He ended up getting a job as cook for the doctor and is still there.

A Mrs. Howard was chaplain at the hospital. She often came to my room to cheer me up and bring me goodies when I had so much pain after surgery. She also told me more about Jesus who loved me. I did not want to hear about that because He was letting me suffer so much now, besides having made me the way I was. I was also very much afraid before each operation. She kept on being very kind to me.

The time came when I did not need any more surgery. Then my doctor fitted me with two braces for my legs and gave me a pair of crutches. I had to learn to walk on only two legs! When I managed that, I was discharged and went back to Dharangaon.

About February 1973, there were special meetings held for the boarding girls. I was listening to all the messages that Mr. Shiwaji Gavit gave, but still resisting God's love. One day he spoke on John 1:12. Then I realized what a sinner I was and that I must believe in Jesus before He could take my sins away. Right there I prayed and confessed all my sins. I knew He had forgiven them. It was on a Thursday at 10:00 A.M. that I became a Christian. Since then God's Word has become very precious to me and I read it every day. I also pray every day. God has helped me ever since and I am so thankful.

When the holidays came I wrote to my parents and told them I could walk on two legs now. Could I please come home to show them how I could walk? They invited me to come and I was very happy. This time my parents came by bullock cart to meet me at the railway station. When I left for school I had to walk on all four for several miles. For the first time in my life my parents hugged me and I saw tears in their eyes. They were so happy and so was I.

When I arrived in the village, a cot was put down for me to sit on. Someone came with a blanket to spread on the cot first. Then I was served a lovely cup of tea. All the neighbours gathered around to look at me and ask many questions. This was not the Payli they had known. I sang some Christian songs for them and they liked it. At night I slept with my grandmother. She had missed me very much. Before I slept I told her I would pray. Grandma was happy that I was happy. Everybody's attitude toward me changed.

I went back to Dharangaon and learned more about God and His Word. When the holidays came I was able to go home like the others. Each time I witnessed to my family and the villagers. Eventually, my parents and Grandma became Christians. Since then a TEAM church has been started in that village. Now I knew it was because of me that they became Christians. Then she ended that part of her testimony by saying that she actually has thanked God many times for allowing her to be born deformed. For it was because of that that she, her parents and the villagers came to know God and believe in Him. Bless her heart! I cried when she read that part and so did some of the girls. From here on, I will tell the rest of Payli's precious story.

As I said, I did not know that part of her life. I met her in Sakri in October, 1975. I only saw her smiling. She needed some help from the other girls but she was always so thankful. There was never a shortage of help for her. In turn she helped them with their Math because she was a very clever girl.

I made it a practice of having calendars in the boarding with a scripture verse for each day, in Marathi of course. I encouraged the girls to be sure to have their devotions before starting the day. If by any chance something unforseen happened and they did not have time I told them that on their way out of their room they might stop by the calendar and read the verse for the day.

It was a July day in 1976, and it was Payli's birthday. I did not know about it. She made a special effort to read the verse that day for it might hold something for her. The verse was from Isaiah 40 part of verse 4, "And the crooked shall be made straight." She took that as a promise that she would be able to walk upright. You see the doctor had given her very short crutches so she had to walk bent over.

As a result the upper part of her body was heavy and strong. Her lower part was very small and thin. The other girls came to tell me that Payli was beginning to tumble over on her head when she walked. They were afraid she might fall in front of a speeding lorry and be run over while crossing the road to school so I began to watch her.

Well, I came to the conclusion that her crutches were too short and made her top heavy. I could easily remedy that by getting her crutches lengthened. I sent a note to the principal that Payli would be staying home because her crutches needed fixing. I sent a man with a note and the crutches to our mission hospital in Chinchpada to have them lengthened by so many inches.

Everything went well and I presented the crutches to Payli. She was all smiles as she tried them out. We had averted what could have been a catastrophe! Then she told me about the verse she had received and how she trusted God to fulfill it. God had honoured her faith she told me. I was delighted to have had a part in it unknowingly.

All went well until Dr. Ormie Uptigrove came by one day on his motorcycle for a drink of water. He was on his way home to Chinchpada. He had been in Dhule. He just happened to see Payli walking with her new crutches. He asked who had given her longer crutches. I confessed and he told me that the doctor in Miraj did not want her to put so much weight on her young shoulders for a few years. I had not known that and felt bad.

He asked that she come over and walk for him on my verandah so he could assess the situation. She came and no peacock was ever prouder than she! Of course, she wore one of her convincing smiles! She walked back and forth a couple of times. Then Dr. Ormie said to me with damp eyes, "Annie, you did the right thing. It has done so much for her morale. It was probably time to lengthen them anyway. It's okay." Both Payli and I were grateful for his gracious words and that no harm had been done. Payli now is probably about 37 years old. She is a telephone operator in a big hospital not far from Miraj.

I forgot to tell you that Payli told me that since the day she read that verse on the calendar, her legs got feeling in them and they got warm. I used to try to get her stockings or socks because her feet were always so cold. That was a miracle because her feet were always so cold they hurt.

Just before I was transferred back to Dharangaon to open the school again, I had prayer with Payli. She told me that she had a burden for people that were handicapped like she was. She hoped she could take a chaplain's course somewhere and minister to handicapped people in various hospitals. She went back to Miraj and took a course in typing and later a telephone operator's course. Her name Payli means feet. If it were a male and his feet and legs were deformed he would be called Payla.

Before I started this story I told you that her testimony afforded a wonderful opportunity to teach the girls another lesson on life. That day at prayer meeting, when Payli finished her testimony the girls asked, "Mai, why did God allow that and similar things to happen to people?"

The first thing I said was a sentence from Payli's own mouth. "If I had not been born like this, I probably would never have heard about Jesus Christ, nor would my family, nor my village. Now I actually thank Him for making me this way." What God allows is for our good and His glory, though we may not understand it now, nor for a long time to come. Someday we will and though we may not understand, we can still trust Him to bring it all out to a desired end. Payli asked God to take her life and later she asked for healing. God did neither but instead He gave her Eternal Life.

Then I thought of Exodus 4:11, where the Lord asks Moses some questions. "Who hath made man's mouth? or who maketh the dumb, or deaf, or the seeing, or the blind? Have not I, the Lord?" It is God that gives life.

I told the girls that we all see how Payli struggles to get along in life. Everything she does is an effort. We all would like to see her healed but we also see the grace that God gives to her each day to put up with her infirmity. Often we cannot change our circumstances or the people we live or work with, and God does not either. He wants to make the change in us, so we can respond properly. There's a big difference between reacting to people and circumstances, and responding to life the way He wants us to.

CHAPTER 33

Arranged Marriages: History and Examples

This is a controversial subject here in the Western World. Most people think it is horrible but after seeing marriages break up here, I think it might not be a bad idea to have parents involved more in the decision making. I have mentioned it to young people and they mostly groan. Some change their mind after I explain the benefits. I am no authority on that subject but I have seen benefits when it's done under the Lord's guidance. Recently a 25 year old young man came to me and said, "I need to and want to get married but it's so hard to find the right girl. Will you pray for me, Annie?" I assured him I would and offered to tell him and any of his friends about how I arranged marriages in India. He has not taken me up on that but I hope he will. Maybe he is afraid I will set something up for him! No fear!

You say that's my view because I am not married, that I have no idea of what it's like. That is very true, I don't dispute that. I have had my opportunities and each time it was not God's will. I am not against marriage at all. It is wonderful to see happily married couples but my slogan now is, "Better be single, than wish you were!" I know plenty of people who wish they were not single and plenty who wish they were. So each must seek God's will in the matter.

What seems so sad to me is to see a couple struggle so in their marriage and finally decide on divorce without ever telling their parents (especially if they are Christians). I have had them tell me about it and then end up by saying, "neither of our parents have a clue about this so please don't tell them. It would break their hearts." Well, it breaks their hearts in the end anyway! I know there is the danger of them taking sides (it is so easy to do) and making things worse. So, they tell their friends instead but we all know that the parents care the most and would do anything to help. May God help our land of the Americas.

In India, especially among non-Christians (and even among some Christians) the question of dowry having to be repaid in the case of divorce, usually keeps the parents very much involved in how the young couple gets along.

The question of a dowry never came up in the marriage arrangements we as missionaries made. Usually when you marry into a family, you marry the whole family. That's true here too, I think. The boy stays with his parents, but the girl leaves her parents to go and live with her in-laws. If the boy is educated and has a job elsewhere, as often is the case in modern India, the couple live by themselves. That means they have room (and money?) to have either hers or his younger sibling(s) live with them. Then the young man has to pay for their schooling and clothes. I never thought that to be a good idea.

In the case of an orphan, they were quite popular, because they knew the orphan siblings would not come and live with them. Nor did I (we) demand things that other families might demand like expensive saris for myself for the wedding, or for the other orphan sisters of the bride. That was much less expense for the boy's parents. Sometimes, the boy's parents paid for the entire expense, for clothes, for both the bride and groom and the reception. Other times, we split all the expenses depending on the situation of the boy's parents. The mission paid for it, not I.

Orphans were also popular because the in-laws to be knew that the girl would not keep wanting to go back home, or run away. That was because as soon as they were all married there would no longer be a home to come back to. Well, there was, as long as I was still there. They also knew I would not always be there because I would retire. The orphans themselves felt so blessed that someone would come and ask for them. Their own parents had given them away and they felt rejected. Now they were happy to have someone they could call Mama and Papa so they usually tried their best to please the husband and in-laws to make the marriage work.

Among the non-Christians often the two young people did not have much or any say, as to who they married. That is how it had always been done. If they objected it usually did no good. Often a young girl would be married to a much older man because he had money. That I think is changing a bit in modern India. More are finding their own mates and asking their parents to arrange it for them.

I often discovered though that they themselves don't expect a 'love marriage' to last, if their parents have not been involved. Sometimes when travelling on a train or bus I'd see a woman by herself with one or two children. No one else. Usually a man or boy accompanies a woman when she goes home to visit her parents. Then one of them brings her back. I'd ask the young mother if she was going home to see her parents. She would say, "yes, I am going to stay with them now. You see my marriage was a 'love marriage.'" It was just a given that those marriages don't work. It signifies something from the movies.

The non-Christians often demand such high dowries that they are unattainable. They send the young wife back to her parents after about a month and tell her she has to return with certain gifts from her parents. Sometimes, it might be a table and chairs(for prestige), a very expensive wall clock or even a scooter. She is told not to return without the item. If her parents cannot fill the bill, the girl feels so scared and helpless that she may kill herself by jumping in the well. Or, if she dares to return without it, they may pour gas on her and set her on fire.

So not all the arranged marriages work well but there is a difference between those and the Christians'. I have heard of instances (among Hindus) where two pregnant women would arrange a marriage between their yet unborn children. Even those people that do not know God, know that an unborn child is a human being.

The abortionists here try to convince people that it's a blob or tissue. May God have mercy! Of course, those two mothers were hoping one had a girl and the other a boy. If perchance, the boy died at birth or soon thereafter, the wee little girl was considered a widow. The child's hair would be shaved and she might have to stay that way the rest of her life. She could never marry and was looked down upon. She may have been the cause of her 'husband's' death.

There are things I could tell you about a widow having to throw herself on the funeral pyre of her husband but this is not a book about running down a country or its customs. I will go on to tell you how we (I) did the marriage arrangements. Not all of us did it the same. For a short time we had a lovely single Christian woman in charge of the orphans so she made some of the arrangements. We were trying to indigenise.

I have mentioned my dear friend and colleague Gladys Henriksen many times (she went to Heaven in May 1999). I wish she could read this book. When Gladys retired I asked her to leave me her 'mantle.' She promised she would pray for me and all the orphans every day. She did that till her dying day. She went very suddenly while in Bible Study at the Home where she was being cared for.

After she retired, it seemed like a whole lot of suitors came. Almost as if a sign had been put up over the door, "Under New Management." It kind of frightened me. Now I had to do it all alone. Yet not alone for the Lord was there to help me.

It was rather sad the way I did it the first few times. When parents came with their boy I would go and ask one of the girls if she would like to be married to him. She said no without even coming to see him. I asked the next one and her answer was the same. I think I went down the list and all gave the same answer so I told the party the answer was no. Well, the next party came and the same thing happened. I think it happened about three times. This was not good advertising.

A custom I was unaware of was that you never tell a man and his parents an outright, "No". You thank them for coming and give them tea. Then you tell them that you will think it over and let them know. Most often that answer meant no and they knew it, but you did not say that word. Sometimes it meant I wanted some time to send a spy, as it were, to find out more about the family. That was necessary because some would lie about their age, their job and whether they were Christians or not. My first item of 'business' was always to inquire about their salvation.

To tell a party no is an outright affront to their dignity. We have all seen here how it affects people when they get ditched by a lover. If you did say no, word would get around and it would be very hard for those parents to find a wife for their son. For sure there must be something terribly wrong or the answer would not have been so harsh. I got guidance from the Christian women regarding customs before I made any more mistakes.

SUCCESSFUL MARRIAGE ARRANGEMENTS

After those initial failures, I decided I'd better get a plan that would work. I called all the orphan girls to my room for a conference. I told them if they always said no, I would not be able to get any of them married. I asked them why they all had said no. Their answer surprised me and made me cry. They said they always wanted to stay with me because no one loved them like I did.

A mother-in-law might not be so good to live with. That blessed my heart.

Then I told them how I appreciated that but I would not always be there with them. The time would come for me to have to leave India permanently. I said I would rather get them all married and settled in their own homes. I'd like to see my grandchildren so I could go to my country comforted that they were all settled and happy. When I'd pray for them, I'd be able to picture them with their husband and children in their homes.

This was my plan, I told them, when someone comes for a wife, I will say I don't have a girl right now. If you decide after what we've talked over now, that you do want to get married after all, then come and tell me.

That made a difference and I believe an answer to prayer. Two weeks later one of the girls came to see me. I asked her what she wanted but she could not voice it. I waited a bit and asked her again. This time very shyly she said, "You asked us to come and see you." "Oh, about what?" I had a pretty good idea but I wanted her to say it. She finally said, "You asked us..if...we.." "So, is that what you want?" "Yes."

"Alright," I said, "I'm glad to hear that. What do you think we should do about it?" "Pray!" We bowed our heads and she said she would pray first. This is what she prayed. "Dear Lord, the time has come for me to get married. But Mai does not know who or where the man is but you do. Mai has brought me up to love you and prepared me for marriage. Somewhere, there is a mother that has brought up a son in the same way. Please send those parents with their son to Mai. Amen." You can imagine how moved I was by her prayer. Such simple faith. I prayed too but with tears of joy. Then I told her that we had told God we would wait and He would answer.

We did not have long to wait. This girl was working in the kitchen in the boarding when they came. After I told them about her I sent my cook to call her. She came right in and asked what I wanted. I asked her if she would go to the headmistress and get a piece of chalk for me. She had no idea what was going on because I often had strangers drop in. While she was gone I asked them if they would be interested in her. When she brought the chalk, they saw her again.

Yes, they were interested so while they had tea I went to the kitchen and told my girl that the people in my living room had come for a girl. They had seen her when she brought the chalk and they would like to see her again. I asked her to do her hair and change her sari and come back. I also asked her to please take a good look at him and his parents when I introduced her to them.

She came back looking so nice. She sat on the chair beside me and I asked her if the cooking was almost finished. I just made talk so they could listen to how she talked to me and see her better. Then I turned to the boy and asked him and his parents some general questions. That gave her an opportunity to get a good look at him and hear his voice.

At the opportune time I told them I would take my daughter to my bedroom and talk to her so they could talk to each other too. I asked her what she thought. Would she be interested in him? I asked her to wait while I went back to talk to them. Yes, they were interested. Would she come back out?

I went and got her for she had said she would be interested. The atmosphere was more relaxed and I had tried to keep it that way from the beginning. Pretty soon we were talking about a wedding date, which I preferred was no more than two weeks hence. First we must have an engagement party that afternoon. So off to town they went to buy her a green sari, some green bangles, sandals, and a blouse piece. I'm afraid I never found out why the colour green and nobody I asked about it knew.

The church board got involved and interviewed the family in a relaxed way. Next we all gathered on my side verandah for a short service during which the pastor announced the engagement, read scripture and prayed for the couple. They sat side by side on a mat on the floor in the front. Then the parents served sweets and tea to the adults that were present,(children did not come for this). The parents and their son went home and came back in two weeks.

In the next two Sunday services, the pastor announced the wedding bands. My job was to get her bedding and clothes ready to go to her new home. I asked the matron to teach her how to take the right proportions of flour, oil, sugar, and spices for different dishes for two people. She had been used to helping with the cooking for nearly two hundred.

All day long I kept asking the Lord to keep us all in His will for these two. If it was not of Him, would He show us. Everything went well, but when I went to bed I asked myself what I had done. What if it did not work out? What if they were not happy? You know arranging for our children's marriages was one of the hardest things I had to do. Before I fell asleep that night, the Lord had restored peace to my heart and mind.

Now a few words about the wedding. Four chairs (usually from my dining room) were placed in the church in front of the platform. That was for the bridal couple, a bride's maid and the best man. Yes, they sat down for the service. One of the bride's older sisters would bring her into the church. The other orphan girls and I followed them. The girls all went and sat down while I stayed standing behind the couple. When the pastor asked who gives this woman away, I came forward and stood in front of the couple. While I said, "I Do" I took her hand and placed it in the groom's hand. That was hard and I always cried. It seemed so final to do that.

A YOUNG BRIDE RETURNED

I am not sure exactly how many marriages I arranged but probably about ten. All had gone well. One day as I was having my morning coffee on the back verandah I saw a couple walking in the direction of our gate. I watched and soon I recognized them. They had been married about six months.

The woman always walks about ten feet behind her husband. That has always puzzled me because anything could happen to her, especially if she is carrying a small child. From what I observed, the man does not take a glance behind him either. Maybe he has eyes on the back of his head like some teachers do! This wife was walking farther behind him than that and I said to myself, "Oh, Oh, trouble must be coming."

I put my cup down and went out toward the gate to welcome them. "Lord, give me wisdom." I prayed. As soon as I got close enough to him, he started to tell me how bad the wife was that I had given him. He was bringing her back and would repay expenses I had for the wedding. I shook his hand and said, "Let's wait with everything. I'll give you both some water to drink. Then we'll make tea. Then it will be lunch time and after lunch the three of us will sit down and talk." That satisfied him. I hugged, kissed and welcomed my daughter and we went into my house. While they had tea, I went into my bedroom for a quick prayer asking God for His wisdom.

During lunch we made small talk about general things like his work. We sat around my table and I told them that I wanted to hear both sides. I wanted each to tell me in front of the other that way there would be no talking behind their backs. I also asked them to please not interrupt the other one. I would hear both out.

He said he would start. He said that his wife does not cook for him and does not wash his clothes. I asked her if that was true. She said it was so I asked for her reasons for not cooking for him first. She told me that because he had been a bachelor, the neighbour women felt sorry for him. When he came home tired from work he had to make his own meal. One or the other of them would bring him his curry every evening. All he had to do was make the chappatis which did not take very long. This was the routine to which they all got used to.

BUT of course, since they were married, she had made the curry and the bread too. When they sat down to eat, she would serve him his food on his plate, as any wife would but then a neighbour woman would still bring a small dish of her curry and set it in front of him saying, "You eat." In order not to hurt her, he would eat it instead of his wife's curry. She finished by telling me that because of this she just cooked enough curry for herself.

I verified with him if that was what was happening and he said it was. I asked him if he saw anything wrong with what he had been doing. He did not. I then told him that before I gave him a girl in marriage I had investigated from the missionaries and nationals as to what kind of man he was. I said because they all gave you a very good recommendation I gave you a very good girl. I appreciate the fact that the neighbours took good care of you because you were going to be my future son-in-law. I would like to thank them.

"However, now you are married, your obligation is to your wife, to not hurt her feelings. Isn't that right?" "Yes." "I do not blame your wife for not cooking for you." I addressed him as Zavai (son-in-law) and said there is something you can do that will take care of it all. "What is that?" "You can go to your neighbours and thank them very much for having brought you delicious curry every evening. Then tell them that you are now married and your wife is cooking for you. They will not need to take such trouble from now on. Can you, and will you do that for your wife and for me?" He agreed that would be good. I pointed out to them both that those women should have known better!! They could bring a taste of curry over once in a while but they should set it in front of her. Then she could divide it between them as was Indian custom.

"My daughter, now that the cooking question is settled, tell me why you don't wash his clothes?" "Mai, this is what happened. As with the cooking, the neighbour women felt sorry for him having to wash his clothes after he came from work...."

Now let me describe what happened. These government quarters had a small corner on the front verandah arranged as a bathing place. A big flat stone was put there on which they sat for a bath. The water would run off through a hole. A flimsy cloth curtain made it kind of private. Across the corner a string was tied over which they would throw their dirty clothes. As soon as he had gone to work, the women came and took his clothes and washed them with their husband's then returned them to the string all clean and folded neatly.

After my girl had done the breakfast dishes, she'd go out to get his clothes and wash them on the stone along with hers. They wash them every day because they do it by hand. The first morning she came out his clothes were gone. She did not know what had happened to them but in the afternoon they'd appear all clean hung over the string. The next day the same thing happened. She told him and he said that was what they had always done for him. She told him she wanted to wash them. Again he said he could not hurt those women. So she said to him if that's what he wanted then they could keep doing it!?!

Again, I addressed my Zavai and asked if that was a pretty accurate account of what had been going on. He said it was. Gently I tried to get him to see how that would hurt his wife. I added that, "I am not married, but if I was, and my husband worked as hard as you do, I would want to wash his clothes. He would be supporting me and I would want to wash that sweat out of his clothes myself not have our neighbour women do it." My voice broke when I said that. I asked him if he could see how much his wife loved him and that she wanted to do his cooking and washing.

Then he started to cry and asked me to forgive him. Joy welled up in my heart that God was working, that a soft chord had been struck in his heart. She began to cry and asked him to forgive her because she should have been a better wife. He was very sorry that he had caused his wife such heartache and me as well. I assured him that I had forgiven him and his wife would too.

Next I asked what we should do. He said to ask God for forgiveness. I agreed that all sin is against God but that He will so gladly forgive when we confess it to Him and to one another. We all prayed through tears.

The wonderful thing was that when the last amen was said we all looked up smiling. God had done a wonderful work. He thanked me, they both did. Then he looked at her and said, "if Mai will give us permission, come let's go home!" I wanted them to stay overnight but he had to be at work the next day. He just took one day off to return his wife! God had other plans. Praise the Lord! They went back home and God has blessed them with three children.

There was one more complaint but not from him. This came in the form of a letter from one of my Zavais. He said he had a very good wife, and he thanked me for her but she spent too much money on food. Especially too much on oil since it was very expensive and rationed but she was a very good cook.

Then I realized that in her case I had forgotten, or neglected, to have the matron teach her before she got married what amounts to use for only two people. She too was used to cooking for so many girls in the boarding. I told him it was my mistake. Since he had been a bachelor for quite a few years, he knew what quantities to use for one. Would he be so kind as to measure out twice that amount of flour, oil, and sugar for her before he went to work for a few days? I told him that I was pretty sure that would help.

Nabhuji and Suvarta Nikhali.

Well, in about three weeks he wrote again. I was not sure if I wanted to open it but he was happy. He said he took my advice and now they had more money but her food did not taste as good as it had before!! We say you can't win for losing, don't we? About six months after that I was going on furlough and I went to visit this couple in their little mud hut. He was a cured leper and a cobbler by trade. He is retired now.

After the meal we sat outside to visit. He started to tell me what a good wife he had. He was the only leper there that had a clean wife (meaning non-leper). That seemed to put him a few notches above the other cured lepers. He got up and went into the hut. He came out with a little hand towel and wiped his tears as he wept and told me how blessed and happy he was. That made his mother-in-law very thankful. They have two boys who are both married. The last few letters have told me that he has cancer of the throat and not long to live. It makes me sad. I pray their faith may not falter.

When he was a baby, he contracted leprosy from his mother. One night she took him to the front door of the Leprosy Hospital in Paratwada and left him there. He does not know his family but like Payli, he thanks God that he got leprosy so that he would be brought to the Christian Hospital where he was raised. Especially because he was introduced to the Lord Jesus. Pray for Nabhuji and his family.

CHAPTER 34

Miscellaneous

On my furlough of 1969, I rented an apartment in Abbotsford in order to be closer to my parents. They were in Valhaven Home on Mt. Lehman Road and had been there for about four years. When I first came home I did deputation work. As time went on Dad's legs gave out because of bone cancer. Mother pushed him to the dining room in a wheelchair for each meal. It was getting harder for her to push Dad because she had a pacemaker. We all wondered what should be done since the Home felt they needed more care than they were licensed to give. While we were praying about this I continued (as all the family did) to visit them. But more about that later.

I also often got a call from someone to go and talk to their relative or friend in hospital who was terminally ill. My doctor at the time, sometimes asked me to talk to his patients who were dying in hospital. It was a joy to be with them when they asked Jesus to forgive their sins and be their Saviour. Quite a few times they died a couple of days later.

I had a neighbour on the floor where I lived who was not a Christian. I will call her Ann. She was very disturbed because her husband, her Mother and her son had all committed suicide. She felt she would too. I talked with her about coming to Jesus but she always said another day would be better.

I had gone to Vancouver to meet some missionaries whose ship was docking there for a day. I could not find them and discovered later that another couple had been there and taken them out for the day. I was disappointed but there was nothing I could do but return to Abbotsford early.

When I got back Ann came out of her room which was next to mine. As it happened(?) she was coming to knock on my door. She had already knocked several times. Now she was going to try one more time. If I still was not back she was going to jump from her fifth floor patio. I had witnessed to her and now she was ready to accept Jesus but because I had not been home she felt God was telling her He did not want her to come to Him.

I invited her into my suite and she asked Jesus to come into her heart. She was so thankful I had come home when I did. I understood then why I was not able to meet those missionaries. If I had, I would have stayed with them all day. Ann was different after that but she still had mental problems. I heard several years later when I came on furlough again that indeed Ann had taken her own life. I was very sad.

Another time when I was locking my door on my way to the hospital, Ann came out at exactly the same time. She asked me if I was going to the hospital to "save" people. It so happened, I told her that I was on my way to visit a friend in hospital. She said, "While you are there, you might as well go and save "Devil Mr. B." She further told me he was 84 years old and was the wickedest person she had ever seen and he was dying. I don't remember what I told her, if anything.

On the way, I asked the Lord to guide me. If I find him Lord, and if you want me to talk to him, have him open the subject. It seems to me they had patient's names posted on the door of each ward so I found him at once. It was a two bed ward and I went in to see which was Mr. B. He was the one in the bed behind the pulled curtain. I was not going to go in thinking the nurse might be with him but his roommate said to go because he kept his curtain drawn all the time.

I walked over and called him by name and asked if I might visit him. He invited me over. I told him that he did not know me and I did not know him. I introduced myself and told him that a friend of mine had asked me to go and see him. So how was he? I saw before he answered that he indeed was gravely ill. He was propped up with a bunch of pillows, his breathing was bad, his lips were blueish and his voice very weak.

His answer to my query came with a lot of swearing. Excuse me, but I will tell you what he said. "God damn the hospital, the nurses, the doctors, the bed, the medicine, and the food. Each category prefaced by those two words. When he stopped, I spoke. "Mr. B. now that you have opened up the subject, how are things between you and God? I can see you are very sick." His answer, "Everything is fine. I have never done anything bad so I am not concerned. God will accept me the way I am when I die."

Oh, Mr. B. I said, "can you really say that? I can't. I have done things I should not have done, and said things I should not have. I have not done things and said things I should have done and said." Then tears came to his eyes and he said I must say the same as you. I am bad. I am too bad for God to accept and forgive.

I did not say anything but quietly started to sing, "Just as I am and waiting not, to rid my soul of one dark blot. But that Thou bids't me come to Thee, Oh Lamb of God, I come. I come." He brought his hands together as if folded in prayer, his lips began to move as the tears ran down his cheeks. He was praying quietly as I sang. I did not even pray with him. I did not need to. As I finished singing, his wife came around the curtain to visit him. I introduced myself to her and left.

That was the only time I ever saw him. I left the next morning for a wedding in Victoria. When I returned two days later the first concern I had was to go to hospital to see Mr. B. When I came to his room, his roommate asked me what on earth I had told him that day. He told me Mr. B. was a changed man. He never swore after that and was gracious to everyone. So I told him about our conversation, how I sang and that I believed he had accepted Jesus as his Saviour. I then asked him if he had done that and he said no, but that he would after I left because he had seen such a tremendous change in Mr. B.

I asked him what had happened to Mr. B. He told me that after supper that day, he had gone into a coma and the nurses moved his bed to another ward. I looked in the paper and there was his obituary. I was at peace that Mr. B. had gone to Heaven.

When I saw Ann again she asked me if I had talked to Mr. B. that day. I told her I had and also told her about our conversation. What's more, I said, I believe he is in Heaven. She was very upset. She said he did not deserve to have his sins forgiven and go to Heaven. He had been too wicked. I explained to her that God is not like we are. His love extends grace to anyone who will ask for it. My thoughts went to Jonah and the Ninevites. They repented and God forgave then Jonah was angry with God for having forgiven them. How human we all are!

STAYING HOME TO CARE FOR OUR PARENTS

I told you my family was concerned about where our parents could go. Well, the Lord had a plan and it happened so naturally. One day I brought our parents to my apartment for lunch in the high rise. Mother was very impressed with the lovely apartment. After lunch she asked if there were any vacant rooms. I told her there were. Then she asked me to take her to the caretaker so he could show her one. He took us to one the ninth floor that had two large patio doors facing east so you could see all of downtown.

She said to him that she and Dad wanted to rent it. In fact, she said she wanted to stay there that night. It was so much brighter than the Home where they were and they had a view. I talked to my sisters about it and they tactfully asked me if I was willing to stay indefinitely to care for them. I said I would because they were both not well at all and I felt it might be a year before they would be unable to stay there. The Lord would take them Home and then I would return to India.

I believe it was three days from then that we moved them into that apartment. They were very happy there and spent most of each day looking out. Dad in his wheelchair and Mother in a rocker. They were so contented. Suddenly, it dawned on me that my desire to care for my parents had been fulfilled! When they really needed me, I was there. God moved all the pieces into place so neatly that I was not even fully aware of what He was doing. He had put that desire there to begin with and now He was fulfilling it. I thank God for it.

That one year stretched out to five years and nine months. I was never sorry and still am not that I had stayed home. It was hard to see them go down slowly. For the first two years or so I slept in my place and was with them all day. Later, I slept in their living room because they so often needed me at night. They enjoyed the visits from the rest of the family there as well as visits from their friends at Grace church. When visitors would ask Dad how he was, he would say, "I am helpless but not hopeless."

Dad's condition worsened and he asked to be moved to the Menno Home. He knew it was too hard for Mother to take care of him any longer. He was there almost two months and the Lord took him Home very suddenly on October 24, 1973. That was three years after they moved into the apartment.

I continued to care for Mother for about two more years. Her memory had deteriorated a lot the day Dad passed away. The shock was too much. One day she said to me, "Child, how long are you going to stay here to take care of me? You go back. Your children in India need you. I will stay one month with each of my other children." She did that but I was not sure if it would work out so I stayed home until the fall of 1975.

ORPHAN REUNIONS

While I was home those years I began to think how good it would be if I could invite all the orphans back to Dharangaon for a reunion when I returned to India. I spoke at a ladies' meeting not long before I left. One of the ladies asked me if there was something special on my heart that they could pray for. At once, I said, 'orphan reunion' and that it was a big undertaking. I did not even know if it would be feasible but that it was a burden on my heart. You see, there was no one that kept in contact with them, for they were scattered all over Maharashtra State after they were married. I had a burden to bring them home to where they had all been brought in as babies so they could see each other.

That lady was Frieda Martens. She told her husband Henry about what I had said. Henry said, "She'll need money if she's going to do that. Give her a cheque for $200." You know it had not even entered my mind that I would need money! So before I called the Martens answered! That proved such a blessing because through it the Lord seemed to confirm to me that the burden I had was from Him.

I was stationed in Sakri but I am backtracking a wee bit. I arrived in Sakri in October 1975. I had decided that Christmas would be a good time to have the reunion so I sent out letters of invitation to them all. I also invited Gladys to return for it from Chicago where she was retired. I felt it would not be complete without everybody's dear Mai.

I had heard that Roy and Adelina Martens (formerly in India) would be visiting some of the churches at the same time. I asked them to join us and Roy to be our speaker. They had both had a lot of input into the orphan boys. I also invited my cousin Iona Heppner and her coworker Margaret Vigeland.

Gladys Henriksen, Iona Heppner and I.

The set day came. I had gone back to Dharangaon a little early to get things ready. I bought rice and grain and had it cleaned and ground. The orphans began to arrive from all directions. I did not know if or how many would be able to come but they came carrying a bit of bedding. It was wonderful to see them all. Some of the older ones I had never met and it had been many years since they saw Gladys.

Some of the orphans had not seen each other since they were married. There were tears and laughter as they met. I happened to see Madhumalti go up to Suniti and ask, "Who are you? Are you my sister? I am Madhu." Suniti gave her name and they fell on each other's neck crying. They had grown up together but not seen each other for forty years! So it brought great joy to my heart to have been able to facilitate it all. Many people in Abbotsford added money to that first $200 donation from the Martens and it was sufficient. To God be the glory!

We had scheduled two meetings a day for three days. On the fourth day everybody left. In total we were about one hundred and sixty people. We had the first meeting on the evening of December 24. Gladys had suggested that since I organized it, I should emcee the first meeting and I did. First I welcomed them all then as I was going to say more I started to cry. All I could think of was the mistakes I had made and asked them for forgiveness.

What happened then was so typically Indian. They started to say, "No, Mai, you loved us. When you punished us it was because we were very naughty." Several of them came up to the platform to wipe my tears with their hands. "Please don't cry. We have not held anything against you. We have our own children now and we almost despair. How could you bring up so many?" That "you" referred to all the missionaries that had a part in their upbringing. Roy's messages were so down to earth and such a blessing. The last regular meeting was on the Saturday night and it lasted till midnight. Many of our children wanted to testify or pray. You can imagine how that encouraged us all. They were such a blessing to one another too. Then Sunday morning we had a worship service which ended with a communion service. It was goodbye for everyone but we had all been enriched by being together.

After I retired, I have been back three times for orphan reunions. The last was in 1997 and I told them all it would be my last trip. But now they are writing again to ask when we are having the next reunion. As much as I would like to go back again, I am not planning on it. I suggested they have one on their own.

The last time I was there, we had the communion service as usual. I had taken the plastic cups from Grace Church (about three hundred that I washed) with me. I announced that they could each take their cup home and put it where they would see it often. It was to remind each of us of the hope we have of meeting again in Heaven and being present at the Marriage Supper of the Lamb. Some of the younger grandchildren were not saved but I gave them each an empty one to remind them of the Blood Jesus shed for them. It was also my prayer that they would accept Jesus as Saviour.

BEING A MEDIATOR

When I arrived in India I soon learned that when there has been a misunderstanding between two people, they ask a mediator to help resolve the problem. At first I thought, "if she or he is really sorry they should go themselves and ask for forgiveness. Why would you want to involve a third party? They can't really be very anxious to get it fixed up!"

I learned however. There was a time when I thought one of the teachers had done something and after praying about it for a month or more, I went to her and asked her. She was in the clear for sure. She took it very, very hard though. She felt so bad that I had thought that of her and I felt terrible too. I could have waited a little longer and the truth would have come out on its own. I would have felt just as bad as she did, if she had asked me the same thing but I could not take my words back. I did tell her immediately that I was so sorry and asked her to forgive me.

The relationship between us was very strained after that. When I went to her classroom to ask a question about the class she would not answer. She told one of the girls the answer who then told me. What could I do?

After about two or three weeks I could not stand it any longer. I wanted to be forgiven. I also wanted her to know I held nothing against her so I went to the Pastor's wife. After I told her what happened I asked her to please mediate between us. She was willing and ready to do that but did not report back to me so I did not know how the teacher had responded. I kept praying.

The next day, the teacher sent one of the little school girls to me with a flower from her garden. She was definitely instructed to say, "Tell Mai, that ——Bai sent this flower to you." Then I asked the little girl to go back and tell her thank you very much. How I thanked God for that olive branch!

I had planned a trip to Jalgaon, which was twenty miles away, on the following Saturday. I sent word to that teacher and the one she shared the house with that I would like them to accompany me. I used to do that with the various workers as an outing and an act of appreciation for their work.

To my great delight, they both accepted and we had a lovely day. Of course, I treated them to special things like tea made with pure milk and ice cream. There was one shop where it was safe to eat ice cream. We just had a very lovely day together. Through that experience, the preciousness of Christ being the Mediator between God and me became more real. Dear reader, has Christ become your Mediator? If not accept His offer today.

Then I had the experience of me being the mediator between one of the orphan girls and the headmistress. I will call her "M". This girl M had been disobeying the rules in school for a long time. The headmistress gave her proper notice and punishment. Each time M asked for forgiveness. She was forgiven over and over again. One day she was expelled from school for three days. The headmistress sent M to me to tell me she had been expelled so I gave M some work to do in the boarding those days.

The three days were up and M came to me to ask if she could now go back to school. I said she could but she must ask for forgiveness before entering the classroom. She did that, but a few minutes later made a nuisance of herself again in class. She was sent back to me. Now what to do? M looked at me as if to ask the same thing I was thinking. I felt like punishing her.

Then the Lord put an idea into my mind. I took her by the hand and said, "Come, I'll go with you." At the classroom door I asked, "Yeu ka?" (May we come in?) We were invited in. I told M that since I had brought her up it looked as if this is how I taught her to act. It made me feel responsible for what she did. I asked her to step back.

I faced the headmistress and as I started to talk, I broke down. I was overwhelmed with how many times God had forgiven me as Jesus had interceded for me before His Father. I told the Headmistress that what M had done was as if I have done it. Would she forgive me? She said she would and had tears in her eyes. Then M took my arm and started to cry and said, "No, Mai you did not do this, I did?" Then she asked both of us for forgiveness. It made a difference in M and I was very thankful. She is married and has a family. She works in a village as sort of a public health nurse.

CHILDREN'S PRAYERS

Howard and Frances Hall's little daughter Judy (from Port Huron, Michigan) prayed thus, "Dear Jesus, bless the orphans that Miss Goertz has, and bless the orphans' parents too."

During the riots and fighting in Pakistan, little orphan Premi (Turab) Moses prayed, "Lord, don't let a war start here. Let it stay where it is, or let it go somewhere else. But please don't let it come here." The idea of a war really scared our little tyke. Premi is married and has a nice family but is a widow now.

I told you about the back pain I had before I had surgery. I was visiting my brother Isaac and Alma and family. Ruth is their oldest child. She was real small at the time. When Alma put her to bed Ruthie prayed. "Dear Jesus make Aunt Annie's back better so she can go back to India again. She wants to go back and tell the people about You. So they may be saved and go to be with You where You are. If they should all be lost it would be so terrible. Oh, Mommy, I just love to lie here and think of Jesus and the Angels. Amen."

A little girl in our boarding was the only surviving child of her parents. They had several little sons but they all died at birth, or soon after. Her parents were Hindus. The little girl soon became a Christian after coming to Dharangaon. It was holiday time in a few months so she went home to her parents. Her faith was so strong in Jesus and she told her parents about Him. She told them that the true and living God answers prayer. With great boldness she sat down beside her Mother and prayed, "Dear God, my parents do not know you. But they want a son so badly. I ask you Jesus to please give them a son. If you do, then they will believe in you. I am sure. In Jesus name. Amen.

She came back to school and in a few months she received a post card from home informing her that her mother was pregnant. The girl's joy knew no bounds. She thanked God over and over. What I did not know, was that a while later they had sent another post card telling her the date the baby was to be born.

She remembered the date and when it arrived she came to me all excited. "Mai, we must pray." She started right in, "Dear God, this is the day the baby will be born. I asked you to give them a son. I know you will. But just in case that's a girl in my Mother's tummy, you had better change it into a boy right now. They will believe in you, if you do. In Jesus' Name. Amen.

Another post card came in due time. And YES it informed her that they had a son. Again she came to me to pray. This time she thanked God for answering her prayer. She also asked God to help her parents believe in Him. Her simple witness was rewarded and her many prayers were answered. Her parents did become Christians. Eventually others in the village did too. A church was started. Praise The Lord! In a real sense some of the girls became church planters.

CHAPTER 35

An Unexpected Visitor on Christmas Day

It was Christmas Day in 1982. We always had a service in church on December 24, no matter what day of the week it fell on. Our custom was to have a love feast right after the service for those that had not gone away for the holidays. The girls and teachers had left but the orphans were there as well as some of the workers and a few Christians that lived off the compound. We must have been close to fifty people. Each family brought as much rice as they would ordinarily use for one meal. We put it all together and cooked it.

Goat meat was bought for the curry. We probably collected money from each family. Sometimes I paid for all the meat. Before we went to church the meat and rice was put on to cook. The stove was three big stones put in a circle. A shallow hole was dug in the middle where a wood fire was built. When we returned from the service it was all ready except for the meat. It had to be taken out of the big kettle, while some spices, cut up onions and garlic were fried a bit. When ready, the meat was put back into the kettle to absorb the curry flavour.

That particular day, some of the women were doing what I have just described when suddenly a jeep drove up. Out jumped about five police officers and then a man decked out in uniform and ribbons. He was introduced to me as the Chief of Police for our area by one of our teachers. He wanted to see me so I invited him into my house and served him tea and cookies. He was very congenial and apologized for coming on our biggest feast day of the year.

Then he asked for my name which I gave him. Then his tone changed and he said, "You are not Annie Goertz." I assured him I was but he said, "You are —— ———." I said, "No, I am not that person." I got out my passport and showed it to him. He looked at it and still did not believe me. I got my residential permit then he said I was using false documents. Next he showed me a letter of accusations against a missionary that had been in Dharangaon at least two or more years ago when I was at home.

I explained to him that the letter was two years old and I knew the people that had written it. They felt bad they had done it and had asked to be forgiven. I said the case should be thrown out because it was so old. He then got up and left. His driver and police followed him into the jeep and away they went.

I thought that was the end of that, but alas, it was just the beginning! That same Chief of Police returned on December 30 accompanied by some local police. He showed me the same letter and left. On April 6, 1983 the local police came to inform me that I was to report to the Chief in his office in ——— on April 7.

I went but I was sorry I had gone. But there was no getting out of it, I knew. He was very angry. First he told me that I had never entertained him and his men in my home with chicken curry and cake. My neighbouring Norwegian Mission friends had done that he told me. I explained to him that was a couple and made all the difference. I further told him that since I am a single woman, I did not entertain men. I asked him what he would think of me if I had parties with all the police? I told him that I guard my character and reputation very carefully.

He left that subject and asked me about some of the teachers that had taught in our school in the past. I told him that I had been on furlough when they left to teach elsewhere and I did not know where they were. He thought we should keep in contact with all of them for years to come. I said that seemed impossible to me. Finally, he said that he would have to see to it that I left the country because I was not cooperating with his office.

I was on the field council and in two weeks we were meeting in Nasik. I had not had a proper vacation so I felt I should get away some place else for a time of rest and prayer. I was pretty sure that the threat would be carried out. I needed to fortify myself in the Word and prayer against what might lie ahead.

After our meetings were finished and since I was already a good third of the way to Kedgaon I decided to go right from Nasik. Kedgaon is a small town near Pune where the Pandita Rama Bai Mukti Mission is. At that Mission they are set up to care for a few missionaries or other guests for a few days. It was just what I felt I needed. They even brought a breakfast tray to my room and an afternoon tea tray. The pampering was good for me.

I later learned that on April 22 (after I left home) the police had sent a summons to me in Dharangaon to be out of the country by April 30. Since I was absent, they showed it to the teachers. I was unaware of it and was innocently resting at Mukti. A few days later one of my teachers sent me a telegram saying, "Return immediately to Dharangaon."

I was very tired and wasn't even sure if this was anything authentic so I did not return. I had received 'Wolf, Wolf' telegrams in the past and thought this might be one. The missionaries there encouraged me to stay because they too had had telegrams that meant nothing serious. It was just a way of getting someone to come quickly.

On April 27 I had a letter from the other teacher. He told me that there really was an order for me from the police. His wife had not stopped crying since the order had come. I realized then that it was serious and I took the train from there that night.

It was a long trip and I did not reach my home until 11:00 a.m. on April 28. The teachers told me that they had read the summons and that I must leave India by midnight on April 30. I sent one of the men to the police station to tell them that I had arrived. No one came. In the afternoon I sent him again but still no one came. By 8:00 p.m. I figured I'd better go myself. I asked the two teachers to accompany me. It was a little over a mile to walk. They confirmed that there was a letter for me but the policeman who was to deliver it to me was out of town. He would not be back until the next morning. There was nothing I could do but wait. I was amazed at the peace I had but isn't that what our Father has promised?

April 29 dawned and I started my day as usual. I had my devotions and as was my custom, I turned the radio on while I had my breakfast. It was always so good to listen to Dr. Warren Wiersbe's "Back to the Bible" program. "What would he have for me this morning?" I thought. I turned the radio on but not a sound! Oh no, the very day I need something special from the Lord, my radio is dead! Usually if there was interference all I could get was static but there wasn't even that. When anything like that occurred I would just switch it off but I didn't that morning and actually forgot that it was still on.

Halfway through my breakfast Dr. Wiersbe's voice came on loud and clear. It startled me for it sounded as if he was sitting right next to me. Are you ready for this? This is what he said, "Missionary, are you being uprooted and sent to another country? Do not fear. God is with you." Then the radio went absolutely dead again. I however, did not need anymore.

Now let me leave the story there for a minute and come back to it. I wrote Back to the Bible and asked them to please send me the tape of the April 29 broadcast. I, of course told Dr. Wiersbe what had happened. They sent it to me but there was nothing on the tape that resembled what I had heard. India is a day ahead of the United States so they may have sent me the wrong tape. Or, did God send an Angel to say that to me that morning? He surely could have. I would love to know. That is something that will have to wait if and until God chooses to reveal it to me. Does it really matter? God did it somehow for me, His child who needed something from Him that day. How He loves His children! That means you too.

You can imagine how wonderful it was to get that message right from the Lord that morning before everything broke loose as it were. Well, at 9:00 a.m. the police came with the letter from the Government of India that told me I had to be out of India by midnight the next day, APRIL 30. I lived 280 miles from Bombay. I had to take two trains with several hours layover between the two. The local police were very sympathetic. They actually felt very bad and told me they knew there was nothing I had done. They suggested I go to —— —— and try to get them to reconsider.

I decided to take his advice and took one of the teachers along for moral support because I had to go back to that same office. This time he was furious as soon as he saw me. He fairly shouted, "Quit India by midnight tomorrow. I will send my men in the jeep to pick you up if you have not gone by then." I did not want to be manhandled by the police. The teacher had tears in his eyes.

We went out into the hallway to try to decide on some plan of action. One of the peons came to me and said, "Don't talk to this man anymore. Go directly to Bombay." Then he gave me the address of the building. One of our orphan girls was working in the office of the Mamalatdar of the district. This man was above the chief. So I asked the peon if he would quickly summon her to my side from another building close by.

She came and wondered what had happened. I held her close and said to the peon, "This is my daughter." Then I had tears in my eyes. He asked her is that was so. She confirmed it by telling him that when she was a tiny baby, her mother died. She had been brought to us by her father and we raised her. I told her briefly what happened and kissed her goodbye, not knowing if I would see her again or not.

There was no time to lose, so the teacher and I went back to Dharangaon. I grabbed my small suitcase and took the midnight train to Bombay. The train was due in Bombay at 6:00 the next morning but they had engine trouble so we arrived at 11:30 a.m. instead. The very day I needed more time, it came up short. I grabbed a taxi and asked him to rush me to the guest house. Fortunately, the government building was only about two blocks from the guest house. The hostess said she would put some soup on while I had a bath and changed. Her husband called the government office and made an appointment for me for 2:00 p.m.

I had not had my devotions on the train, as far as reading the Bible and Our Daily Bread. I had prayed you can be sure as I sat up all night on the train. I had a few minutes to spare after my soup and before my appointment so I knelt by the bed to read.

As I started to read the portion in the Daily Bread, it seemed so far from what I needed but I read on. Richard DeHaan told the story of two men that were taking a shortcut through a farmer's field. As they walked and talked they heard what they thought sounded like the hoofs of an animal running behind them. They looked and it was an angry bull charging after them. They started to run but they knew they could not outrun the bull. John called to his friend, "Pray." He yelled, "You pray, John." John called back, "I don't know how to pray. You pray." All out of breath and still running he starts to pray, "For what we are about to receive, Lord, make us truly thankful." That's what he had heard his Father pray before meals.

Then DeHaan made the application: "Servant of God, can you kneel down and thank God for what you are about to receive? You may soon receive bad treatment. Can you be truly thankful?" Unknown to him, I was about to go through a hard trial. I was greatly strengthened through that reading. While I was still on my knees I did thank God for what was ahead because He was already there.

Then it was time to hurry to the office and I did not know what would happen. At that very moment God's presence flooded my whole being and the room. He was so close to me. I got off my knees, reached for my passport and the deportation order and said out loud, "Let's go, Lord."

Let me tell you what happened in me just at that time, in a split second. I had always been scared to die. Oh, I knew I was ready to go to Heaven, but the dying part scared me and especially dying alone in India. My family might never know how I died or from what! Now suddenly, all fear of dying was gone. I thought if God can be this close to me now, how much closer He will be when the most glorious moment of my life comes, the minute He takes me Home to be with Himself! The day He sends the Angels to carry me Home! So if for no other reason during this experience, I truly thank the Lord that He took that fear away. Besides, if dying is really as bad as we think it is, why is everybody dying?

Back to my story. I only needed to walk a short distance, as I said. The Holy Spirit crammed an awful lot of verses into my mind. Here are some of them:

- 1 Sam. 8:7, "For I am the one they are rejecting, not you."
- Then one sentence from the Living Bible: "He works without regard to human means."

- Ex. 14:14, "The Lord will fight for you."
- Amos 5:14, " The Lord God of hosts will truly be your helper, as you have claimed He is."
- Zech. 2:8, "he who harms you, sticks his finger in Jehovah's eye."
- Zech. 4:6, "...Not by might, nor by power, but by my Spirit, saith the Lord of hosts."
- Matt. 10:18,19, "And you shall be brought before governors and kings for my sake, for a testimony against them and the Gentiles. But when they deliver you up, take no thought how, or what you shall speak: for it shall be given you in that same hour what ye shall speak. For it is not ye that speak, but the Spirit of your Father which speaketh in you."
- Col. 3:17 (LB), "Whatever you do or say, let it be as a representative of the Lord Jesus."

Now wasn't that a quiver full? The last one especially hit home to think that I was in Government House as a representative of the Lord Jesus! When I arrived at the building I was told where to go. It was quite a high one. In one room was a long bench where everyone sat to wait his turn. The last one always sat at the other end. The officials office was off this room. I introduced myself to the peon and told him my work was urgent, so would he please make sure I got in on time. Yes, yes. I waited until my turn came but then he took the one that came after me. He kept doing that so I talked to him again. He motioned for me to wait.

I was concerned because the next day was a holiday and then Sunday. Four o'clock came and the peon left. I quickly called to him and he said the official had gone home for the weekend. The other offices closed at 5:00 or 5:30 p.m. So I asked him what I could do because midnight was my deadline. He then motioned for me to go to the office across from the room where we had waited. I then realized what had happened. I had seen all the men shaking hands very warmly with the peon. I got it. If you "greased" his hand, you got to go in. So he controlled who got to go for an interview and who did not. I would not have done it anyway, even if I had known what was happening. I never did.

This official was like a bear. I showed him my paper and all he said was, "Go home." I said I could not. So I just sat there. Others came and went and he signed all their papers. I did not say a word, just sat there. Finally he got tired of seeing me so he dinged his little bell. A woman came from another office. He told her to go and find my file. She brought in every file that began with a G, but not mine. Then he told her to take me into her office.

I followed her and she gave me a chair and she sat behind a desk. I noticed there was an official sitting behind a screen in the same office but he said nothing. She asked me why I was there. I told her and she said, "They are very strict. They won't change their order. Take your purse and go to the Airport." I told her I had no money for fare. I also told her I had done nothing to warrant such an order. She never did find my file and they wondered if I was even registered with them! I told her there must be a misunderstanding.

"Lord, what shall I do? Time is going." Then it came to me to ask her what she would do if her boss told her to take her purse and go to the Airport and fly to London, England." She said she could not. I asked why not and she said she had a two year old daughter at home. She would go home first and take her with her. I then told her the truth is that I have brought up many children and they seem like my very own. How can I leave from here without ever saying goodbye? Their hearts would break and mine too. Then I saw a tear in her eye but that was it. I sat some more and they had to sit with me. I felt sorry for them because they were not the ones that got me into this.

The lady suggested to me that I go home and come back on Monday. Then they would see what could be done. I asked her to remember that my stay in India would run out in a few short hours. I cannot step out on to the sidewalk. You can have me arrested on the street but the Indian flag flies on top of this building. As long as I stay in this building I am safe. Please go home and I'll stay here till you come back on Monday. I was praying like crazy that they would not take me up on it.

Next the man spoke up and asked me what I hoped to accomplish by sitting there. I said, "To tell you the truth, I am waiting for a miracle." He asked me how that was possible. I told him that I believed in the true and living God. I belonged to Him and I served Him. He wondered how that could happen and where. I said I did not know how but that the miracle would, "take place in your heart." He only smiled.

We all sat quietly. Then the Lord impressed on me to go to the man and ask for mercy. So, I got up, walked over to him, folded my hands (as they do when making a request) and addressed him. "Sir, each time I make application for a residential permit, I always sign where it says that I will leave the country anytime I am asked to. I still mean that. I will leave but not now. I need time. So, sir, all I ask is for mercy. Nothing less, nothing more-just mercy."

When I said the word MERCY I realized afresh how much mercy the Lord had extended to me all my life. It so flooded my soul and for a second it seemed I was standing before God, instead of this man. I broke down and cried. The gentleman did not like my tears and asked if eight days would be enough time. I said it would not. Two weeks? I said no. Six months? I replied, "Sir, it is not enough. I have done nothing amiss. I retire in two years. I would very much like to stay until that time and complete my work here and go home in peace."

Talk of a miracle!! He said, "Madam, I will write out a new order." When he said that I really sobbed. "Madam, I told you I would write out a new order, so why are you crying?" I said simply, "Because you are extending mercy." He was relieved and told me to sit down while he wrote it out. Of course, I had no idea what he was going to write but I knew God was in charge.

He quickly wrote it out and came over to hand it to me. The lady intercepted it and said, "We need several copies. We need some too. In fact we need six in all." He said all the typists had gone home, all the offices were closed.

I reached out and said I would type it. Once again he was going to hand it to me. Again, the lady said, "That's not right. We cannot make her type her own order. That does not beautify us.(literal translation) Give it to me, I'll see if I can find someone to type it."

She came back in half an hour waving the six copies! She told us she had found one lone typist who was working overtime. I said thank you quietly to the Lord. The man separated them and signed each one. Then with a smile he gave me two copies, one for me and one to take to the office in ——.

Then he spoke most kindly to me. Now please don't go back home. You have been under great stress. Stay at the guest house and rest till Monday then go home. We shook hands and parted as friends. I apologized profusely that they had to stay with me for several hours after the office closed. As soon as I was outside the building I looked at my new order. This is what it said. "The above mentioned Canadian National is permitted to stay in India till further notice." How I praised the Lord.

The couple at the guest house had been quite concerned because I was gone so long. They prayed during that time. After that I applied each year for a residential permit as I had for 34 years. I never heard from the government again. They never sent me a renewed permit either. I stayed in India till March 1984 which was when I was scheduled to retire. When I left Bombay, immigration should have taken my "new order" from me but they did not. I still have it as proof of the miracle that God performed.

This has been a long and detailed story of God's faithfulness. Had not God forgiven my sins? Had not God let me know they were forgiven? Was anything too hard for Him after that? No, nothing has ever been too hard for Him and it won't be. Praise the Lord! I can trust Him with everything and so can you.

It was of interest to me that a missionary from a neighbouring mission had a 'Quit India' notice too. He checked with me as to what my outcome was. He had been there much longer than I but he was allowed to stay without any ado.

Another couple, related to this man, was given ten days notice to leave. They tried their best to get it overturned but as far as I know they were not even given a hearing. They had to leave.

It makes one wonder how God decides those things. He allowed two of His servants to continue on, yet the couple had to leave. We cannot understand His ways because they are so much higher than ours. And His thoughts higher than ours. God was just as good to that couple as He was to the two of us. We can trust Him completely. He answers all our prayers. The answer may be yes, no or wait! We are inclined to think that only yes is an answer to our prayer.

CHAPTER 36

Various Topics

In a previous chapter I told you that I retired from India in March 1984, officially on June 30 after a three month furlough. While I was preparing to go home I had a burden to pray that the Lord would give me something worthwhile to do here at home. I did not want to just retire. I longed for a ministry. I had been in India longer than anywhere else.

I knelt by the chair with the striped cover on it. The man in the black suit is Rev. Gavit, he is also my son-in-law. My granddaughter is putting a garland on my neck.

At the end of every furlough, a church had a re-commissioning service for me. That was always a blessed time. I might be asked to give a brief testimony then the pastor would give the charge to me to be faithful in my personal walk with the Lord, to keep in the Word and in prayer for my own growth. To be faithful in giving out the Word of God and also to write to the church regularly.

Now I had a burden that the Indian Church might commission me for my retirement. I wanted the blessing of the Indian brethren. I wrote to one of the pastors, Rev. G. C. Gavit. He was very much in agreement. A date was set and the pastor and his wife came. Leslie and Verna Buhler came too, in fact they brought the pastor in their jeep. It was a very blessed service. I have been aware of the answers to the prayers that were prayed that day as I knelt by a chair.

It seemed that illnesses among the boarding girls came by seasons. A lot might have Pink Eye (sore eyes) or scabies. Of course those two were very contagious. Colds and flu spread quickly too. I ran a little clinic several times a day for the girls.

When they came for medicine, there might be up to thirty or more sometimes. The easiest way was to have them stand in groups according to what was wrong. Sore eyes in one place, colds in another, earache, scabies, headaches, toothache and slivers to be removed. That way I did not have to go from one medicine to the other and it saved time. It also kept me from spreading the disease from one to the other.

How well I remember one evening, when the sick girls were gathered into groups as usual. One girl was left standing by herself. I asked her which medicine she needed. She said none. She had come to talk to me. She patiently waited till I was finished. I asked her what she wanted to talk about and she said she would tell me after we went to my room.

We both sat down. Then she asked, "What does vishwas mean?" That word in English is faith. I breathed a prayer for wisdom then I asked her if she would please go and sit on 'that' chair. She did and I said she had demonstrated faith. She wondered how. I explained that if she had thought that chair would break when she sat on it she would not have done it. She agreed. I said that was faith. You knew I would not ask you to sit on a chair that would break, didn't you?.

Her face lit up and she said, "That's all I wanted to know." I asked her why she wanted to know. She said I had told them in Bible Classes that we must have faith in Jesus that He will forgive our sins if we ask Him. I told her that was true. We must believe that Jesus will do what He says He will do. She stood to her feet and said, "thank you, Mai, now my salvation has happened!" Bless her heart. She became a child of God right there. We then thanked Jesus. She was only about seven years old. It was good to see her grow in her faith. She still loves the Lord and lives for Him.

When I left India for my second furlough, I was able to come by ship all the way to Vancouver. Our last port of call before Vancouver was Honolulu. That's my first and only visit to that State. The first thing we wanted after we docked was an ice cream cone.

Several American missionaries and I were travelling together so we took a few tours that day and saw a lot. The one thing that stands out in my mind though was a visit to a Buddhist Temple. We had seen them in India but here we saw American men sit lotus fashion on the floor. They were chanting just like we had heard them do in India.

We talked to one of them and tried to witness to him. He was not interested and told us how glad he was that he had been enlightened. He was brought up in a Christian home. He said in Sunday School he used to sing, "Jesus Loves Me" but now he sings, "Buddha loves me.." It made us feel so sad. We had never seen American people do that. I thought about how great is that darkness when people turn their backs on the true Light.

About twenty years later, I was to see many foreigners come to India from many countries. Many dressed in saffron robes, some came to become followers of Buddha, Sai Baba, and Hari Krishna. Some became true followers of the religions of India and turned their backs on their families and homelands. Of course, most had to turn all their money and passports over to their Religious Leaders so they had to stay. After a while some became disillusioned and went back home poorer than when they came.

One young man from the USA was asked (for his initiation), to sit on the floor, Lotus fashion, in the middle of a bare room. They placed an apple in front of him and he was told to look at that apple all day to teach him meditation. He did that faithfully for two days. Then he decided he could look at an apple at home if that was what he wanted so he told them he was leaving to go back home and he did.

Some of them got very lonesome and went to visit the missionaries and several accepted Jesus as their Saviour. Praise The Lord!

THE HOLY SPIRIT-Misconceptions

About all I knew about the Holy Spirit before I was saved were some songs about Him that we sang in church. I also knew that when people were baptized the minister would baptize them in the name of the Father, the Son and the Holy Ghost. Most likely more was taught by our preachers but I probably just did not understand it.

You remember that I attended Prairie Bible Institute very soon after I received assurance of salvation. There we received wonderful teaching. The first truth about the Holy Spirit that Rev. Maxwell was able to bring home to my heart was that the Holy Spirit is not an "IT". He is the third PERSON of the Godhead.

Our beloved Mr. Maxwell also taught that the Holy Spirit indwells us from the moment we accept Jesus as our Saviour. It is a once for all coming to dwell within us. He will never leave us. We cannot receive the Holy Spirit over and over again, just as we cannot accept Jesus over and over again. I have had people tell me how they accepted Jesus over and over again, after they sinned.

We were taught from the Scriptures that there is only one baptism of the Holy Spirit but many fillings, namely daily fillings. My idea of that was, was that I must know when I am being filled. I must be conscious of it. So in India, I often worried about being filled. I always asked the Holy Spirit to have His way and guide me each day. Looking back, I know He did use me but I wanted to know for sure that I yielded to Him.

I remember a few times going out at night, in India, and looking up at the sky. The moon and the stars were so bright. I'd talk to God about wanting to be filled with the Holy Spirit. Not only did I talk to Him, I begged Him! Nothing ever happened that I was aware of. Oh yes, a few adults were saved, and many girls were. The girls also grew in their Christian walk as I taught them but I wanted more.

I believe it was when I came on my second furlough that there was so much talk about the Holy Spirit. There were quite a few charismatic conferences where there were special manifestations of the Holy Spirit, I was told. I was not searching for such outward manifestations because I had witnessed them in India and they were scarey. They also were not Scriptural but I wanted to see for myself what went on here at home. I attended a Women's Rally held by a well known woman preacher.

She started right in about the manifestations that should be visible and audible if one were truly filled with the Spirit. Then she talked at length about it being impossible to be a child of God and not speak in tongues. I knew that was not correct. After a while she had question time. I got up and told her what I had understood and that I had never spoken in tongues. I asked her if she would say that I was not born again. She told me very emphatically that I was not. Now I was hearing something contrary to the Word of God so no more of those rallies for me.

I still wanted to be sure though that I had been or was filled with the Holy Spirit. About that time I attended a fall Missions Conference at Prairie in

Three Hills. I had come hoping to hear something that would help me in regards to that.

One afternoon when the Tabernacle was completely empty because people were resting, I went and sat down on one of the benches. I prayed, "Dear Lord, I don't want to be struggling about this forever. Let me know what I must do." So very clearly the answer came to me at that instant. "Annie, you take it by faith, just like you did when you received assurance of salvation."

What a release that was for me! I praised God that I did not have to go by feelings again. I had wanted to feel filled by the Holy Spirit. Do you see the mistake I made? I had begun by faith, now I was going back to feelings. Feelings change so often. I needed to trust the Word of God which never changes. 1 John 5:14,15.

Later I did talk to Mr. Maxwell about the struggle I had gone through. He then said something that hit the nail on the head, as we say. He explained so plainly that it is never a question of how much do I have of the Holy Spirit but how much does He have of me! I have all of Him the minute I am born again but He does not get all of me that minute. In our new found peace and joy of sins forgiven we may think he has all of us. It is also our sincere desire that He should.

As we grow in grace and knowledge of the Lord, we soon discover that the Holy Spirit does not have all of us. It is a daily committing ourselves to Him and asking Him to guide us. I once heard a speaker say that it is like putting a glove on our hand. The glove can do nothing. It cannot move its fingers. When the hand is inside the glove, the glove does what the hand wants. We are the glove and the Holy Spirit is the hand inside.

So at the beginning of the day we ask the Holy Spirit to empower us to do His bidding. We ask Him to take control of our day and of us. Then we get up from prayer and take it by faith that He will. It gives us a quietness of spirit and peace knowing that the Lord has heard us and is in control. He will bring things to pass so naturally. At the end of the day we can thank Him for His guidance.

When we go to bed the Holy Spirit is still in us. The next morning we do the same as we did the day before. We say, "Lord, here I am again. I am available for you to guide me, and to give me discernment. Encourage someone through me today. Show me if there is a person that I need to talk to about his soul. Help me to show forth the love and joy of the Lord today." Then we believe that He will do what we have asked of Him, because He has said He would.

CHAPTER 37

Poems

On my furloughs people often asked if I was going back to India. I always said I was. Then I came across a poem which says it so well. I will quote it here. I do not know who the author is, so I cannot give credit.

WOULD YOU GO BACK?

If you had been to heathen lands,
Where weary souls stretch out their hands
To plead, yet no one understands,
Would you go back? Would you?

If you had seen the women bear
Their heavy loads with none to share,
Had heard them weep, with none to care.
Would you go back? Would you?

If you had seen them in despair,
And beat their breasts, and pull their hair,
Had heard them weep, with none to care,
Would you go back? Would you?

If you had walked through India's sand,
Your hand within the Saviour's hand,
And knew He'd called you to that land,
Would you go back? Would you?

If you had seen the glorious sight,
When heathen people, in their night
Were brought from darkness into Light,
Would you go back? Would you?

* * * * *

"Were the whole realm of nature mine,
That were a present far too small;
Love so amazing, so divine,
Demands my soul, my life, my all."

* * * * *

Some of you will remember that I printed the following lines from a song on every prayer card I had made. I give it here:

"He was not willing that any should perish;
Am I His follower, and can I live
Longer at ease with a soul going downward,
Lost for the lack of the help I might give?

Perishing, perishing! Thou was not willing;
Master, forgive, and inspire us anew;
Banish our worldliness; help us to ever
Live with eternity's values in view."

A CRY FROM HEATHENDOM.
Why didn't you tell us sooner?
The words came sad and low,

O ye who knew the Gospel truths,
Why didn't you tell us sooner?
The Saviour died for those who sin,
He died to save from woe;
But we never heard the story,
Why didn't you let us know?

You have had the Gospel message,
You have known a Saviour's love;

Your dear ones passed from Christian homes,
To the blessed Home above.
Why did you let our fathers die
And into the silence go?
With no thought of Christ to comfort,
Why didn't you let us know?
We appeal to you, O Christians,
In lands beyond the sea!
Why didn't you tell us sooner,
Christ died to set men free?
Nineteen hundred years have passed
Since disciples were told to go
To the uttermost parts of the earth and teach,
Why didn't YOU let US know?

- *G. P. Turnbull.*

* * * *

"The very air teems thick with beleaguered friends;
Each word we speak has infinite effects;
Each soul we pass, must go to Heaven or to Hell...
Be earnest, earnest, earnest— mad if thou wilt:
Do what thou doest, as if the stake were Heaven
And this thy last deed 'ere the judgement day!"

-from Borden of Yale.

The school girls in front of the hostel. Some of them are my grandchildren.

The school in drill hour.

CHAPTER 36

Not What Billy Graham Says!

I was staying with Howard and Frances Hall in Port Huron, Michigan while I was speaking at the Ross Bible Church. Frances decided to invite some ladies in for coffee and have me speak to them. It seems to me about seven ladies came. I don't remember what I told them but after it was over and we had our coffee one of the ladies asked Frances to show us the newly decorated den.

So we all marched in behind Frances and I was the last in line. Before we got into the room, a lady by the name of Fran (don't get her mixed up with Frances) who was just ahead of me turned around to talk to me. She put her hands on her chest and said, "Annie I have very bad pain in my chest all the time." I asked her how long she had it. "For two years," she told me.

I asked her if she had been to her doctor. She had. I advised her to go to a different doctor, you know, get a second opinion! She had. Then I said she might ask to see a specialist. She had. She had been to seven doctors in all and no one could find anything wrong. The last one sent her to a psychiatrist who told her that it was all in her head. Again Fran put her hand on her chest and told me she had constant pain and she was afraid.

Fran evidently expected me to do something. "Oh, Lord, give me wisdom." Then I said to her that it sounded to me as if it might be a burden of sin. She wanted to know why I thought that. I told her, "because I had one too." "Well, if it is, what can I do about it?" I answered, "Just kneel by your bed and ask Jesus to take the burden of sin away."

That's as far as I got, for the ladies had finished looking at the den and now were ready to go home. The one that gave Fran a ride, came by took her by the arm and pulled her toward the door. She said she was in a hurry to get home and they left as quickly as that. I was left with my mouth open. After they were all gone I told Frances what had happened. I told her I should have told her more and prayed with her. Frances said that would have been good because she could have taken her home. We could not change that now so we sat down and prayed for Fran.

Three or four days later I was asked to speak to Howard's Sunday School class one evening. As we came into the foyer of the church, Fran walked up to me all happy and said she had done what I told her to. She was not a church goer but she had heard I was going to be there so got a ride. It was all so sudden and I asked her what I

had told her to do. You asked me to kneel by my bed and ask Jesus to take my burden of sin away, and I did that. I asked, "You mean, you got saved?" She had never heard that word before and said, "Ya, if that's what you call it!" We could not talk anymore just then because they called it was time to begin the meeting but I was dying to hear more.

Before I began to speak, I told them that there was a lady there by the name of Fran. She had told me in the hall that she had just been saved a few days ago. I wondered if we could give her a few minutes to tell us about it. Everyone readily agreed. Once she started she could not stop. She kept telling it over and over again. She was bubbling over with joy. After about 45 minutes, I spoke up and told her how wonderful it was to hear her story. It seems to me, we just had prayer and went home. It could be I spoke a few minutes too.

Anyway, here's what she told us. When she came into her home that day, she put her purse on the table and threw her coat over a chair. She rushed straight to the rug by their bed and knelt down. She said, "Jesus, Annie told me to ask you to take my burden of sin, will you?" At that moment her chest pain was gone. She did not know what to do next so she looked up and added, "Jesus, Annie did not tell me what else to say to you. But anyway, there you have it!"

She got up off her knees and the first person she wanted to tell was her daughter. She phoned her and told her that Jesus had just taken her burden of sin and now she had no more chest pain. The daughter asked, "Mom, you did what?" So she told her again. The daughter said, "Mom, that isn't how you do it. Billy Graham says you have to go a meeting and go forward." Fran said, "I don't care what Billy Graham says, I did what Annie said and it worked." She added that she would not complain to her anymore about chest pain.

Fran wanted to call her friends and tell them what had happened but she wondered what they would say. Well, the Lord took care of that. The daughter was so shocked, she called her Mom's friends and told them. The daughter and the friends decided they had better go over and see for themselves if the pain was really gone.

Now Fran had an audience and she took great joy in telling them all. Some of the friends had tears in their eyes when she told them what Jesus had done for her. She was sure they wanted the same peace but there were others that got upset and left immediately. In fact no one stayed very long. She asked me why they would do that. I explained to her that Satan blinds the eyes of people so that they decide they do not want Jesus. That was very hard for her to understand.

Then her husband George came from work. I dare say that she did not have supper ready. What did supper matter as compared to her joy? She greeted him by the door and told him what Annie had said and what she had done. She talked so fast and was so excited and happy. He did not know what to make of this sudden change in his wife. She took him by the hand and led him to the rug in their bedroom. Then she put her hand on his neck and tried to push him down into a kneeling position. That did NOT work. He thought she had gone nuts. I imagine they eventually had supper, maybe he had to make it. Bless his heart!

She started going to church and told everybody about her Jesus but George could not get excited. He had to admit his wife was different since her chest pain was gone. It took about two years before he became a Christian. Then they were both baptized. Fran became a vibrant person. Both she and George have gone to be with the Lord.

During the years since then, I have often told the story of Fran. On several occasions, someone in the audience had a burden of sin too. They went home and did what I had told Fran to do. If the Holy Spirit has spoken to you through this story, why don't you kneel by your bed and pray the same prayer? Oh, the exact words don't matter. Just get the sin question settled before it is too late. If you do, would you please let me know? Thanks.

SURGERY POSTPONED

During my second furlough I needed major surgery. My family doctor was in Vancouver so that is where I would have the surgery. I saw him on the first of the month and he said he would book me for the thirtieth of that month. I was disappointed that I had to wait so long because I wanted to do deputation work.

The thirtieth of that month came and went and no call from my doctor so I called him. He apologized profusely for he had completely forgotten to call the hospital and book me. What now? He calmly said that he would book me for the thirtieth of that month so it meant another month of waiting. I felt I was wasting my time. I have come to know the Lord better since then and know that God never wastes our time. He is in control when we leave it to Him. He rules and overrules even when someone else makes a mistake, and when we do.

That month passed and I was admitted to hospital. The nurse gave me a pill to relax me, so I would sleep and not worry about surgery the next day. I took it and was beginning to feel groggy. Just then they brought a new patient into my two bed ward. She moaned and at times screamed. She was tied down in bed and tossed her head from side to side constantly. This was not the usual patient.

When the nurse came to my bed, I asked her what was wrong with the woman. The nurse was a Christian and whispered to me that she had tried to kill herself. I did not want to go to sleep for thinking that she might try it again after she was discharged and succeed.

So I got up, as dizzy as I was (from the pill), went over to her bed. I brushed her hair from her face and told her that Jesus loved her. She said nobody loved her. I told her again that indeed Jesus loved her. Also that I had no idea what was troubling her but if she would only call on God He would surely help her, because He has promised He would. Then I gave her a kiss. She looked at me so shocked. She asked why I did that. I told her that even though I did not know her I loved her because God did. I barely made it back to my bed and fell asleep till next morning.

When I came to after surgery, I looked for that woman. The nurse said she had slept soundly all night so her doctor had discharged her in the morning while I was in surgery. I think she must have called on the Lord and probably was saved but I don't know that for sure. At least the Lord met her need whatever it was.

It was then I felt that the Lord was behind it all. He allowed my doctor to forget to book me, in order for me to be there that very night when this very troubled woman came in! One soul, every soul is worth so much to God. He will do anything to get the message of His love to a needy soul. I never got her name but God knows who and where she is. I pray for her whenever I am reminded of her.

The Queen Mary moored at Long Beach, CA. Edwin took me there on September 20, 1990 for a nostalgic lunch.

Riding a cycle rickshaw in Mathura, U.P.

CHAPTER 39

Retirement

In an earlier chapter I told you of some of the difficulties a missionary faces when they retire. We eventually get adjusted and the Lord leads us into a ministry or ministries where we can continue to serve. Our friends, family and churches may have a hard time adjusting to us too!

While I was on vacation in India a missionary loaned me Chuck Colson's first book, "Born Again." I love to hear how people were saved. When I came to that part in his book, I cried all the way through it. The Lord gave me a real burden at that time to want to visit prisoners after I retired.

I had visited many in India, in a town called Erandol, seven miles from my home. The Taluka office was in that very tiny village. That is where I had to apply for ration cards for myself and the boarding for commodities such as kerosene, wheat, jowari, sugar, and cooking oil. The jail was right next to the office building. Their plight was so bad. I do not think they had many re-offenders. Each cell was about six by six feet. There were a row of them with just a wall between.

Sometimes I saw three to one cell, and the next one might have six. Each cell held as many as was necessary. A cell had only three walls made of bricks, the floor of stone slabs. The front was open to the public, just iron bars from the ceiling to the floor with a small door made of heavy iron bars. There was no toilet, no chair and not even a mat to sit or ly on. I thought it was merciful that they faced north. That way they did not get the hot sun most of the day. Their food was handed through the bars.

If I had to wait for my appointment or for a bus I would go and talk to the men. I'd ask what they were in for. I also asked them if they had ever heard of Jesus Christ. None had. After my first visit to them, I would bring gospel tracts in their language the next time. I thought our prisons here were something like that but I found out that they are much different.

When I arrived in Abbotsford, I heard of a prison ministry called M/2 W/2 Christian Association. M/2 stands for two men, one man visiting a male prisoner. Likewise W/2 stands for two women visiting. I applied to be a visitor to women and was accepted. I had the joy of seeing two of them make a profession of faith in Christ. There's no way for me to follow up after they leave so I do not know if they are following on or not.

For a few weeks I took a prisoner from the Haney Women's Minimum Security Institute to the Maple Ridge Hospital to visit her boy friend. He had fallen asleep while driving all night to come and visit her. He broke several bones when he rolled over. The brother of the patient had been told that a missionary was driving her and that she was in the lounge writing letters.

I was astounded when he came to me and asked if I could possibly tell him how to find God. He was at wits end and no one so far had been able to help him. He sat down and I explained the way of salvation to him. He seemed very moved and said he would accept Jesus as soon as he got back to Vancouver to his apartment. If he did or not I may never know. It was another time when a seed was planted in a heart and God knows if it sprouted or not. All you and I can do is plant the seed and we want to be faithful at every opportunity the Lord gives. I was with this organization for about five years. I quit when the women's prison was moved to Burnaby. It was too far for me to drive at night.

My church has a Missions Committee that serves our missionaries. They screen candidates and mission boards and encourage the missionaries. They see that they get letters regularly from our members here. This committee also organizes our yearly missionary conference. It was a great joy for me to serve on that committee for about seven years.

Another opportunity at church that I enjoyed very much was helping out in Junior Church. Some of the little ones were so wiggly and squirmy I wondered if they ever heard anything. I was always amazed and overjoyed when they could tell me what the story had been the Sunday before. I probably helped out in that department for about two years. Occasionally, I did substitute teaching in Sunday School or in Pioneer Clubs.

Probably, the greatest joy was to be the speaker several years at Children's camps run by the Canadian Sunday School Mission in Peachland, BC. At each camp it was wonderful to pray with the children as they came (to my trailer) to be saved. Many were from unsaved homes, and not just unsaved but very difficult situations. It was like sending lambs among wolves. The administrators, Jake and Lillian Esau used to follow up most of the children during the year, as much as was possible. That was a comfort.

Since I still enjoy good health I have been able to help my senior friends and some of my family with their shopping. Some of these folks live in Nursing Homes while some are still able to be in their own homes. They are not able to drive anymore so they don't need help with just their shopping, but for doctor's visits, to banks and getting toe nails cut as well.

The most blessed has been to become good friends with several who did not know the Lord. He allowed me to have a small part in their accepting Jesus as Saviour. Now they are in Heaven with the Lord. There is no greater joy and satisfaction than that.

As I said before, there are all the orphan families in India I keep in touch with through letters. I write to each one at least twice a year. That is, a general letter, which I write in Marathi and then make copies of. Then each one gets a personal note on the back of the letter. A couple of times I have sent three in one year when something very important has happened.

Some of them have a phone now and ask me to call them but it is too expensive. I'd write more often but I am afraid I am losing my Marathi. I have forgotten the genders of words. So, I make most words neuter gender. Shame on me! I have bewailed my plight and told them that I am ashamed to make so many mistakes. I have also asked them if I might PLEASE write in English. Their answer always is, "then it's not you, if you write in English. We can read your letters easily." Bless their hearts. Most do not read any English.

I had great plans for doing a lot of reading after my retirement but I haven't. I think it was Brother Bach that used to say, "to retire means they just put new tires on you!" I think that is what has happened here and I love it. I love to visit friends in the Nursing homes and that takes time. I also try to see my remaining family as often as possible because I was away for so many years. The rest of the time I guess I'm just busy.

When I had enough miles for a free trip I went to China, Hong Kong and Taiwan. Another time a trip to Italy with a friend, (also on free miles) to visit her son (an MK) who is a missionary there.

I have already told you about my trips back to India for the Orphan Reunions. The dates are as follows:

1. November 11,1987 to March 11,1988.
2. October 28 to December 2, 1993.
3. November 1 to 26, 1997.

You can see each one was shorter than the one before. It was hard on my health, especially the last one.

That pretty well gives you a bird's eye view of my sixteen years of retirement up to March 30, 2000. My heart is full of praise to God.

Before we entered the Taj Mahal, we had to rent cloth covers for our shoes or else take them off.

Mailing a letter to my parents.

CHAPTER 40

Conclusion

Now what conclusion can I draw from my 81 years (one month short as of the day of this writing) here on earth? Maybe a better question would be to ask you what conclusion you have arrived at after reading my story? That is if you stuck with me to the end! Thank you, if you did. My desire and aim in writing it has been to demonstrate that God is faithful to His Word. If we desire to know Him, He reveals Himself to us through His Word and by the Holy Spirit. He is not as hard to find as we think. We just have to come on His terms.

I guess the first statement I want to make is that I am glad I was born! I have truly enjoyed my life. That does not mean that I have enjoyed every day of it and that there have been no problems. There have been plenty but joy always followed. I have learned to trust God in the dark as well as in the light. If I do not know Him in the light, then I will not be able to trust Him in the dark.

Sometimes, I was inclined to panic until I learned that God never panics. We panic because we think that the outcome depends on us. I never heard God say, "Oh dear, look what has happened to Annie! What will I do now?" He has it all under complete control all the time. Sometimes I expected God to do something right now, either for me or someone else. "Lord, can't you hear the clock ticking away? Do SOMETHING!" From somewhere these printed words came across my desk (I don't remember who said them or who sent them). GOD IS NEVER LATE, BUT RARELY EARLY. We can go right down to the wire and know God will be there.

I have learned that peoples' hearts are the same the world over. The colour of skin does not matter one bit. Rev. Henry Unrau once said in his sermon at Grace Church that, "God is God, even when people are people." I think it is very important to keep that in mind.

I am thankful that our parents taught us to work and to work hard. I have worked hard and enjoyed it. Hard work does not hurt us. Of course, it has to be within limits. Not all work is pleasant. It was up to me to teach the girls (the akkas) how to wash diapers so I washed them and had them watch me.

Sometimes, they were not careful and let the children play with toys while they were on the pottie. They did it because it kept them seated!! There was nothing wrong with that except that the floor sloped towards the toilet which was even with the floor. If they dropped the toys, they naturally rolled into the toilet. That plugged it and it overflowed! I had warned them about it and each time called the sweeper from town to retrieve the toys. It was costly and often they could not come immediately. I learned that if I required something difficult from the girls I'd better be willing to do it myself first. I must be humble enough to do any task. I felt it was very important.

So I asked the akkas to come and watch me retrieve the toys. I say "Ughh" before I tell you about it. First, I put a gunny sack on the floor and rolled my sleeve up right to the shoulder. Then I reached in just about to my shoulder and got the toys out. It was not pleasant, to say the least. I washed in disinfectant at once then I told them to do it next time if they would. You may be sure no toys ever fell in again! And I really did not want them to have to do it (it was gross, as the kids say!). If you come to serve, you must serve, not just tell others what to do.

There were mornings when I succeeded in getting out of bed only after two or three attempts. My blood pressure and my haemoglobin were too low. I learned then that the promise in Deuteronomy 33:25 is true, "..and as thy days, so shall they strength be." Not a day according to our strength, but strength according to the need. God always poured in strength until I could get medical help.

Jesus told His disciples, "and you shall be witnesses unto Me.." Acts 1:8b. We are inclined to think that missionaries do witnessing, emphasis on the do. That is, that they go out to do missionary work. I learned it is more "to be" than to do. People watch more what we are than what we say. The same is true of all of us believers wherever we are. I am so thankful that He lets His light shine through when we are completely unaware of it. I will give two examples.

First on one of my flights back to India we stopped in Frankfurt, Germany because of engine trouble. It was about 2:00 a.m. and we were all so tired. I planned to lie back and sleep while they fixed the problem. Then we heard the loud speaker crackle, "Everybody has to get off. As you exit, you will be given coupons for coffee and doughnuts in the terminal." The last thing I wanted was food but I dutifully took it and walked toward the far end of the room to sit down by an empty table. A very well dressed business man followed me and asked if he might join me. I welcomed him. He put his food down, and told me he had been watching me since we left New York. He was scared to death to fly and asked me how I could be so peaceful. I asked if this was his first time to fly. I was badly mistaken for he told me he had to fly almost every day. Flying was torture because he was afraid every minute he was in a plane.

He asked me again how come I could be so peaceful. I told him that as a missionary I was required to fly. I had been afraid at first but not anymore. I too did not want to think of going down in a plane, but if it went down I would go up! He wondered how that could be. I gave him my testimony as to how the Lord forgave my sins and that I had the assurance of going to Heaven. We probably talked about an hour. He was so open. I told him how he could have the same peace that I had but I did not ask him to make a decision.

A seed was planted though, in a stranger's heart. In due time the Lord could cause it to bear fruit. He asked me where I was heading and I told him Bombay. He surprised me when he said that he was inclined to change his flight and go to Bombay as well. From there he'd continue to his destination.

When I asked him why, he answered that he wanted to be on the same plane as I as long as possible because no plane would go down on which I was a passenger! I was very humbled by his words. I knew my attitude had not been right when we had to deplane. Nor am I justifying that at all. What I learned was that in order for God to get a message to a prepared heart he will bypass me completely and allow His peace and light to come to the fore. Praise be to Him.

Secondly, my travels had brought me to Colorado Springs, Colorado where I was visiting my colleague from India, Augusta Swanson. Before I left, there was some concern as to whether I would make my flight from Denver to California. I don't remember the reason for that but Augusta was especially concerned. During the night I heard loud moaning from her bedroom. Thinking she was sick I tiptoed to her door. She was praying over and over, "Dear Lord, help Annie to catch that flight." The Lord had heard her prayer, all was in order at the airport. I checked in and waited for the call to board. The call came and we stood in line at the gate. There was a gentleman just ahead of me and I was the last in line. Suddenly, the stewardess put out her hand to stop the man ahead of me. She apologized profusely to both of us but he was very upset to say the least. Our next flight was in the morning and he practically threatened her for having done that.

There was nothing to do but to sit down and try to get some sleep. I was not disturbed at all. Augusta had prayed so earnestly and since the Lord saw fit to not answer there must be a very good reason. I did not want to be on any plane I was not to be on. I did not realize the man was watching me.

After a few minutes he came over and said that if I had kicked up a fuss too, they probably would have found two seats for us. "Anyway," he said, "it makes me mad that you are so peaceful through all this." I invited him to sit down and told him that I was a believer, a missionary. I told him about Augusta's prayer. The Lord's answer had been no, so why would I want to be on that plane? I told him that I had turned my life over to God and I knew He was in control, even now. There must be a good reason for the Lord to allow it.

Tears came to his eyes and he said he must be that reason. I was surprised at the sudden change. He was running away from his wife and family, he told me. He was going to go as far away that night as he possibly could and never return. I looked at him and prayed quietly. I searched for words but none came. He too sat quietly as tears came down his cheeks. The Lord was speaking to him I knew.

He was in great turmoil. After some time he turned to me and told me that he too was a believer and what he was doing was wrong. "The Lord has used you to speak to me. I am glad we missed that flight. I am turning in my ticket and I am going back home. Thank you so very much Ma'am. God bless you." And he was gone.

We never introduced ourselves but God knows his name, his family and where they live. I rather think that they are happy in the Lord. I tell you this story to encourage you. The Lord has probably used you in a similar way and you were not aware of it. I did not know I looked peaceful! I was so very sleepy.

As to prayer, I thank God that He answers the cry of my heart and not always the words of my prayer. He knows my deepest longing to want His will and so answers accordingly. My life would be in complete chaos at times if He always answered the very words I say in prayer. I may think I know what His will is but I don't. He knows what the result would be if He answered all my prayers with a yes.

Oft in danger, is what the Apostle Paul wrote. I am not comparing myself to him by any means. I have not been in the same kind of dangers, nor as often or as severe but I have learned as Paul did, that the safest place in all the world is in the centre of God's will.

If I were to live my life over again, would I choose to follow the Lord to India? Yes, many times over. I have probably had some of my happiest and hardest times in India but I would do it again.

What would I change? What would I do differently? That's hard to say. I am human and might make the same mistakes. I would hope that I would follow the Lord more closely, be more patient, laugh more, take myself less seriously, pray more fervently, speak more tenderly, encourage others more and trust the Lord more completely. And I'd better start right now!

Yesterday's gone, tomorrow may never be mine,
But we have this moment today.